STORM ON THE
HORIZON

The New Age, UFOs, and
the Cosmic Christ

Sylvia McKelvey

LifeRich Publishing is a registered trademark of The Reader's Digest Association, Inc.

LifeRich Publishing books may be ordered through booksellers or by contacting:

LifeRich Publishing
1663 Liberty Drive
Bloomington, IN 47403
www.liferichpublishing.com
1 (888) 238-8637

Scripture taken from the New King James Version of the Bible unless otherwise indicated.

ISBN: 978-1-4897-2420-5 (sc)
ISBN: 978-1-4897-2421-2 (hc)
ISBN: 978-1-4897-2419-9 (e)

Library of Congress Control Number: 2019910356

Print information available on the last page.

LifeRich Publishing rev. date: 08/19/2019

Dedication

For Gerry

Contents

Preface

There are two popular views about UFOs running simultaneously today. One view takes the scientific approach with little regard for reported UFO sightings by the general public, opting instead to rely on scientific data—a signal or sound, for example, captured by any of the enormous radio telescopes stationed at strategic points around the globe. These huge scopes are not only listening, but also actively sending signals from Earth to the outer regions of space. This, of course, is in the hope that such signals will be picked by any spacefaring life forms capable of intercepting such a message. Should a signal be picked up from either side of the scope, our science and reality would change in an instant. Governments would be notified, and official committees formed. Space protocols would be enacted and the world's populace informed of the incredible event should extraterrestrials lock on to Earth's coordinates and pay us a visit. Many scientists believe that contact with extraterrestrials is only a matter of *when*, not *if.*

When they think of UFOs, most people imagine flying saucers, alien beings, advanced technology, and amazing spacecraft. An essence of superiority permeates our impressions of UFOs, due in part to the inability of our governments and military to catch them, control them, or coerce them into landing and presenting themselves to the world—at least for now. However, if contact with alien life forms has already been made, as some believe, the US government is not forthcoming with information. Only denials are offered, despite evidence to the contrary provided by pilots, astronauts, and other highly credible people.

In reality, UFOs have been seen by people from all walks of life— royalty, presidents, celebrities, clergy, and citizens in countries all around the world. Many of them have shared their stories, evidence, and impressions of who and what the aliens are and why they are here. And yet we get no official word from the governments of the world and no disclosure of information. Some of these individuals—scientists, politicians, and laypeople alike—are among those who believe that the truth is out there and it is only a matter of time before we see ETs for ourselves. Others scoff at the very idea of UFOs or choose to simply wait and see.

The second view of UFOs involves a much more spiritual application. Many people believe that a brotherhood of celestial beings will soon come to Earth to assist in our planetary evolution and membership into an interstellar society of united planets. Some people see aliens as space brothers, spirit masters, saviors of the world, helpers, teachers, protectors of the planet, our ancient alien ancestors, or even the gods of old. Aliens are viewed as benevolent benefactors of humanity who will show us how to lead kinder, gentler lives and develop an all-inclusive united society of planetary people. But it goes deeper than that. Some people look also for a new type of leadership on Earth and are actively working to bring it about. A movement is poised to welcome a global leader, be it from this world or another.

I would like to offer a third view that incorporates Bible prophecy and the arrival on Earth of something or someone that could manifest the most incredible deception our planet has ever experienced. Could such an alien appearance be part of the great end-times deception talked about in the Bible? What could so amaze our highly technological world of advanced science and weaponry that we would feel so insignificant as to offer any resistance? What could cause superpowers to lay down arms, wealth to lose its importance, and corporations to stop conducting business? What could cause governments of the world to unite—or surrender?

It has become apparent from my own investigation that a diabolical plan has been in the works for a long time, a diabolical plan that would set upon this Earth a great deception from the farthest corners of the globe to the infinite expanse of space. Changes in politics, religion, and education all appear to be headed toward the acceptance of a united world and a possible intergalactic governing body. Perhaps this will come as the result of our world's continued upward technological spiral into new and uncharted realities of science and beyond. But the spiritual values of humanity cannot be ignored, even if science advances an evolutionary hypothesis to explain humankind's place in the universe. Our innate desire to worship something of greater moral value outside ourselves must be satisfied. We cannot establish a new and global spirituality alone, but indications suggest that a base of unseen forces, even benevolent ETs, is helping it along. Spirit masters with their "Plan of the Ages" advocate for the establishment of a new world teacher, new Christ, and new global leader—even a cosmic one.

How then does one merge the two beliefs of science and the supernatural and unite people who accept the existence of an alien brotherhood with scientists who continue to troll the outer regions of the universe in search of bona fide life? First of all, one would have to establish a protocol and methodology that would ultimately lead to the discovery of extraterrestrial life through acceptable scientific data that would appear nonthreatening to mainstream society. One would then have to present viable evidence of the reality of the paranormal, especially in regard to unseen beings or other life forms. If both exist, then one theory could not overrule the other and they would have to work together. But one first has to prove that both exist. That's perhaps where I come in.

I can attest to the existence of the supernatural and UFOs based on the evidence I have collected as a Christian investigator through my own personal experiences and photographs. UFOs and spirits exist, and here's the evidence.

In many ways this evidence has served as the impetus of my becoming a Christian researcher by looking into why and where these things occur and what significance they have in people's spiritual beliefs, none more so than with those promoting a new Christ, the one some call Maitreya.

What happens when the spirit realm is not a secret anymore? What happens when you have valid palatable evidence of its existence? My experiences have caused me to think in much different ways—not about God, for my faith is still strong, but about *them*. Knowing that the Bible tells us these entities exist, what part might they play in future events? One answer might surprise you.

In providing such evidence, however, I don't mean to encourage anyone to seek them out, but rather to expose them. Whether posing as guides, masters, angels, or aliens, these entities are real, but in knowing this, we can know too that God is real. Thus Jesus is real, and He is going to return just exactly as He promised, and that's the main point.

Through Jesus, we are not in bondage to these unseen forces, nor should we fear them, but we certainly need to be aware of them and respect their power. God provides us the protection we need to keep us from their deceptive influence, but that doesn't mean they won't try. Dubious spirit beings masquerade in any number of forms, as spirit guides, ghosts, angels, and even extraterrestrials.

I have been a Christian researcher for over thirty years. I provided background research and appeared in the 1982 Christian documentary *The New Age, A Pathway to Paradise?* produced by WCFC Christian television in Chicago, Illinois. The documentary dealt with the growing New Age movement and included interviews with Christian authors Constance Cumbey and Dave Hunt, whom I had the privilege of working with.

Additionally, I have been a field investigator and state section director for the national Mutual UFO Network (MUFON) for Santa Clara County, California, and have spent many hours investigating reported UFO sightings. What I have learned along the way is that many paranormal experiences that people have in some New Age groups are nearly identical to what people are experiencing with UFOs. And I have had my own sightings.

It is my hope that the history and evidence provided here will lead you to a better understanding of our current times, the conspiracy against humanity, and the global deception it is bringing with it. I don't believe anyone likes to expose his or her life for public consumption, and writing about my own is something I have stubbornly fought against for years. But finally it all came down to one very important question. What would I say if God asked me, "If you knew and had evidence, why didn't you say something?" That was a sobering and frightening thought. So, I'm saying something.

The need is real. According to a January 2014 article by journalist Michael Snyder, data from a *National Geographic* survey showed that 77 percent of Americans believe that space aliens have visited Earth, but only 68 percent believe that Jesus is God or the Son of God. "With each passing year, the frequency of UFO sightings seems to keep increasing," Snyder said. Movies, television shows, and even video games have been keen to capture the extraterrestrial genre, and their popularity is growing. Is it a fad or something more? Snyder continues, "It is almost as if the population of the planet is being primed for something. Could this phenomenon be the 'strong delusion' of the last days talked about in the Bible? And if there are beings out there that are not human, what is it that they want? Could it be that they have an extremely insidious agenda?"[1]

Looking back to the two popular viewpoints regarding UFOs, there is an obvious common denominator with both views: *anticipation*. The question that must be asked is this: What are we waiting for?

Acknowledgements

I give a special thank-you to all those who have contributed to the completion of this project. First of all, to my Lord and Savior Jesus Christ, I give a thank-you for *His* service. Then to my amazing husband, Kim, for his love and support throughout this project. To my daughters, Amy and Ginny, for always having faith in their mom. Additional thanks goes to my brother Brian, to friends Connie and Naomi, and especially to Jim and Marcia for their Christian wisdom and support. And finally, a thank-you goes to Constance for nudging me to complete this book and to all those who shared their stories in confidence. You know who you are.

Introduction

Voices

- The internet went slightly more bananas than usual last weekend over the *New York Times'* story implying that extraterrestrials are real and the U.S. government has been tracking them for years.
— Jeff Wise, *New York* magazine, December 26, 2017

- I believe that these extraterrestrial vehicles and their crews are visiting this planet from other planets, which are a little more technically advanced than we are on Earth. I feel that we need to have a top level, coordinated program to scientifically collect and analyze data from all over the Earth concerning any type of encounter, and to determine how best to interfere with these visitors in a friendly fashion.
— Astronaut Gordon Cooper at the United Nations, 1985

- Two Jefferson County air unit police officers, described by their lieutenant as 'solid guys,' swear that they had a two-minute dogfight with a UFO during a routine helicopter patrol Friday night. Two officers on the ground said they, too, spotted the object. The UFO, a glowing pear-shaped object about the size of a basketball, literally flew circles around the helicopter, even though the fliers say they were moving at speeds approaching 100 mph.
— Gardiner Harris, Louisville *Courier-Journal*, March 4, 1993

- Maitreya's "star" is not a star, of course … It is one of four spaceships … They are in each of the four corners of the Earth—north-south-east-west … The Space Brothers are totally involved in Maitreya's

emergence. These four craft have been specially called upon. They are huge, each about the size of five football fields put together.
— Benjamin Creme, *The Gathering of the Forces of Light*

• A wave of unprecedented appearances of UFOs in the skies of Israel has stirred up UFO enthusiasts and several thousands of other people who have been witnesses to unforgettable sights. The mounting reports in recent weeks leave no room for doubt in the minds of many that UFOs have invaded Planet Earth!
— Israeli journalist Iris Almagor, March 1997

• Over a two-week period in late 2004, an unknown, 45-foot long Tic Tac shaped object played cat and mouse with the U.S. Navy off the coast of California. The mighty U.S.S. Nimitz aircraft carrier, and its support ships including the U.S.S. Princeton, carrying the most sophisticated sensor systems in the world, repeatedly detected recurring glimpses of the Tic Tac but were unable to lock on. On November 14, F-18s were ordered into the area and saw it up close. Dave Fravor, commander of the elite Black Aces unit, says the Tic Tac reacted to the presence of the F-18s and then took off like a bullet fired from a gun. "It takes off like nothing I've ever seen. One minute it is here, and off, it's gone," said retired Navy pilot David Fravor.
—George Knapp, Las Vegas Now May 18, 2018

We propose to send a message to any extraterrestrial civilization(s) that might be listening stating that we are ready to communicate with them and inviting them to respond.
— The Search for Extraterrestrial Intelligence (SETI), http://active-seti.info

• Almost twice as wide as the dish at America's Arecibo Observatory, in the Puerto Rican jungle, the new Chinese dish [named Fast, the five-hundred-meter aperture spherical telescope] is the largest in the world, if not the universe …

- In the techno poetic idiom of the 21st century, nothing would symbolize China's rise like a high-definition shot of a Chinese astronaut setting foot on the red planet. Nothing except, perhaps, first contact.
  — Ross Anderson, *The Atlantic*, December 20, 2017

- The first-ever observations of merging binary stars stunned the astronomy community last year, but not quite as much as the first-ever signal from extraterrestrial life might someday stun the world.
  — Megan Bartels, *Fox News*, August 28, 2018

- "We cast this message into the cosmos. It is likely to survive a billion years into our future, when our civilization is profoundly altered and the surface of the Earth may be vastly changed. Of the 200 billion stars in the Milky Way galaxy, some—perhaps many—may have inhabited planets and spacefaring civilizations. If one such civilization intercepts Voyager and can understand these recorded contents, here is our message: This is a present from a small distant world, a token of our sounds, our science, our images, our music, our thoughts and our feelings. We are attempting to survive our time so we may live into yours. We hope someday, having solved the problems we face, to join a community of galactic civilizations. This record represents our hope and our determination, and our good will in a vast and awesome universe."
  — Jimmy Carter, former president of the United States of America, on the occasion of the launch of America's Voyager 1 spacecraft into space on June 16, 1977.

What would happen if the record came back?
What if it were hand delivered?

CHAPTER ONE
That No One Deceives You

Jesus Christ was only one week away from being crucified, and His final hours were ebbing quickly. One can only imagine His frame of mind, for He knew what lay ahead for His disciples and all believers. In those final days, those final hours, what would He tell them? What message or words of encouragement could He leave with them? What sense of urgency did He feel? The days were evil, and all that was prophesied about the Savior was about to be fulfilled. What was on His mind? Would He challenge them with a new parable or comfort them with more beatitudes? In actuality, what He told them involved the future and a dire warning. He knew what was going to happen, and He knew it was paramount that they know as well. Matthew 24 details the serious tone of Jesus's message to His disciples, including the prophetic events that lay ahead and the strong warning He gave them.

Jesus and His disciples had just left the temple in Jerusalem, and as they walked, the disciples became awestruck by all the beautiful buildings around them. What pride they must have felt for this magnificent place of worship. But their enthusiasm was short-lived. Jesus said to them, "Do you not see all these things? Assuredly, I say to you, not one stone shall be left here upon another, that shall not be thrown down." (Matthew 24: 2) That statement by Jesus no doubt caught them by surprise and riveted their attention. Was He talking about a warring nation and a future invasion? Why so dismal? Although Jesus had told them repeatedly that He was going to leave them, the disciples did not fully understand.

Jesus knew that He was meant to be the ultimate sacrifice, not only for His disciples but also for all those who would believe in Him to be saved.

He was going to die, He was going to live, and He was going to win. The devil was going to be defeated in all matters of life and death, including his own destruction, but he was not going down without a fight. Jesus knew this. Although Jesus was going to leave this earth, He assured them He would return. This no doubt left the disciples with a lot of questions, for they were troubled in their minds and in their hearts.

Later, when they had gone to the Mount of Olives, the disciples approached Jesus in private and asked Him, "Tell us, when these things will be? And what will be the sign of Your coming at the end of the age?" (Matthew 24:3).

Understanding the seriousness of the situation that the disciples and all believers would be facing, Jesus was earnest in His warning to them. "Take heed that no one deceives you. For many will come in My name saying 'I am the Christ,' and will deceive many." (Matthew 24:4-5) And He told them too of the tumultuous times to come:

> "And you will hear of wars and rumors of wars. See that you are not troubled for all these things must come to pass, but the end is not yet. For nation will rise against nation, and kingdom against kingdom. And there will be famines, pestilences, and earthquakes in various places. All these are the beginning of sorrows. (Matthew 24:5-8)

Such sorrows would undoubtedly include a reprobate world that would rise up with the devil and his angels stirring the pot of hatred against all believers because of Jesus. It would not bode well for some. "Then they will deliver you up to tribulation and kill you, and you will be hated by all nations for My name's sake. And then many will be offended, will betray one another, and will hate one another." (Matthew 24:9-10) The chaotic times to come will no doubt stress humanity to the breaking point and leave the masses naive and vulnerable. "Then many false prophets will rise up and deceive many. And because lawlessness will abound, the love of many will grow cold." (Matthew 24:11-12)

It is hard not to see our current time in this analogy: rebellion and restlessness, a desensitizing toward the loss of human life, and an increase in senseless crimes. Conditions of love growing cold have become the mainstay of news reports in our current society. The stirring up of emotions to divide people has moved dangerously close to the point of murderous rage. Derelict human rationale for eradicating and preventing opposition to people with differing opinions is becoming an accepted norm, and hive mentality is circumventing individual thought. How much more must occur before standards of behavior are put in place and enforced with the actions of each individual scrutinized and evaluated by an electorate ruling class? Thumbs up or down? It is not difficult to imagine that difficult days may lie ahead.

But there is hope.

"He who endures to the end shall be saved." (Matthew 24:13) Jesus promises. But first the gospel must be preached to the world as a witness to all the nations, and then the end will come. No doubt the Internet and mass communication have been, and will continue to be, substantial factors in accomplishing this goal. Today news and information can be transmitted around the world in a matter of seconds. What's left?

Unfortunately, things are going to change for our world—and not for the better. According to scripture, an upheaval in our current global political structure is coming, bringing with it *someone* who will be the antithesis of all that is godly and holy, a self-proclaimed god, and an abomination.

"Therefore when you see the 'abomination of desolation,' spoken of by Daniel the prophet, standing in the holy place" (whoever reads let them understand), "then let him who are in Judea flee to the mountains." (Matthew 24: 15-16) Certainly this will be a time of great upheaval when this abomination appears and people flee for their lives:

> "And let him who is in the field not go back to get his clothes. But woe to those who are pregnant and to those who are nursing babies in those days! And pray that your flight may not be in winter or on the Sabbath. For then there will be great tribulation, such has not been since the beginning of the world until this time, no, nor ever shall be. And unless those days were shortened, no flesh would be saved; but for the elect's sake those days will be shortened." (Matthew 24:18-22)

It is important to note that Jesus gets even more specific. "Then if anyone says to you, 'Look, here is the Christ!' or 'There!' do not believe it. For false christs and false prophets will rise and show great signs and wonders to deceive, if possible, even the elect." (Matthew24:23-24) Now, having given the disciples adequate warning of the deceptive times that lay ahead, and a warning for all future believers, Jesus reminds them in no uncertain terms, "See, I have told you beforehand." (Matthew 24:25)

Heads up.

CHAPTER TWO
An Inconvenient Plan

"If men look for the Christ who left His disciples centuries ago, they will fail to see the Christ Who is in the process of returning... The Son of God is on His way and He cometh not alone His advance guard is already here and the Plan which they must follow is already made clear."[2]
—Alice A. Bailey, *The Externalization of the Hierarchy*

Bailey's statement is as fresh in my mind today as it was in 1981 when I first read it in the booklets that were being distributed at a local library. *The Reappearance of the Christ, Preparation for the Reappearance of the Christ,* and *World Goodwill* were the titles. Within these pages were instructions on how one should adequately prepare the way for the return of the Christ. This literature was being distributed by an organization called Lucis Trust, then headquartered at 666 United Nations Plaza in New York. The literature had a solid agenda for the promotion of a returning Christ, who incidentally will not be Jesus. Although Lucis Trust's address has changed over the years, its New Age/New Christ agenda has not.

Lucis Trust has had an ongoing association with the spirituality of the United Nations as a longtime participant in the activities of the United Nations Meditation Room. However, it has broadened its participation to include a global prospectus, and through the spirit-inspired writings of Bailey, it now has "a plan." It continues to expand its New Age/New Christ theology on a global scale, thanks in part to the advisory position it holds within the United Nations, particularly its consultative status with the UN's Economic and Social Council (ECOSOC) and World Goodwill,

Lucis's nongovernmental organization. Naturally, such strategically based operations could only serve to benefit a world teacher or Christ as time and opportunity present themselves, and I believe they will.

Although Lucis Trust has decided to serve as a sounding board to announce to the public the return or reappearance of the Christ or a facsimile, it can't do it alone. Many New Age groups openly endorse the Alice A. Bailey writings.

Having its roots soundly in theosophy, Lucis Trust—along with other like-minded New Age groups—has gone one step further in preparing the way by conditioning the minds of receptive individuals everywhere to the idea of a soon-to-be seen new Christ for a New Age. They believe that we have somehow transitioned from the astrology-not-science-determined age of Pisces to the current astrology-not-science-determined age of Aquarius. Although time and dates of such occurrence are highly debated, even among astrologers, it appears by popular consensus that the time is now.

In an obvious attempt to gain credibility by interjecting Bible prophecy into their writings, they have unabashedly misapplied and reinterpreted biblical scripture in an attempt to give legitimacy to this New Age Christ. Pisces hands off to Aquarius and it is all things new again. According to "the Plan," however, the new Aquarian era would naturally require changes in politics, religion, and education, according to their standards, and through the incorporation of a new view of our world from a global—if not cosmic—perspective.

Interestingly, claims of extraterrestrial enlightenment for the good of the planet have made their way into various levels of world governments, and in the case of the United Nations; E.T. has not left the building. Some advocacy groups have petitioned for disclosure and acceptance of extraterrestrials globally, while others want to shove the entire topic under a rug. But ignoring it won't make it go away, especially if one looks to the advice and guidance received from an extraterrestrial impetus. Therefore, there must be a plan—and they have one.

Lucis Trust, originally called Lucifer Trust and amended to Lucis (I would think for obvious reasons), along with their arcane school, Triangles meditation groups, and World Servers, has established several public outreach programs that have found fertile soil among many New Age groups. Particularly interested are the groups dedicated to the proposition of establishing a new world order and the new Christ for whom all nations are waiting—the Messiah of the Jews, Krishna for Hindus, Maitreya Buddha for the Buddhists, and Imam Mahdi for the Muslims. To simplify the matter, the new Christ will be referred to as simply the World Teacher. Why is this important?

The main impetus of this spiritual campaign, again, comes from the writings of Alice A. Bailey, who claimed to have been "overshadowed" by a spirit master named Djwhal Khul, aka the Tibetan or simply DK. Along with other spirit masters who have purportedly been around for millennia, DK has enlisted the help of conscripts who readily allow the overshadowing of their bodies and minds in order to put on paper the spirit masters' agenda—the "Plan"—for the New Age. And the masters have to make good on who they say they are; in other words, they must appear.

One occult belief is that once a student of the occult is ready, a master appears, sometimes without warning. As inductee Alice Bailey wrote, "I heard what I thought was a clear note of music which sounded from the sky, through the hill and in me. Then I heard a voice which said, 'There are some books which it is desired should be written for the public. You can write them. Will you do so?'"[3] Of course, these books dealt with a new plan for humanity that Bailey could help initiate. Now, it is one thing to suspect a plan; it is another to get it in writing. Bailey would eventually write twenty-four of these books, which are of interest because she did not write from her own inspiration; *she took dictation*. She was following the path of another spirit master contactee, the Russian occultist and New Age matriarch Helena Blavatsky, who several years prior had taken dictation from her disembodied "secret chiefs" or spirit masters. These "inspired" writings became the tenets of Theosophy, a belief system based on the teachings of these ethereal beings and concerning a new Christ for a New Age, sans Jesus.

Helena Blavatsky, upon meeting her own spiritual masters and while under their tutelage, wrote *The Secret Doctrine*, seen as a primer for New Age spirituality. Equipped with this esoteric knowledge, dredged heavily in Eastern mysticism, and the framework for the global plan for humanity, she founded the Theosophical Society in the United States in 1875. From there, Bailey branched out with her own form of anti-Christian, anti-Semitic, pro-new Christ esoteric writings provided to her by the masters via her pen. But there is more than spiritual chumminess at work in these teachings.

Fast-forward to 1970 when Earth Day sprang into being and the 1980s when the Harmonic Convergence drew crowds, in the minds of many aspirants, the New Age was dawning at last. Through the efforts of these New Age artisans, the world was quickly changing into a Gaia-centric endeavor of light, love, and oneness. Festivals such as Peacequake, Harmonic Convergences, and Earth Day were filling the bill.

I had the occasion to attend the 1982 Peacequake in San Francisco—a gathering of artists, mystics, robed followers of the Guru Bhagwan Shree Rajneesh, and smatterings of political action groups advocating the same old message of anti-war, anti-bombs, anti-Christian, anti-Jew, and anti-government sentiments mixed with mystic crystal revelations. All in favor of the New Age, say "om."

Based on the stacks of literature that were freely distributed, we can assume that some of the psychic personalities in attendance must have been channeling inspiration from Karl Marx. Eager to rally around the socialist propaganda, one small boy wore a button that read, "Eat the Rich." This rehashed anarchy was no doubt by design. Dave Hunt, who investigated the spiritual and political workings of the New Age, saw it as nothing more than a rebirth of Marxism: "Clearly Marxism has an important part to play in 'The Plan' to establish the New World Order that H. G. Wells, Alice Bailey, and others wrote about. Marxism and the New Age Movement share the common goal of a socialistic world government."[4]

Constance Cumbey delved deeper to show that the movement is nothing short of Nazism when you peel through the layers of "light" and "love": "New Age esotericists believe in the existence of 'masters' who are organized in a 'Hierarchy' headed by a New Age Messiah. The Nazis likewise believed in the existence of a hierarchy of 'masters' headed by a New Age Christ whom they considered to be their very own Hitler, as Hitler himself believed."[5]

Sound diabolical? It is. Repackaged for universal consumption, now comes the call for earth's transformation into an all-inclusive global society stripped of all divisions of borders, politics, and religious affiliations. However, it still adheres to some semblance of religion through the propagation of a world teacher or new Christ, born from the twisting of biblical scriptures and prophecies from multiple religions. Convenient. To give adequate hutzpah to the fulfillment of prophecy, the inclusion of extraterrestrial forces giving notice to the world of "the Coming One" might culminate in the future grand event. It's just the beginning of "the Plan."

Apparently lacking originality in their own teachings, the Lucis Trust and other New Age groups have customized Bible scripture to meet their requirements for what a new Christ or world teacher would look like in order to be palatable to the religions of the world. They have long offered programs and training to further desire for and acceptance of a new world teacher, a man who would hold the office of the Christ, the man who would be Christ Maitreya rather than Jesus Christ. Why is this important?

The New Age globalist directives, which the master DK wrote through Alice Bailey, harbored a blatant anti-Christian, anti-Semitic doctrine deemed necessary to seed the minds of the youth of every generation. The message was that old values needed reforming and that reformation could be accomplished through the efforts of world servers and global citizens, specifically in the aforementioned areas of politics, religion, and education. These changes would be based on the spirit masters' socialist mandates and disdain for the filthy lucre of capitalism. If the social upheaval of our current age is any indication, it appears they may have accomplished much already.

The expectation is not just of a "coming one," but of global transformation, with the help of other participants, such as the Space Brothers, to effectively set up a world system that the world's populace could get behind and support. Of course, adding extraterrestrials to the plan—and they do—results in a compelling agenda for global change.

To assist this transformative agenda, in the spirit of light and love, DK has given to the world, through Bailey, a world prayer. It is officially known as "The Great Invocation," but I prefer to refer to it as "The Great Invitation" because that's exactly what it is. The prayer, which is meant to be a unifier of all beliefs, is a petition to (their) Christ to return to earth, at least according to the third stanza, which was released to the public in 1945. In the first (1935) and second (1940) stanzas, the language is much bolder, with petitions for a "Rider from a Secret Place"—the "Coming One"—to come forth and fulfill his mission. "Let Light and Love and

Power and Death fulfill the purpose of the Coming One," says the Tibetan through Bailey in one book titled, ironically, *Ponder On This*.[6]

If such a global plan exists, and it does, it far exceeds the flash-in-a-pan announcements of other Christ figures or spiritual leaders. It has organization, participation, staying power, and growth, both domestically within the United States and by active participation in the United Nations. Additionally, such propaganda has firmly planted the idea of a new leader for a new age. Perhaps then it is the idea that is the "idea" itself, and all ideas need to be promoted.

Enter Benjamin Creme. If the world is on course for global and galactic transformation, perhaps a spokesman was needed, so one was provided. The late Benjamin Creme, an Englishman who ardently followed the teachings of Alice A. Bailey, devoted a large portion of his life to announcing to the world the return of a Christ, the one he called Maitreya.

In the 1980s, Creme was at the pinnacle of his calling. In April 1982, an all-out media campaign was launched to announce the return of Christ, the world teacher who was about to make his appearance on the world's stage. That is, of course, after the clamoring believers enticed him enough and the world's media gave him adequate press time.

Full-page advertisements appeared in several languages around the world, flyers were dropped off at every available public venue, and multiple radio and television announcements were carried over the airwaves. Massive efforts orchestrated globally by the Tara Center and Share International wrapped up the grand announcement by issuing a request to the world's media to seek out the Christ. Few did. Many of the faithful waited with bated breath for the "Day of Declaration" of the Christ, only to be informed that his appearance had been put on hold awaiting a better opportunity, i.e., more press coverage.

It's been more than thirty years, and the faithful are still resonating in assuring tones the appearance of this unusual man, believing that he will soon make his presence known. For now, however, he chooses to remain in the background, languishing in unidentified locations around the world and making incognito appearances with talk show hosts and media types who ostensibly remain unaware of his true identity.

Grabbing onto Bible prophecy once again in an attempt to validate his claims, Benjamin Creme remained stoic in his dedication to the "plan for humanity" as fostered by the masters, some of whom he allegedly became acquainted with as early as 1959. In 1972 Creme began his crusade for Maitreya, which he revealed through his own written word, *The Reappearance of the Christ and the Masters of Wisdom*, released in 1979.[7] The stage was set. Invoking the assistance of the Space Brothers, a.k.a. Extraterrestrials, the plan was moving forward on a wing and a prayer—or invocation, literally.

Public outreach remains an all-important factor in establishing a vision of a reformed world in the minds of people everywhere. Meditation or getting in touch with these ethereal forces can't hurt either. According to Bailey, "Forget not that meditation clarifies the mind as to the fact and nature of the Plan, that understanding brings that Plan into the world of desire, and that love releases the form which will make the Plan materialize upon the physical plane."[8] In other words, mental conditioning is important, something apparently akin to the Space Brothers, as according to Bailey, "The objective of all the work to be done at this time is to educate public opinion and to familiarize the thinking people of the world with the urgency and the opportunity." According to Bailey, the ETs were working hard for the opportunity as well: "Thus will the work of the Hierarchy be facilitated and the door opened to the regenerative forces of those extra-planetary Beings Who offer their help at this time." [9]

The spirit masters offered help as well as channeled messages, a reality not lost on idle talk or fantasy by the select few. The widespread influence of their channeled messages is evidenced by New Age enthusiasts such as Shirley MacLaine, who was forthright about her indoctrination: "I turned my attention to the more modern channelers and the entities who communicated through them. Best known of the current channeled spiritual entities appeared to be a spiritual master known as DK, channeled by Alice Bailey, and later by Benjamin Crème."[10]

Benjamin Creme was no stranger to the teachings of Bailey or the Space Brothers. The Space Brothers or Space People as he often referred to them, he described as etheric beings who are able to lower their vibrational rate and that of their spaceships in order to be seen in our physical world. This is something he explained that the masters also can do and as such could appear to look like anyone of us at any time. Creme had a large interest in UFOs. He was secretary of the UFO-focused Aetherius Society under the leadership of "ET contactee" George King, and he was a friend and colleague of George Adamski. Adamski, another early contactee of the Space Brothers, claimed to have been welcomed aboard spaceships for friendly get-togethers with Nordic-looking space people. Adamski was also a follower of Tibetan mystical teachings that often run parallel to the Space Brothers' dogma, which has been updated and redistributed for today's consumers. One UFO investigator of recent times who was well known among many UFO communities was Wendell C. Stevens, a follower of the Alice Bailey teachings and an acquaintance of Benjamin Creme. In *Angels in Starships*, Stevens writes, "Benjamin Creme informed us that Lord Maitreya had told him that all the angels of all the mythologies and histories of our world were simply extraterrestrials or extradimensionals, or both, and that they have come and gone ever since humanity came into being on this planet."[11]

Looks like they're back. A star shines brightly in the night sky overhead, but it isn't a true star. Maitreya has air support, as Creme explained: "Maitreya's 'star' is not a star, of course ... It is one of four spaceships ... They are in each of the four corners of the Earth—north-south-east-west ... The Space Brothers are totally involved in Maitreya's emergence. These four craft have been specially called upon. They are huge, each about the size of five football fields put together."[12]

There seem to be a definite connection between spirit masters and UFOs. Many progressive New Age inductees willfully expect the appearance of the Space Brothers on our planet, and many established New Age organizations are on board, including Findhorn, one of the most notable New Age communities. The founders of the Findhorn community in Scotland have long claimed many communiqués with aliens. While Findhorn was under the leadership of founder Peter Caddy, an ardent believer in the alien brotherhood, a large UFO landing pad was constructed on the property in expectation of the Brothers stopping by.

So why doesn't the public know about *them*? Are the governments of the world keeping something from us? Mr. Creme thought so. "The governments will only act when they are forced to do it. When Maitreya [the world teacher] is known openly, He will be asked questions ... and the truth of the relationship between this planet and other planets will become known. Then the people from other planets will land [openly] and the reality of their existence will be known."[13] Mr. Creme, whom a reporter once called the "Herald of the Cosmic Christ," passed in 2016.[14] The cosmic Christ, however, lives on, and the Space Brothers continue to use the sky as a message board to the world.

Surely those who reference Bible scriptures should know there is another one who will come, the "instead of Christ," and that there are diabolical powers, principalities, rulers of darkness, and spiritual hosts of wickedness in the heavenly places (Ephesians 6:12). Heavenly places? What is up there that we should be aware of? What do the skies hold in store for us? Something has been a long time coming, with many active participants and a history all its own.

CHAPTER THREE
Space Brothers and Others

It may be the prelude to the big day when, knowing that
their presence will now be accepted without panic or fear,
our cosmic colonizers will face us, like a father to a son,
and say: "Sons of earth, it is time for you to know the facts
of life, galactic life, that is."[15]
—Otto Binder, *Flying Saucers Are Watching Us*

So what do the Space Brothers have to do with the New Age? Plenty. A
long lineage of New Age globalist teachings has been disseminated early on
through the topic of UFOs, most notably through the contactees. While
Kenneth Arnold was stirring the pot of UFO enthusiasm with claims of
flying saucer sightings, others were stirring the pot with claims of contact.

In 1950, journalist Frank Scully laid claim to evidence of the spacefarers
transportation that were about to come crashing down, one in Arizona and
another in New Mexico. In *Behind the Flying Saucers*, Scully reveals claims
of Scientist X, aka Dr. Gee, later thought to have been a con artist, who
had given him details of three allegedly captured saucers, á la Roswell.
Each saucer was metallic in composition, and crew members measured
thirty-six to forty inches in height. Although rumored to have crashed
somewhere near Denver, their homeport was Venus. An interesting aside
is that the disc sizes varied significantly; one was 99.9 feet wide and 72
feet tall, another was 72 feet wide, and the third was 36 feet wide. All
three diameters are divisible by nine, possibly indicating the use of human
measurement in their construction. Of course, such claims have never been
verified, nor have the stories.

Scully's book was one more in a seemingly unending line of publications that would stoke the flames of saucers and their occupants visiting planet Earth. In the exponential and sometimes amusing expose of credibility, or lack thereof, reverse engineered technology was obtained by the unfortunate downing, accidental or otherwise, of alien craft. Scully, having no firsthand experience with the non-terrestrial types, based much of what he wrote about the spacecrafts on the testimony of others. "I have never seen a flying saucer," he wrote. "I have never joined in any mass hysteria on the subject, and to the best of my knowledge and belief, I have never participated in the perpetration of a hoax on flying saucers." Regarding the spacecraft itself, "I have talked to men of science who have told me they have not only seen them but have worked on several."[16]

Less scientific are the unmitigated claims, made by Borderland Sciences Research Associates (BSRA) and its directors N. Mead Layne and Max Freedom, about ether ships manned by Etherians. Scully notes that the scientific credibility of BSRA research specialists—consisting of "metaphysicians, theosophist, mediums, trances, and students of the occult"—flew out the window when they obtained their information regarding the origins of the ether ships from medium Mark Probert and the "other side." Scully pointed out that although the communiqués came from the other side, the ether ships, according to BSRA, were originating from a mother ship at least ten miles long and traveling five hundred miles above Earth at great speed. Apparently such information is derived from *Oahspe*, a book describing Etherians as ancestors of both the Chinese and Aryan races, the "Originators of the Sanskrit language, but long removed as taxpayers on this earth."[17]

Such claims are part of a series of theatrics embracing all things otherworldly as belonging to science, if not ancient science, and the predecessor of our modern technology—or at least the idea sounds somewhat convincing.

What was happening in the 1950s was only a continuation of what had been conceived and propagated by early theosophists, particularly Bailey and the Space People. Theosophy would broaden its horizons, and so would the followers of the ETs' plan.

George Adamski. Perhaps no one was better known in that same era for making headlines with his claims of contact with beings from the planet

Venus. The Venusians, with whom he hooked up in a California desert in 1952, obligingly took him into their spacecraft, often offering him onboard meals and entertainment. Adamski claimed a close association with one particular brother from space, a Nordic-looking humanoid with long blond hair and blue eyes, named Orthon. He would later meet another crew member named Firkon. Years later, in *Angels in Starships*, authored by Giorgio Dibitonto, William T. Sherwood, and Wendelle C. Stevens, Dibitonto claims to have been taken aboard a spaceship by his own ET contact, Raphael, and introduced to Orthon and Firkon. Small universe.

Adamski soon became indoctrinated in the "save the planet—save yourselves" rhetoric delivered by Orthon and company and chronicled in his 1953 *Flying Saucers Have Landed*, cowritten with British journalist and occultist Desmond Leslie. However, Adamski had earlier been indoctrinated in the teachings of Tibetan mysticism, which he propagated and profited from with his Royal Order of Tibet organization, his bread and butter during the 1930s. That organization's teachings came straight out of the writings of theosophists H. P. Blavatsky, Alice A. Bailey, and Annie Besant.

One chapter in *The Flying Saucers Have Landed* is about "Vimanas," ancient flying boats, and others things such as ancient Aztec discs. These boats or ships were thought to be powered by Vril, sometimes referred to as the etheric force, and by harmonics, such as the Hindu word *om*, which uses the power of sound. Desmond Leslie concurred: "I have other records on my files of flying saucers that produced a strange musical note, described by observers as unlike any sound they had ever heard." Leslie uses as an example the claims of occultist and alleged witness to Adamski's desert meeting with the space folk, George Hunt Williamson.[18]

Williamson claimed that on September 27, 1952, he saw an enormous saucer pass over his house that was generating a noise "more powerful than a jet; musical, rather like a huge swarm of bees."[19] It is interesting that noises, even musical strains, have been associated with spirit contacts and saucer sightings. Sound and music, the simplest forms of communication, from the beating of drums to the ringing of bells, capture our attention. Likewise, the method used to communicate with the aliens in the movie *Close Encounters of the Third Kind* was musical notes.

Williamson, his wife, and friends Alfred and Betty Bailey were regular visitors at Adamski's Palomar Gardens commune in California, and they had become members of his Theosophy-spinoff cult, the Royal Order of Tibet. The couples spent many hours trying to contact the Space Brothers via automatic writing and Ouija board while Adamski telepathically channeled messages from the Brothers, including those from one referred to as the Venusian Sanat Kumara, a.k.a. the Lord of the Flame. Of this extraterrestrial eminence Adamski wrote, "With His Lords and helpers He 'projected the Spark' that stimulated men to rationality, and lived among them in physical form for countless millennia, teaching and guiding the huge black creatures who worshipped Him as the 'Holy of Heaven.'"[20]

It's not clear whether the "huge black creatures" were also a Venus export, but it is interesting that the Venusians associated their leader with the title of Sanat Kumara—or simply Sanat. By rearranging the *t* and *n*, the name becomes *Satan*. Just saying.

Dr. Mead Layne surfaces in *Flying Saucers Have Landed* with an explanation of why it is so difficult to have a literal hands-on with Venusian folk. According to Layne, their entire existence is etheric in nature, which allows them to appear in "solid or semi-solid forms, as they will." Whether solid or not, the important thing, as Layne expresses, is that they exist.[21]

Master, oh my master. Surfacing too, not surprisingly, was the Master DK, who explains through *his* writings via Alice Bailey that the vibratory principle used by the ancients was a combination of light and sound that allowed for the erection and movement of tall monolithic structures, presumably even those in existence today. Seconding that revelation, Adamski references theosophist Annie Besant, expert in arcane knowledge, who explains that movement of mega stones can be achieved by use of the "force of terrestrial magnetism," which would allegedly cause the object to become weightless and then, in a Jedi move of sorts, be moved by the touch of a finger to its destination.[22]

Adamski, having been moved emotionally by meeting "a human being from another world," becomes more candid about his conversations with the Venusian, especially concerning their concept of God. As it turns out, the word *God* is not in their vocabulary. They prefer to reference the "Creator of All" as their overlord, and they fault us for not adhering to the "Laws of the Creator instead of laws of, of course, materialism as Earth man does."[23]

Philosophically we weren't getting it, but physically they were getting us. When asked if any Earth people had been taken away in a spacecraft, Orthon became less forthright. However, and I quote, "He smiled broadly, and in a half-way manner nodded his head in the affirmative, although I felt that he was not to willing to give that information."[24] Adamski was told not to mention it further. Further increasing the sense of intrigue, he says that Orthon told him several other things he couldn't mention either— the same admonition previously given to Benjamin Creme. Although Mr. Creme said that he could vouch for the authenticity of Adamski's association with the Space Brothers, he didn't have the liberty to speak of his own Space Brother involvement: "The nature of this work I am afraid I must not reveal, but many misconceptions about them and their activities which I had held were rectified at this time."[25]

Williamson, on the other hand, was not so confined to secrecy. He was an open follower of the American prewar activist, anarchist, and occultist William Dudley Pelley and Pelley's Hitler-loving Silver Shirts clan, who were seen as the American complement to Hitler's Brown Shirts. Pelly's anti-Semitism and fascination with the occult fit nicely with the Master DK, via Alice A. Bailey's anti-Semitic, anti-Christian teachings.

Pelley, who claimed to have gone to the "other side," dove headfirst into the occult sciences from which he would establish Soulcraft, a religion consisting of a mixture of Theosophy, Jainism, Spiritualism, and Hinduism. Central to the Soulcraft teachings is the belief that "star guests," as Pelley called them, were responsible for creating the human race on Earth. It's funny how God can get the word out on who created us, but apparently star guests 'fess up only in private.

In the Soulcraft journal, *Valor*, Pelley openly hailed the arrival of UFOs and enthusiastically embraced the ufology movement. Pelley even claimed to have seen a UFO in October 1953 and regularly published reports of sightings by Soulcraft employees, one being George Hunt Williamson. Williamson, who by then had gained notoriety from his association with George Adamski, became an active promoter of the Soulcraft religion. While Pelley seized the opportunity to use UFOs in his Soulcraft religion, Williamson first concentrated on the spacemen and then incorporated UFOs into the religion. A space-based vision of a new world was set in motion.

Scott Beekman, writing of William Dudley Pelley in his book by the same name, elaborates: "Like Pelley, Williamson stressed reincarnation and a golden 'New Age' that will dawn after the apocalyptic battle that inaugurates the Aquarian Age."[26] Beekman believed that much of Pelley's religious ideas continued to circulate in various offshoots, long after his Soulcraft religion had waned, in a "Bastardized Liberation-Theosophy" version seen in such spiritual descendants as Bridge to Freedom, Summit Lighthouse, Christ's Truth Church, the Aetherius Society, and the "I AM" theology of Guy and Edna Ballard.[27]

Williamson, like Adamski, would go on to establish his own career as a UFO investigator and contactee. However, Adamski was far from drifting out of the public's view, nor was he lacking in the public's opinion of him. To be continued.

Meanwhile, across the pond the Findhorn community was abuzz with channeled messages from Venusians who were obligingly ready to take advantage of the landing pad, but apparently had not been able to do so because of inclement weather conditions. In 1954, Peter Caddy, his wife, Eileen, Anne Edwards (the psychic Naomi), and company were now fast on their way to learning the secrets of the universe. They had been receiving channeled messages from Lukano, a captain of a Venusian vessel that had been cruising the neighborhood. Lukano connected with Caddy just in time to issue a warning of an impending catastrophic event of such magnitude that some of the locals, the chosen ones, would have to be picked up by the good-natured saucer people and taken out of harm's way.

When that didn't happen, possibly because of landing conditions again, another message was received that led Caddy to believe that umpteen flying saucers from Mars and Venus were headed our way on a mission to touch down and tell the Earthlings that we were, once again, on the brink of disaster. According to Andy Roberts, Caddy told reporters that "The main thing is to be nice to them … they have to be met with friendship. They are trying to help us."[28] Otherwise it was a no-go for a ride out of the impending holocaust, I assume. It didn't happen. One has to wonder if the ETs were having a chicken little syndrome about the sky falling, had poor timing in estimating disasters, or were playing these people like a fiddle.

This type of scenario is played out over and over today with other contactees, as if the ETs are striving to present themselves as heroes whom we should respectfully welcome to Earth. They may be coming from Mars, or they may be coming from Venus, or they may be here already.

Back to Adamski. Bubbling up from the cauldron of knowledge comes a surprising revelation. According to theosophist and author Gerard Aartsen, Adamski realized later in life that he wasn't simply the *contactee* of a Venusian—he *was* a Venusian. That must have been a jolting surprise. Although Adamski's awareness of his Venusian identity may have occurred later in his life, preparations for his enlightenment began early on.

Furthering his claims about Adamski's specialness in *George Adamski: A Herald for the Space Brothers*, Aartsen relays an odd story. At just four years old, while waiting with his family at a pier for their trip to America, Adamski had a strange encounter. According to Aartsen, a strange man approached the young boy, walked off with him, and minutes later returned him "a different child than his previous self."[29] No comment.

The voyage was a life-changing event for Adamski. Aartsen refers to the account given by author Henry Dohan. In *The Pawn of His Creator*, Henry Dohan writes that while under way to Dunkirk, New York, the Adamskis were approached by a "tall man with dark features" who struck up an immediate friendship with the family. The new acquaintance, whom Dohan has named Uncle Sid, spent quite a lot of time with the young Adamski during the voyage.[30]

After their arrival in America, the friendship with Uncle Sid continued for many years with frequent visits to the Adamskis' home. Upon the death of George's father, Uncle Sid took over the parental duties of raising the boy, even persuading George's mother to allow the twelve-year-old to go to a private school, a Lamas monastery in Tibet. Uncle Sid offered to personally sponsor George, and Mrs. Adamski agreed.

Adamski spent three years in Tibet learning the spiritual practices of the East, mastering meditation techniques, and "acquiring yogic abilities and healing powers."[31] It was on no mere whim that Adamski followed the teachings of Blavatsky, Bailey, and the masters, as according to Gerard Aartsen, "Uncle Sid was in fact a Space Brother."[32] Of course.

Benjamin Creme, who met Adamski in 1958, became totally convinced that all of Adamski's claims of meeting the Space Brothers were true. Although he knew Adamski at that time, he had already developed a comradeship with another UFO contactee, George King (1919–1997).

King was the founder of the Aetherius Society, another Theosophy-based UFO organization for which Benjamin Creme served as vice president from 1957 to 1959. The society was formed in 1955 and named for King's Venusian master, Aetherius. King, who was reportedly born psychic, became the "primary terrestrial mental channel" for this master, possibly thanks to his longtime practice of yoga.

In *Contacts with the Gods from Space: Pathway to the New Millennium*, cowritten with Richard Lewis, King writes of his calling. On a Saturday morning in 1954, King heard a disembodied voice abruptly commanding him to "Prepare yourself! You are to become the voice of Interplanetary Parliament."[33] He heard nothing further until days later when, just after he completed a session of yoga breathing, something unimaginable happened. According to King,

> A man walked *through* my locked door, across the creaking boards beneath the faded grey carpet, and sat down opposite to me! The battered old chair creaked as it supported his weight! He was dressed in spotless white robes, which seemed to gleam in the green meditative light I was using. But they were real enough. I had heard the faint swish they made as he crossed the room. I recognized my visitor immediately as a modern leader of Spiritual thought in India. He is very much alive at the moment—living in a somewhat rotund physical body in the Himalayas.[34]

Nice trick if you can pull it off. But according to King, this house call happened just as he claimed. The "Swami," after delivering a pep talk to King about being worthy of the command given by the Master Aetherius, made his exit—again *through* the locked door.

King became the conduit by which Master Aetherius gave his teachings. These teachings, like those of other masters, centered on the beliefs of reincarnation, the Akashic record, karma, Space Brothers, the energies of the masters themselves, and the Great White Brotherhood of spirit beings (which would be deemed racist today). Then there was *King's* special calling. In yet another reflection, ad nauseam, of an alleged coming new era, coauthor Richard Lawrence emotes, "Sir George was born under the sign of Aquarius—fittingly since one of his tasks has been to pave the way for the Aquarian Age."[35] He would have company.

Howard Menger, another contactee, came on the scene in the late 1950s with his own claims of meeting extraterrestrials. Menger conducted "Adamski-style" chats with the friendly Venusian brothers and documented these encounters in *From Outer Space to You* and *The High Bridge Incident*.[36] Not unlike other contactees, Menger claimed to have met his first space being in the woods near his home in Hunterdon County, New Jersey, at the age of ten.

Then there was Daniel Fry, who had been employed as an engineer at the White Sands Proving Ground in New Mexico. Fry claimed that after boarding a remote-controlled spheroid- shaped spacecraft in the desert on July 4, 1949, he flew to New York and back in thirty minutes. That flight and Fry's contact with the pilot, Alan (pronounced *a-lawn*), are documented in *The White Sands Incident*. Although many of his claims raised eyebrows, he managed to gather around him a faithful following and establish an organization called Understanding. The membership would grow internationally with a focus not necessarily UFO or mystical in nature, although it allowed for both. According to a 1973 report by University of California professor Robert S. Ellwood, who researched Fry's organization and their member meetings, there was no particular religious practice connected with the meeting. The only exception was the New Age prayer, "The Great Invocation," from the Alice Bailey writings.[37]

Other 1950s contactees such as George Van Tassel and Truman Bethurum joined the book circuit and publicity campaign with their own Space Brother contacts. The world was a kinder, gentler, place back then. Friendly extraterrestrials arrived on a meet-and-greet basis, warning us of our ability to destroy the earth by nuclear energy and weapons (something we had obviously figured out for ourselves), yet offering no solutions to these problems other than to say it was up to us. Would advanced beings so concerned about our welfare travel across the universe to simply shrug their shoulders at our imminent demise?

Some believe the Space Brothers will play an important role in the transitioning of Earth to a more wholesome, all-inclusive habitat. According to popular belief among many who want to believe that our extraterrestrial friends are here on some type of "benevolent mission for the Galactic Federation," as expressed in an article on skygaze.com,[38] the Brothers view Earth's inhabitants as warmongering primitives with atomic weapons. Many believe the Brothers, as good parents, will step in to save us from our own annihilation with an all-too-familiar frame of reference. Although various scenarios could play out, the common theme is that when Earth is on the eve of destruction, our galactic Brothers will step in and offer their services to save us—including, if necessary, relocating people to more stable surroundings by granting passage, aboard their spaceships, to another planet or celestial location out of the danger zone.

One cannot help but smell an extraterrestrial rat in all this—secretive abductions, a new age with intergalactic promotion of socialism, mimicking Christian Bible prophecy intermeshed with undisclosed secrets of things to come, via the Space Brothers and others. With spiritual trappings from the Far East and their own exalted godhood, how can we lose?

Whether these accounts are real or made-up, they serve the purpose of implanting the idea of space people as our intermediaries in a far advanced galaxy of enlightened beings, such as the ancients who have been here before and will be here once again.

Who are they? Where are they? Will they be coming back? What do they want? There is more at work with these aliens than most people realize, or at least other people hope so. In the end, will we see them as teachers or our spiritual better half? David Whitehouse believes the latter: "One day we may converse with an alien. A future Pope and it may discuss questions of faith."[39]

And what would such a being tell us? For a land-based pilgrim of truth, not much is lauded as unique or exceptional. It is as if humankind has lost interest in any terrestrial guidance, opting to reach out to the stars for the ultimate definitive explanation of who we are and where we came from. Certainly the fascination with the heavens transcends all generations with an overwhelming desire and aspiration to seek whatever is out there, and to leave our earthly confines to go up to the clouds and soar among the heavens. And in time, humankind will.

What is the longing, the fascination with what's out there, that has so enraptured us? Why do we seek answers from the outer regions of space? What is this desire to ascend to whoever or whatever is out there, or to bring whatever down here? To reach out and touch something outside ourselves as evidence of our own being? Are we alone? In reality, we have already received our answer. Do we not care—or can we not fathom the idea—that an extraterrestrial traveler has already come to us, an envoy from heaven, the Son of God Himself, the one we know as Jesus? Jesus never told us that we were silly in our assumptions of life out there. In fact, He confirmed it—*and* provided a way through Him to go there.

This off-planet divine being, Jesus, taught us, lived among us, died among us and for us, and yet lived. It was an act of redemption for those who will understand and believe who their Creator is. There are creatures and masters from other realms who victimize Earth and choose to dwell here, but for believers in Jesus, they are an active yet already defeated foe.

Jesus promised to return to this planet someday to reclaim those among this creation who know Him and believe in Him. Jesus Christ completed His mission, His sacrifice, and returned home. And although we don't know where He went upon leaving Earth, we do know the direction He took—*up*.

CHAPTER FOUR
Up

In the year 22, third month of winter, sixth hour of the
day, ... it was found a circle of fire coming from the sky.
—Pharaoh Thutmose III, 1460 BC[40]

Religious conflict was not the only issue facing the ancient Egyptians
during the time of the pharaohs. But for many rulers and kingdoms of
the day, conflicts that could not be settled by reasonable means led to war,
and Egypt was no exception. Divide and conquer was a near standard
throughout the ancient world, and warfare between those who would be
king was undoubtedly a primary concern of every pharaoh. Battlefield
training was an important leadership skill of the pharaohs, as with any
ruling monarch, and Thutmose III excelled at it. He is considered by many
historians to have been the Napoleon of Egypt, having captured 350 cities
during his reign and most of the ancient empires spanning the region from
the Euphrates to Nubia.

One battle, however, might have gone in favor of Egypt's archenemy,
the Nabians, had it not been for some unexpected help of such peculiarity
that it left even the pharaoh dumbfounded. One ancient report describes
a bloody battle that was raging on both sides, with the Nabians gaining
ground on the Egyptians. During the heat of battle, when all seemed lost,
something quite unexpected happened. A brilliant star descended from the
sky and began to advance on the Nabians, radiating such brilliance that
it blinded the Nabians so that they could no longer continue to fight. The
Nabians became so terrified that they gave up the battle and retreated with

haste to the surrounding mountains to hide from the terrifying object, thereby giving the victory to the Egyptians.

Unexpected help from above was not limited to the Egyptians. In 329 BC, Alexander the Great wrote of having his army buzzed by *silver shields*, causing an entire regiment of soldiers, elephants, and horses to frantically disperse in all directions. As if that wasn't troubling enough, Alexander's army encountered unidentified flying objects during the siege of the Phoenician city of Tyre in 332 BC. Both armies were fighting to the death, but the fighting abruptly stopped when soldiers on both sides were stunned by a strange spectacle in the sky above them. Peter Brooksmith writes of this incredible event:

> Soldiers on both sides watched in astonishment as a large flying shield, moving in formation with four smaller shields, circled over the city. Suddenly the large UFO shot a beam of light at the city wall in front of the army and drove a hole right through it. Further beams were fired from the UFO and these shattered towers and other defenses of the citadel. Alexander's troops quickly took advantage of the situation and poured into the city, and the UFOs remained overhead until the army had fully secured the town. The UFOs then took off together and disappeared.[41]

No one could have expected that armed reinforcements would come from the sky to give Alexander the victory and command of the city. Many ancient cultures reported fast-moving stars, unusual lights, and burning torches in the sky, but it is remarkable to read of shields that could not only fly in formation, but were armed and dangerous. Apparently what was *up there* was intrinsically interested in what was going on *down here*.

Of course this is not the only account of lights being involved in the affairs of humans. For example, the Bible tells of the Children of Israel being led through the wilderness by a pillar of light by day and a pillar of fire by night. There is no reason to assume, however, that the lights were UFOs as we think of today.

Even the Roman emperor Constantine had his run-in with a strange object in the sky. On the eve of battle, Constantine and his men were suddenly dumbstruck by unusual objects hovering in the sky above them. And as if to deliver a message to the emperor, these objects came together in the form of a cross. The shaken emperor was awestruck by the sight, and his resulting zeal and euphoria led him to order his entire army to paint crosses on their shields before marching into battle—a battle they would ultimately win. In the aftermath of that incredible event, Christianity through Constantine became the official religion of Rome.

These incredible encounters decided the outcomes of wars and conflicts among men, but they apparently resulted in conflicts among the nonhuman entities themselves. In 103 BC, for example, there was a well-documented report of shields clashing in the night sky above the cities of Amelia and Todi in Italy. According to researcher Jacques Vallee, "It was reported that at night there had been seen in the heavens flaming spears, and shields, which at first moved in different directions, and then clashed together assuming the formations and movement of men in battle, and finally some of them would give way, while others pressed on in pursuit, and all streamed away to the westward."[42]

A similar aggressive event took place in England in October 1253, when a large bright star suddenly appeared out of a black cloud within close range of two smaller stars. According to the report from Nicholas of Finder, "A battle royal soon commenced, the small stars charging the great star again and again, so that it began to diminish in size, and sparks of fire fell from the combatants."[43] Another report from England in 1660 told of a dogfight that took place between two large spheres and lasted nearly two hours. The European continent didn't fare much better. A celestial fracas broke out in Languedoc, France, in 1395, when five small stars were observed attacking one big star.

It would be difficult to say *what* was present during these encounters other than bright stars, lights, and brilliant objects appearing in formation. The one common factor was that they all appeared unexpectedly and were observed in the sky over land. However, that was not always the case. The famed explorer Christopher Columbus made notation in his ship's log of observing a strange light while at sea on the evening of October 11, 1492. He described this unidentifiable light as best he could for the era, as "a small wax candle that rose and lifted up." His son Ferdinand, who was present with him on deck and saw the light, also described it as a candle that went up and down.[44]

Until Columbus's time, these strange lights or stars seemed to show up at times of important events such as travel, wars, and exploration. They were recorded as interacting with the affairs of men on occasion, but there was no explanation of the strange interactions between the objects themselves. One event that challenged the typical order of things occurred in Germany in the city of Nuremberg on April 4, 1561. The residents of the city awoke to a frightening event taking place in the early morning hours, high above their city. Hundreds of local residents witnessed one of the most astounding events to take place in broad daylight and in plain sight.

Odd-shaped objects were streaking back and forth across the sky as if engaged in combat with one another. These objects were of a variety of sizes, shapes, and colors—black cylinders, blue spheres, red crosses, globes, and one large object that appeared to contain smaller globes that shot out of it and immediately joined in the fray. The entire incident was documented in a written report by a local printer, Hans Glaser. Newspapers of that time were called broadsheets because of their large size, which made it easy to post in public for all to read. Included in that broadsheet was a drawing of the fierce battle, and an English translation of Glaser's report reads as follows: "In the morning of April 14, 1561, at daybreak, between 4 and 5 a.m., a dreadful apparition occurred on the sun, and then was seen in Nuremberg in the city, before the gates and in the country by many men and women. At first there appeared in the middle of the sun two blood-red-circular arcs, just like the moon in its last quarter. And in the sun, above and below and on both sides, the color was blood, there stood a round ball of partly dull, partly black ferrous color."[45]

Everyone's attention was riveted on the skies above them. More citizens began to gather in great numbers to observe the blood-red floating balls that began to take center stage in the furious fighting. Some flanked or circled the object described as the sun. Many balls appeared in formations, such as three in a line and four in a square, while others flew alone. Between the balls could be seen a few large red crosses intermingled with large rods and globes, which began to fight among themselves, especially the globes. "The globes flew back and forth among themselves and fought vehemently with each other for over an hour."[46] Then, as if they could fight no longer, some began to burn and to fall to the earth, wasting away in intense smoke. "After all this there was something like a black spear, very long and thick, sighted; the shaft pointed to the east, the point pointed west. Whatever such signs mean God alone knows," wrote Glaser.[47]

This bizarre battle lasted for over an hour and in plain sight of many witnesses, so one would be hard-pressed to doubt the accuracy of Glaser's report, documented further by a woodcut depiction of the fight. Although the people got no answers to their questions about who or what was in their skies that day, there is little doubt that *they* were there.

Approximately five years later, a similar scene played out in Basel, Switzerland, on August 7, 1566. Again it happened at dawn, when the town was besieged by massive numbers of *black spheres* darting across the sky. Just as at Nuremberg, the people were dumbfounded by what they were witnessing as the strange event unfolded before their eyes. One local resident, Samuel Coccius, chronicled the action: "At the time when the sun rose, one saw many large black balls which moved at high speed in the air toward the sun, then made half-turns, banging one against the others as if they were fighting a battle or a combat, a great number of them became red and igneous, thereafter they were consumed and died out."[48] Like Glaser, Coccius documented the event with a woodcut picture of the battle scene. Spheres or balls, stars, and shining shields would continue to be reported throughout the Middle Ages and beyond.

Fast-forward to September 1786, when a huge ball of fire and brilliant light manifested during a hurricane that hit England. At first many witnesses would have thought it a fireball or even a ball lightning, except for the fact that the event lasted forty minutes. In 1779, large numbers of luminous globes filled the air over Boulogne, France, on the same day that an earthquake struck the city. These early reports might be seen as precursors of strange anomalies that seem to occur during times of crisis, affecting people and the earth itself.

One modern example is the well-documented Foo Fighters of World War II. Described as spears or orbs of light, these fearless orbs appeared mysteriously alongside bombers and other aircraft of Allied and Axis forces alike. Both sides thought they were secret aircraft deployed by the enemy, and both sides denied it.

More recent accounts include orbs that were caught in photographs and film as New York's Twin Towers fell after the horrific terrorist attack of September 11, 2001. Additionally, orbs were seen and captured on film flying over the surging waters flowing over the debris field in the aftermath of the 2011 tsunami that struck the east coast of Sendal, Japan. One can't help but wonder if these objects were the same anomalies seen during ancient times.

Globes, spheres, balls, stars, shields, and lights seem to have monopolized the type of aerial phenomenon reported since ancient times. In even the earliest reports, such sightings appeared to be a hands-off type of encounter limited to aerial sightings, leaving the witnesses bewildered yet unscathed, still not knowing what or even how to adequately describe what they were seeing. After all, in ancient times no one had seen them except from the ground up, but with time and technology, things would change.

In 1782, the Montgolfier brothers were hard at work in France on a project that would change the world: the hot air balloon. The following year, the brothers made their first successful launch, carrying aloft a sheep, duck, and rooster. There would be no turning back. Humankind would soon be consumed with the idea of staking our claim in the heavens. It wasn't long before men were taking to the skies in large numbers, as a new mode of travel began to take shape in rapidly expanding avenues of use.

In 1793, Jean-Pierre Blanchard was first to make a manned flight of a balloon in America. He took off from within a prison yard in Philadelphia, Pennsylvania, and landed in Gloucester County, New Jersey. It is reported that President George Washington himself witnessed the takeoff.

Hot air balloons could be free sailing or tethered, and the coarse, basket-woven gondolas could easily carry people and equipment. It didn't take long for the military to realize the tactical advantage of the view from *up above,* and these balloons quickly became strategic airborne observation posts during many war campaigns. The first use of hot air balloons by United States military was the Union Army Balloon Corps in 1861, during the American Civil War. That war served as a stepping-stone toward another advancement, the airship.

In 1863, while the Civil War raged on all fronts, a young German officer, having obtained permission from the German Army, traveled to America to serve as a military observer. The twenty-four-year-old officer requested and obtained a formal meeting with President Abraham Lincoln, after which he was granted privileges to move freely from one post to another within the Union Army. His name was Ferdinand Adolph Heinrich August, Graf von Zeppelin. After a brief tour of duty with the Union Army, Graf von Zeppelin—or Count Zeppelin, as he was more commonly known—left the war theater to see more of the country. His travels took him to St. Paul, Minnesota, where he had a fateful meeting with a former Army Balloon Corps member, John Steiner. In *When Giants Roamed the Sky*, Dale Topping writes, "Steiner had an idea for a 'long and slender' balloon with a rudder, which would enable it to 'reach its destination more smoothly and more surely.' This could only have been a dirigible balloon."[49]

Count Zeppelin was highly impressed, and he would credit Steiner with his inspiration to build such an airship of his own. Years later, on July 2, 1900, the Luftschiff Zeppelin 1 (LZ1) was released from her moorings on her maiden flight at Lake Constance, between Germany and Austria. In the late 1800s, however, while Count Zeppelin's first dirigible was still several years away, stories began to trickle in with descriptions of strange airships both at home and abroad.

On the evening of March 23, 1909, a London police constable had an amazing encounter with a long cylindrical object with bright lights that was emitting a whirring sound as it moved at high speed across the sky. While walking his patrol along Cromwell Road in Peterborough, Constable Kettle heard what he thought was a car approaching from behind him. He turned to see the approaching vehicle, but there was nothing there. He then realized the sound was coming from above him, and he looked up to see a large object blotting out the stars as it moved across the sky. It had a bright light attached to it, and the whirring noise it made was quite audible. His report made all the local papers, and soon there were widespread reports of people sighting similar objects all over England. Referred to as the "scare ships," they appeared to be of the same description as was seen by Constable Kettle. No one knows for sure what was being seen in those early days, but it was quite apparent that they were seeing *something*.

England seemed to be under attack by mysterious airships in the late 1800s, but the United States was not faring much better. Reports were coming in all across the country of strange airship activity, causing widespread panic among the populace.

One particularly odd report comes from a Mr. Robert Hibbard, of Sioux, Iowa, who in March 1897, claimed to have had his pant leg snagged by what he described as an anchor lowered from some type of airship. In April of that same year, Kansas rancher Alexander Hamilton claimed to have witnessed a rather large airship with strange beings on board slowly descend out of the night sky over his ranch and carry off one of the cows from the corral. Although the truth of his claim is highly suspect, even thought by some to be an absolute fraud, it did serve to plant the idea of possible cattle rustlers from the sky, as did thoughts of visitors from the sky from a report of a crashed spacecraft in Aurora, Texas in April of that same year. Townsfolk reportedly buried the pilot. These eyewitness reports weren't limited to the Eastern or Southern areas of the country. Many of the strange airships were heading west.

Cowboys and ETs. As if the American West wasn't wild enough in those days, there were stories of visitors to the western plains who were not settlers. Strange objects were seen soaring through the skies of the Old West, and many a witness was hankering for a chance to talk about them.

John LeMay and Noe Torres have written an interesting and insightful book, *The Real Cowboys and Aliens*, that documents some of the earliest reports of unknown flying objects in the Old West. Although the term *flying saucer* has been associated with a modern-day description, the term was used much earlier. According to LeMay and Torres, "Strange flying ships seen in the sky were first called 'flying saucers' in the 1940s. But long before that, back in 1878, a farmer in North Texas saw something in the sky that he described as a 'large saucer.' It was the first time in history that the word 'saucer' was used for a UFO."[50]

Giving credit where credit is due, we can see some similar descriptions that nicely match descriptions of UFOs today. Newspaper clippings from the late 1800s report unusual objects in the western skies, strange glowing lights, cigar-shaped craft that hover and then take off at great speeds, expanding and contracting airships, red fireballs, and other airborne objects that left cowboys and townspeople confused and apprehensive. UFO reports flooded the newspapers with wild descriptions of the anomalous objects, and read much like what is reported today—and like today, many of those objects remained unidentified.

The late 1800s, however, defined our advancements in knowledge and technology. The machine age was well under way and the sky literally was the limit. Static film cameras gave way to moving picture cameras, offering silly, often bawdy entertainment. Some early motion pictures captured the realities of life: wars, love stories, fantasies of ancient kingdoms, and historical pieces such as depictions of the Civil War.

The 1800s also capitalized on the public's fascination with the wild imagination of Jules Verne in *Twenty Thousand Leagues Under the Sea* in 1870, followed by H. G. Wells's sci-fi classic *The War of The Worlds* in 1898. The thought of *something else* out there, whether friend or foe, left the public thirsting for more. *Off-worldly* fantasies gave way to *otherworldly* offerings, which spiked public interest in spiritualism and theosophy. The enticement to contact departed loved ones opened the floodgates to more dances with the devil in the form of spirit boards and table tipping, all meant to heighten the desire for more contact with an obliging spirit host.

Come the 1900s, a genuine desire to ascend to the heights of the heavens, sans spirits, was taking hold of the scientific minds of the day and inspired showmen. There was an undeniable rise of interest of what was *up there*, not only in our skies but in our universe as well. Humans looking from the ground up were no longer content to be observers. One of history's earliest silent films, *A Trip to the Moon*, produced in 1902 by French director Georges Melies, tells the story of space travelers being launched via a canon-propelled capsule to the moon. These early astronauts of the cinema are met and captured by lunar inhabitants called Selenites. The ever-resourceful earthlings escape captivity and return to Earth with one captured Selenite in tow. Although this film was meant as science fiction fantasy, including the moon as a giant face of a man, it instilled the idea of space travel as a dream that could be achieved. But first humankind would have to figure out how to do it, and it would take more than a lighter-than-air Zeppelin.

Through the minds of dreamers and soon-to-be aeronautics engineers, progress was made. The industrial age was about to get wings. Orville and Wilber Wright, after years of experimenting with kites and full-sized gliders, a popular fascination in the 1890s, made the first successful flight of a motorized airplane. The prototype plane took flight on December 17, 1903, in North Carolina, as Orville Wright soared over the fields at Kitty Hawk for an entire twelve seconds. After that first baby step, humankind soon mastered the airspace with speed and agility never before experienced. Whatever might be up there in the skies would now have company. In a real sense, we had gone up to *them*.

Soon followed the manufacture of airplanes on a large scale, with Germany, France, and England taking the lead. From the flexing of innovation by the new airborne additions to military might, combined with social unrest, it appeared that Europe was priming itself for war. Sure enough, hostilities broke out in Europe on July 28, 1914, and brought into play new battlefields that now included the earth *and* the sky.

Although airplanes were quickly becoming a valuable resource that would later replace Zeppelins as scout ships, those airships had not lost their appeal. Zeppelins, blimps, and large rigid airships were still making their way through the skies around the world, and although their use was primarily commercial, it was not difficult to see the military applications. Germany pounced on the idea, and bomb-deploying Zeppelins were quickly on the scene.

German bomber blimps became a formidable threat during the war with their nonstop bombings over England. The dirigibles were large, dangerous, and feared by many. Lookout posts, which consisted of large balloons and gondolas, were set up to scan the horizon and signal the approach of enemy blimps, while dual-winged biplanes waited at the ready to intercept. Perhaps something *other* was up there as well. Humankind was about to make aerial contact with unidentified flying objects on their own turf.

In *UFOs in Wartime*, Mack Maloney describes one such encounter that occurred in the night sky over London by British Royal Naval Air Service sub-lieutenant J. E. Morgan on January 31, 1916. Flying over London, Morgan was on the lookout for German Zeppelins when he spotted something strange in the sky above him. Maloney provides the details of the sighting, as first documented in 1925 in a book by Captain Joseph Morris titled *German Air Raids on Great Britain, 1914–1918*. Maloney writes, "Morgan had ascended about a mile above London when he saw a bizarre object flying slightly higher than him. He described it as having a row of lighted windows and looking something like a railway carriage with the blinds drawn."[51]

Morgan, thinking that he had indeed come upon a German Zeppelin, closed in for the attack. Maloney tells us, "The mysterious object was about 100 feet above him when Morgan first spotted it. Again, still thinking it was German blimp, he drew the only weapon he had—his service pistol—and began firing at it. Suddenly the object shot straight up at tremendous speed and disappeared into the night. The object rose so quickly in fact, that Morgan thought his own plane was actually losing altitude. This disorientation caused him to crash land in a Marsh."[52]

Although it is difficult to determine exactly what Morgan was firing at, we do know by this account that it was startling enough to cause an experienced pilot to crash his plane. Things on the front were beginning to wind down and an armistice ending WWI was reached on November 11, 1918. The war ended, but not the sightings. Even America's World War I flying ace Eddie Rickenbacker would later say, "Flying saucers are real. Too many good men have seen them, that don't have hallucinations."[53]

As the decades progressed, more mysterious objects were being sighted—in natural settings and performing unnatural feats. Peter Brookesmith gives an account of an object seen in the skies over Sausalito, California, in 1927 when writer Ella Young while sitting outside the Madrona Hotel reported seeing a cigar-shaped craft shoot out of a cloud beyond the bay, and across the sky toward Tamalpais. It was not shaped like any airship she knew. "It was long and slender, of yellow color, and traveling at great speed … it seem to progress alternately contracting and elongating its body."[54] This is undoubtedly an early observation of a shape-shifting UFO.

A wave of sightings washed over the continents, and reports of the odd airships began to come in from all over the world. As more modern airships were built, it seemed the unidentified flying objects began to grow and transform in tandem. Were they going stealth by mimicking the design and technology of our aircraft? Or maybe vice versa?

The modern dirigible was the standard for intercontinental travel in the 1920s and 1930s. Their enormous size and opulence offered many tourists the advantages of flight and the inspiration of sightseeing from the air. The dirigible was also the inspiration for another craft, a mother ship.

Could the event that took place in the skies over Germany in the 1500s be the inspiration for a new group of dirigibles? Floating aircraft carriers were about to make their debut.

In the mid-1930s, the United States Navy began the manufacturing of large ridged dirigibles to serve as airborne aircraft carriers. Carrying an onboard squadron of planes would allow for longer air patrols, as well as the ability to quickly deploy fighter planes from a large hanger bay for defense or observation. Only twenty feet shorter than Germany's *Hindenburg*, the large airships soon took to the air on coast-to-coast maneuvers. Airships such as the USS *Akron* (ZRS-4) and USS *Macon* (ZRS-5), for example, measured an enormous 785 feet in length. On board was a crew of one hundred men and five Curtis Sparrow Hawk biplanes. The Sparrow Hawks were equipped with two .30in M1919 machine guns, and they could be launched from and retrieved into the airships' large internal hanger bays. These carriers could float, hover, or fly through the air at eighty miles an hour. The dark, imposing shadows of these huge ships cruising through the skies could be seen traversing the landscape all across the country. Although these mother ships could master the air, in the end they could not master inclement weather. The *Akron* and *Macon* were both lost at sea because of storms that sent them crashing into the ocean. We still had a lot to learn.

Dirigibles were not the only aircraft to hover and fly. In 1930, a rather unusual object caught the eye of the world-renowned astronomer and discoverer of the planet Pluto, Dr. Clyde Tombaugh. This is from the account documented by Paris Flammonde:

> At 4:47, on the clear, bright afternoon of July 10, while driving down a New Mexico highway with his wife and two daughters, he observed a "curious shiny object, almost immobile." It appeared to have a wobbling motion. The shape was elliptical, the surface seemed polished, and the outline was defined. Shortly after it was initially noticed the unknown moved up into a cloud cluster. Reemerging, it began to rise at an accelerating speed, which the astronomer estimated to be from six to nine hundred miles an hour. In reporting his sighting to the military,

Professor Tombaugh concluded: "The remarkably sudden ascent convinced me it was an absolutely novel airborne device." [55]

If you can't trust the observations of an astronomer, whose can you trust?

In 1930, airplanes didn't have this type of speed and maneuverability. Especially since the country was suffering from the stock market crash of 1929, it wouldn't have been feasible to make money available for any type of aircraft prototype. In the United States and Europe, times were hard and people were just getting by. The prohibition of alcohol in the United States would give rise to gangsters and bootleggers, such as Al Capone and John Dillinger, and crime was on the upswing. Although crime syndicates would eventually be reined in by the FBI, Americans were feeling uneasy, and reports of large unidentified flying objects were only adding to the tension.

Things were not much better overseas. Between 1932 and 1937, Scandinavians were spooked by low-flying unidentifiable aircraft they called ghost fliers. These craft were described as gray single-winged machines with multiple engines, which would have been unconventional at the time. This was enough to cause alarm in Sweden, Norway and Finland, while the United States was about to experience a major alarm of its own.

Far from the madding crowd, Americans were spending many leisurely hours at home. The radio was the focal point for news and entertainment for the entire family, who listened to favorite weekly broadcasts of live music bands, comedians, serials and dramatic plays, including those of the science fiction variety. The public's imaginations and suspicions of an impending invasion by Martians or evil moon dwellers would, ironically, seem to come to fruition on the evening of October 30, 1938. If the idea of some threat from *out there* was not in the minds of many people, it would be now. Strange things were happening in Grover's Mill, New Jersey.

Grover's Mill became ground zero in an 1938 radio broadcast by Orson Welles, in the Mercury Theater's live on-air presentation of the H. G. Wells novel *War of the Worlds*, in which Martian invaders land on a farm in New Jersey and begin a merciless invasion of Earth. The play begins with an interruption to their regular radio broadcast to inform listeners of the report of a Martian landing taking place at the Grover's Mill farm. Actor reporters read their lines, and phony eyewitness accounts were broadcast of ruthless aliens deploying hellish spindly-legged machines in an all-out invasion of the Jersey landscape. Martians were wreaking havoc and running roughshod over the citizens of Grover's Mill. Pretend witnesses gave testimonies of family and friends being picked off by the blasts from the ray guns of the soulless, murderous Martian creatures. It was meant as a Halloween entertainment—but it wasn't.

Listeners who had not heard the opening disclaimers by the station, saying that it was only a theater performance, were moved to mass hysteria. Some listeners called local authorities or talk shows, frightened mobs formed in city streets, and other people—in a mad frenzy—packed up their belongings and left their homes.

The reaction of terrified listeners showed just how vulnerable we are to the power of suggestion. The producer, John Houseman, remarked about how quickly our minds could accept an entire series of events in just a short amount of time. He would later write, "Our actual broadcasting time, from the first mention of the meteorites to the fall of New York City, was less than forty minutes. During that time, men travelled long distances; large bodies of troops were mobilized, cabinet meetings were held, savage battles fought on land and in the air. And millions of people accepted it, emotionally if not logically."[56] This is important. The idea of creatures from space was amusing to most listeners, but the experience proved that people do indeed believe in the possibility of aliens from space coming to our earth.

Another stage was being set—not in space, but in Europe—and it was no theater performance. In the late 1930s, Europe was in a political uproar once again. Hitler and his Nazis were making a move on the nation-states of Europe, and soon the saber rattling of 1939 had erupted into full-blown war unlike any war ever seen in centuries past. Europe had witnessed the rise of a monster called Adolf Hitler. The United States, like Europe, was still recovering from the devastating depression of 1929, and Americans were in no mood for war. But with Hitler declaring war on the world, it was only a matter of time.

While the world was at war with the Nazis, cinema heroes such as Flash Gordon were duking it out with thugs emanating from all points of the universe. Still our minds were heading off from the realities of wars to the consolation of being rescued from the threat coming from the skies. That threat was real.

The 1940s would see considerable advancements in aerodynamics and shipbuilding, and not a moment too soon. Europe had launched itself on a path to total annihilation on land, on sea, and in the heavens above us. The skies over Europe echoed with the roar of B17 bombers and P51 fighter planes locked in combat against Germany's best. Day after day, night after night, flight crews endured the stomach-churning bombardment of exploding flak, machine-gun fire, air-to-air combat, and the horrific and indelible pictures of planes plummeting nose over tail.

Both Allied and Axis pilots were alerted to possible danger lurking in the skies over the European continent, and all eyes scanned the horizon in earnest to identify any aircraft. However, less identifiable airborne objects began to appear in the latter years of the war. These evasive, mysterious spheres or orbs of light, whose exploits startled and confused flight crews on both sides of the conflict, came to be called Foo Fighters.

Allied forces believed these mysterious craft—or spheres—were a secret weapon of Hitler's Axis powers, while the Axis believed them to be a secret weapon of the Allied forces. The bright orbs of light would appear suddenly and keep pace with aircraft, flying alongside or to the front or back of planes. Pilots named them after Foo, a popular British cartoon character, but there was no *foo* about these fighters. The bright round objects could easily keep pace with any aircraft and then bank away at tremendous speeds.

Sightings of these strange objects were not limited to the European war theater; the objects were appearing in Asia as well. Reports came in to military high commands on the Asian front of mysterious bright objects appearing to the front, sides, and rear of their fighter planes and bombers. The spheres would often conduct benign flybys, but they could be menacing as well. Mysterious things were happening.

One event took place in the Pacific on August 28, 1945, involving twelve airmen from the Fifth Air Force intelligence group aboard a C-46 en route to Tokyo. Flying at ten thousand feet and rapidly approaching Iwo Jima, the crew became startled by three brilliant lights. According to researcher Richard Dolan, "As the plane approached Iwo Jima at ten thousand feet, the crew saw teardrop-shaped objects, brilliantly white—'like burning magnesium'—and closing on a parallel course to the plane."[57]

What happened to the plane next was unexpected and terrifying. "The navigational needles went wild, the left engine faltered and spurted oil, the plane lost altitude, and the crew prepared to ditch. Then, in close formation, the objects faded into a cloudbank. At that moment, the plane's engines restarted, and the crew safely flew on."[58]

The war front was nervous and jittery, but the home front was on edge as well. Since November 1944, the Japanese had been gifting the West Coast of North America with incendiary balloons. They had calculated that hydrogen-inflated paper balloons equipped with incendiary bombs could be launched from Japan and drift along air currents all the way to the United States, where they would land and explode on impact. Most of the balloons, an estimated seven thousand, never made it, but a thousand or so did, resulting mostly in forest fires. A pregnant woman and five children died tragically when they came across one of the balloons in a picnic area near Bly, Oregon. Needless to say, the balloons put the US military on high alert for unknown aircraft and objects entering US airspace, where they would trigger an immediate defensive response. One such scenario played out in Los Angeles in the early morning hours of February 25, 1942.

At approximately 2:25 a.m., air raid sirens began to blare throughout the city of Los Angeles. Frightened residents jumped from their beds to see searchlights fixed on a large object moving through the dark sky over the city. A barrage of antiaircraft fire soon followed, filling the air with the thunder of bursting shells overhead. Despite a salvo of 1,430 pounds of explosives, no object was brought down, but several homes and buildings were destroyed and six civilians were killed. Upon review of the early morning assault, it was decided that the object had not been a Japanese plane, and the invading object has never been officially identified.

Another incident occurred just a month before atomic bombs were dropped on the Japanese islands of Hiroshima and Nagasaki, ending the war in the Pacific and resulting in catastrophic loss of life. In July 1945, Navy Pilot Roland D. Powell, who was based at the Naval Air Station in Pasco, Washington, and five other pilots responded to an alert of an intruder in the airspace over the secret Hanford nuclear plant on the Columbia River. The pilots scrambled their F6 Hellcat Interceptors in pursuit of the intruder and soon caught sight of a large object hovering at sixty-five thousand feet above the facility. According to Jerome Clark, "The pilots, who had never seen anything like this, communicated their puzzlement and confusion to each other. The object was oval-shaped, with a streamlined appearance resembling a stretched-out egg. A pink color, it emitted a vapor from its outside edges, leading Powell to suspect that it was trying to create a cloud in which to hide itself."[59] *Cloud cigars* became a common descriptor of these large obscure objects, which in this case was thought to be the size of "three aircraft carriers placed side by side."[60] But before the pilots could close the object, it shot straight up and disappeared.

As World War II came to an end, reports of Foo Fighters began to wane. Concern over the strange lights in the sky became a moot point relative to the postwar recovery efforts. We had dropped the bomb, and the world was changed forever.

Just two short years after the war ended, another conflict in the skies began to take place over North America. This conflict would change our concept of aerodynamics, shatter our sense of security, and bring our feelings of superiority down to a new low. *They* had arrived.

CHAPTER FIVE
The Unknowns

On April 17, 1952, near the Canadian air base of North Bay in Ontario, several "red spheres" flew by at supersonic speeds and subsequently crossed over the southeastern states at the same high speeds. The next day air defense headquarters for the eastern United States released a statement to the press from Newburgh, N.Y., saying that the detection system had developed a pattern of unknowns in both the northeast and northwest, which appeared potentially dangerous.

—Renato Vesco[61]

Washington, DC. At approximately 11:40 p.m. on Saturday evening, July 19, 1952, air traffic controller Edward Nugent was at his station at Washington National Airport when seven objects suddenly appeared on his radar screen. The unknown objects were only fifteen miles south-southwest of the nation's capital and closing in fast. Nugent immediately became concerned, since there were no known aircraft in the area at the time and he was not able to identify these fast-moving objects.

Nugent immediately notified Harry Barnes, his supervisor, of the objects intruding into DC airspace. Not only were they unannounced, but they also were not following normal flight paths as conventional aircraft would be expected to do. Barnes quickly confirmed the objects on radar and agreed that it was out of the ordinary and that the objects appeared to be moving in an unconventional manner. That was just the beginning of the evening's events. After confirming that Nugent's equipment was functioning properly, Barnes called another of National Airport's radar centers, where controller Howard Cocklin said that he, too, had the objects on his scope *and* that he was staring out the tower window at a bright orange light. Barnes and Cocklin didn't know what the objects were, but they did know for sure that the objects weren't hiding.

Tensions rose to nail-biting level as the controllers watched the objects, which were now passing over the White House and Capitol. Barnes was immediately on the phone to Andrews Air Force Base, and although Andrews was only ten miles south of the airport, they were not initially seeing anything on their scopes. Then William Brady, an airman on duty in the tower at Andrews, sighted an orange ball of fire that took off at tremendous speed. Then Staff Sergeant Charles Davenport observed a red-orange light moving erratically, stopping abruptly, and changing course and altitude several times throughout the night.

Back at National Airport, things were escalating. The control tower reported seeing an orange disc moving along at a three-thousand-foot altitude. Capital Airlines pilot S. C. Pierman was on the runway in his DC-4 ready for takeoff when he observed six "white tailless, fast-moving lights" over a period of fourteen minutes.[62] Those white lights appeared on the tower's radar as well. Sightings continued throughout the night, with all three towers locking on to them at the same time and then watching them vanish off scope.

Around 3:00 a.m. two F-94 fighters from New Castle Air Force Base in Delaware arrived over Washington, only to find that the objects had vanished from view and radar. They continued their patrol until low fuel levels forced them to return to New Castle. Immediately upon their departure the objects returned, leaving the controllers to surmise that the objects possessed intelligence and could monitor radio transmissions and air traffic.

Former Air Force Captain Kevin D. Randle recounted what Barnes, in a calmer state of mind, would later write of the unusual behavior of the objects witnessed that night:

> (The UFOs) became most active around the planes we saw on the scope … (They) acted like a bunch of small kids out playing … directed by some innate curiosity. At

times they moved as a group or cluster, at other times as individuals over widely scattered areas … there is no other conclusion that I can reach but that for six hours there were at least ten unidentified flying objects moving above Washington. They were not ordinary aircraft. I could tell that by their movement on the scope. I can safely deduce that they performed gyrations which no known aircraft could perform. By this I mean that our scopes showed that they could make right angle turns and complete reversal of flight. Nor in my opinion could any natural phenomena such as shooting stars, electrical disturbances or clouds account for these spots on our radar.[63]

The following day, media frenzy was in full swing with reports of the strange objects. "Saucers Swarm Capital Air Force Interceptors in Hot Pursuit" declared one headline, while similar headlines peppered the front pages of newspapers across the country. I am sure the air controllers would have preferred that night to have been a once-in-a-lifetime event, but it wasn't over.

While the air force was fresh from an investigation under the direction of Captain Edward Ruppelt regarding the sightings of the weekend of July 19, the objects returned: "The first round of the second wave of sightings over Washington, D.C., didn't begin at night, nor were they first seen by the radar operators at National Airport. At about two thirty P.M. two radar operators at Langley AFB, fairly near Washington D.C., watched an object on their radar scope for about two minutes. They estimated that it approached Langley from the south at a speed of 2,600 miles an hour at an altitude just under 5,000 feet, and disappeared from the radar scopes when it was only eight miles away."[64]

Twenty minutes later another object was sighted, and further sightings would continue well into the evening hours, seen by both civilian and military pilots from different sectors over Washington, DC. One pilot reported that he was in pursuit of what looked like a brilliant white star that shot past the nose of his plane. A commercial airline crew reported glowing objects in the airspace around them. Interceptor jets were scrambled with the same results—there was no catching the objects. Even though the order had been given to "shoot them down" if they could not talk them down, the pilots were unable to accomplish either directive. They were completely outpaced and outmaneuvered.

Again, a media frenzy ensued, and the public more than ever was riveted by the astounding stories of saucers over the nation's capital. Yellowed newspaper clippings of the events that I found in an old book tell the story:

- "Saucers Seen Near Washington Airport" (Associated Press, July 21, 1952): "The Air Force today said it has received reports of the sighting near Washington National Airport of seven to ten unidentified aerial objects around midnight last Saturday ... Earlier the Air Force said it is receiving flying-saucers reports this Summer at a rate higher than at any time since the initial flood of sightings in 1947."

- "Ghosts in Sky Over D.C. Elude Chase by Jets" (U.P. July 27, 1952): "The Air Force reported today that jet fighters spent several hours last night chasing ghostlike 'objects' over the skies of the nation's capital ... 'We don't know what they are' an Air Force spokesman said, 'We have no concrete evidence that they are flying saucers. Conversely, we have no concrete evidence that they are not flying saucers.'" The article goes on to confirm that the Air Force responded to the Civil Aeronautics Administration's radar report of 12 unknowns. "Officials notified the Air Force and two jet interceptors climbed to meet the strange objects. The jets raced to the area of the 'unknowns,' which they reached 11:25 P.M. One of the pilots, who was not named, almost immediately spotted four lights in the sky ahead of him. He said he tried to overtake the lights but was unable to reach them. He said they were about 10 miles ahead of him and he was unable to decrease this distance. When the objects were picked up on the radar screen, their speed was estimated at 100 miles an hour. On the basis of the Air Force report, the top speed was in excess of 550 miles an hour inasmuch as the jets, which are capable of 600 m.p.h. could not catch up with them."

- "Jets Lose Race With Glowing Globs—Mystery Lights Again Streak Over Capital" (July 28): "The Air Force, which always has maintained a skeptical attitude about flying saucers, said today that it was investigating the unidentified objects as glowing white lights, that were spotted by radar and then visually by Air Force and commercial pilots Saturday night."
- "Mysterious Sky Riders Return to Washington—Swoop Over Washington for 6 Hours. Not Hurting Anybody So Jets Let 'Em Alone" (July 29)

The pilots in pursuit had become less panic driven, but that did little to calm the heightened state of uncertainty and foreboding that was spreading across the country like wildfire. It was by this time quite apparent that *something* was up there, and the public wanted the government and military to figure it out. But leave them alone? The July 29 article goes on to say that when the Civil Aeronautics Authority was asked why Air Defense Command had not been alerted, especially after radar had tracked as many as twelve objects for six hours, the response was mind numbing: "We were too busy with other things, and besides, those objects aren't hurting anybody."[65]

The country, just recovering from a world war, was struggling in the throes of a cold war. So this flip remark did not sit well with the nerve-racked public, especially coming just one day after the Air Defense Command had ordered jet pilots to take off immediately upon sighting any of these objects anywhere within the country. Regardless, there were plenty of excuses.

Was it possible that Air Defense Command, despite the command to shoot the objects down if they did not comply, found themselves in jeopardy because they did not know the objects' identities or intentions? One thing was for certain—in 1952 they knew they were up against something quite advanced. "Sightings so far unexplained and increasingly regarded as physical phenomena 'shown in pattern which would indicate that the objects are being controlled by a reasoning body' the Air Force said."[66]

Although the UFO flap of 1952 has become largely identified with Washington, DC, it did not start there. In fact, several events caught the public's attention in 1952. In February, Princess Elizabeth of York became Queen Elizabeth of the United Kingdom, and Prime Minister Winston Churchill announced to the world that England had an atomic bomb. The war with Japan formally ended with the signing of the peace treaty in San Francisco in April, and the Korean War began in June. Rounding out the year, in November the United States exploded a hydrogen bomb at Eniwetok Atoll in the Marshall Islands, while UFO flaps around the world filled newspaper columns throughout the year.

Hollywood had already taken the UFO flap and run with it all the way to the bank. The release of genre movies such as *The Day the Earth Stood Still*, *Earth vs. the Flying Saucers*, and *It Came from Outer Space* repeated the familiar, foreboding theme of what might be lurking in the skies above. Box offices were booming with ticket sales, but so were the newspapers. Sometimes the truth is stranger and more frightening than fiction. Sightings of unusual objects were being reported around the world.

January 1952 was a turning point for public opinion regarding any chance of a saucer invasion on the home front. Remember that in September 1950, the Soviet Union conducted their first A-bomb test. With tensions high and the Cold War raging, concerns of invasion, whether by flying saucers or otherwise, were foremost in the minds of many people. Serious concerns were being raised and opinions voiced by many people, perhaps most importantly by former air force scientist Anthony O. Mirarchi. As early as February 1952, news articles appeared across the country trumpeting Dr. Mirarchi's call to action regarding the threat of saucers. Headlines flashed across the nation's news services: "Savant Asks Spotters to Warn of Saucers" and "Scientist Fears Flying Saucers Portend a Worse 'Pearl Harbor.'"[67]

Mirarchi had taken issue with a report issued by another air force scientist, Dr. Urner Liddel, who supported the explanation of balloons being misidentified as flying saucers. Based on his own research, Mirarchi thought the unidentified objects displayed behavior that indicated some type of preprogramming, which could indicate something else, even guided missiles. Mirarchi feared that the flying saucers could be an experiment by a potential enemy of the United States: "If they were launched by a foreign power, then they could lead to a worse Pearl Harbor than we have ever experienced."[68] He ultimately urged that a considerable appropriation of funds be granted the air force to set up photographic, radar, and spotter tracking points to study the phenomena.

The wheels were set in motion. Anxious civilians vigilantly scanned the skies in search of unidentified aircraft. Reports of strange lights and unusual aircraft swept across the nation and around the world at an alarming rate. 1952 reaped a bumper crop of reports, and the unknowns were making themselves the daily topic of discussion. In the months leading up to the Washington encounters, news wires were pumping out saucer stories in record numbers: "Flying Disk Made Pass at U.S. Jet Over Japan" in March, "Saucer Stories Still Send AF Into the Wild Blue" in April, and "Air Buzzes with Reports of Saucers" in May.

On the morning of June 1, just one month before the Washington, DC, sightings, technicians at the Hughes Aircraft Company in Los Angeles picked up a fast-moving object that was displaying speed and maneuvers far beyond the capability of a conventional aircraft. In July, this headline ran in Miami, Florida: "Two Saucer-Eyed Pilots Report 8 Flying Disks. Pair Doubt 'Any Human' Steered Formation of Supersonic Mystery Craft."[69] Also in July, a photographer for the United States Coast Guard took a picture of four unknown objects in a V formation over Salem, Massachusetts. By then President Truman had met with military advisers to discuss the intruders that were unabashedly entering the airspace over the nation's capital. The mood was serious.

On July 28, 1952, newspapers printed the air force's position in a statement from information officer Lieutenant Colonel Moncel Monts. Saying again that the jet pilots are, and have been under orders to investigate unidentified objects and to shoot them down if they cannot talk them down. In his well-researched and aptly titled book, *Shoot Them Down!* Frank C. Feschino Jr. writes of the statement's aftereffect:

> After this shoot down order against UFOs appeared in newspapers, it prompted an alarming public disapproval in America. On July 29, Robert Farnsworth, president of the United States Rocket Society, sent a telegram to President Truman, the Secretary of Defense, the Secretary of the Navy, and the Secretary of the Army concerning this statement. In part, he suggested, "no offensive action

be taken against the objects reported as unidentified which have been sighted over our nation. Should they be extraterrestrial such action might result in the gravest consequences." On July 30, the Associated Press and United Press wire services released the telegram story. Several other newspapers carried the story, one such headline read, "Don't Shoot."[70]

Meanwhile the air force was not talking about the mysterious jet fighter accidents. Noting Ruppelt's lack of coverage of this important factor, Feschino writes, "Moreover, in 1952 an outstanding amount of mysterious fighter jet accidents also occurred over America that involved devastating crashes. Fighter jets were dropping out of the sky over America in frightening numbers, especially during the summer of 1952."[71] Although the air force was quick to dismiss such pilot encounters as misidentified balloons or planes, it was obvious that the encounters with the *killer balloons* were not going away.

In 1953 and 1954, there were more sightings, airplane escorts, and near collisions with the unidentified flying objects globally and at home. Many of the objects were seen over US military bases and hovering over nuclear facilities. There were reports of multicolored objects, bright glowing objects, large saucer-shaped objects, including large objects of various and unusual shapes and sizes that could maneuver and separate into two or more objects at will. Most importantly perhaps was and that many of these objects had a propensity to follow or buzz airplanes.

Earlier concerns had already led to the formation of the US Air Force's information-gathering team in 1947 known as Project Sign, Sign became Project Grudge in 1949, which, like it's predecessor, did little to shed light on the unknown objects. In 1952 Grudge turned into Project Blue Book, in an attempt by the US Air Force to continue the investigation into the reports of unidentified flying objects sweeping the nation. The Blue Book project convened in 1969 with no official position by the Air Force on the matter of UFOs except to conclude that the anomalous objects presented no danger to the country, could not be proven to be advanced technology and presented no evidence that they were extraterrestrial in origin.

However, it was obvious that the "in your face" maneuvers on the part of the unknowns were meant to get attention, but for what? If the government and military therefore, were not forthcoming with an acknowledgment of their existence, then perhaps others would be.

CHAPTER SIX
Something's Out There

I don't believe in fairy tales, but when I got into flying and
military aviation, I heard other pilots describe too many
unexplained examples of UFOs sighted around Earth to
rule out the possibility that some forms of life exist beyond
our own world. I had no evidence at the time that these
examples conclusively proved anything, but the fact that
so many experienced pilots reported strange sights that
could not easily be explained only heightened my curiosity
about space. And then—I had my own UFO sightings.
> —Astronaut Gordon Cooper[72]

Recently the *Seattle Post-Intelligencer* ran an Associated Press story from
Pendleton, Oregon, retelling the story of pilot Kenneth Arnold sighting of
nine saucer-like objects flying at incredible speed. Arnold was sincere in his
assessment told a reporter, "It seems impossible", he told the reporter, "but
there it is." [73] His 1947 encounter had generated worldwide publicity and
launched a flying-saucer frenzy. Rewards had been offered for evidence. A
pastor had said flying saucers signaled the end of the world. A man found
bleeding from the head had claimed that a flying disc hit him. All this
hoopla had resulted from an event that took place in the summer of 1947,
an event that would forever change our world.

Washington State, June 24, 1947. Thirty-two-year-old businessman
and pilot Kenneth Arnold of Boise, Idaho, had just finished a delivery of
fire equipment to Chehalis, Washington, and was on his way to Yakima.
Arnold had recently heard about a C-46 marine transport that had gone

down in the mountains, and a five-thousand-dollar reward was being offered for the discovery of the downed craft. Although he had already set a flight plan, Arnold decided to take his CallAir A-2 off course for an hour or so, to help with the search in the area thought to be where this plane might have gone down.

At approximately 2:00 p.m., Arnold had been cruising at an altitude of about nine thousand feet over a mountainous area near Mount Rainier in his single-engine CallAir. Suddenly he was startled by a bright flash of light. To his amazement, he saw nine odd-shaped objects flying in formation and moving at high speed. He described the objects as half-moon shaped, resembling a pie plate cut in half, and moving like a saucer skipping across water.

That was the first official report of unidentified flying objects to make national headlines. It forever etched the term *flying saucer* into the minds of the general public, and it gave credence to the argument that unidentified flying objects (UFOs) were a reality and not just a rumor. The press made the most of it through the news services, with front-page headlines in newspapers spanning the entire country. The public wanted more—and they got it. Within days, eyewitness reports of similar objects began pouring in from all parts of the country. Discs of all shapes, sizes, and colors were being reported hovering in the skies, flying at tremendous speeds, making inconceivably sharp turns, and darting straight up in the blink of an eye—feats that no known aircraft could have achieved in 1947 or today. Was our coming of age the coming of *them*?

There was no doubt that the strange aerial objects had caught our attention, and it was quite obvious that we had caught theirs. The press extolled them, the government denied them, but the public embraced them with wonderment and lots of questions.

The summer of 1947 proved to be a hallmark time for sightings. On June 27, a Washington State housewife saw silver discs flying over the Cascade Mountains. On June 28, Air Force Lieutenant Armstrong sighted five or six flying discs north of Lake Mead, Nevada. On June 29, at White Sands Proving Grounds in New Mexico, scientists saw a silvery disc in the sky. On June 30, a navy pilot observed two gray spheres near Williams Field, Arizona. However, July proved to be even more significant. Who and what were these strange craft, people were asking, and who or what were flying them? Perhaps we were about to find out.

On the evening of July 2, 1947, Roswell merchant Dan Wilmot and his wife were sitting on the front steps of their home, looking up at the night sky. It was approximately 9:50 p.m. when they sighted a large, glowing object resembling two inverted saucers faced mouth to mouth streaking through the sky at terrific speed. That same evening a thunderstorm was brewing over the Foster Ranch, seventy-five miles out of Roswell. However, over the claps of thunder, rancher Max Brazel heard something like an explosion.

The next morning Brazel rode his horse to a remote section of the ranch, where he came upon metallic debris strewn over a section of land four hundred feet wide. The silver metallic debris was of all shapes and sizes, like foil to the touch, and unlike anything he had ever seen. Then he noticed that a flock of sheep making their way to a near-by watering hole had stopped dead in their tracks on one side of the debris field. The jittery sheep kept their distance, refusing to cross through the debris field or go anywhere near it. Tired of their nervousness and refusal to cross that section of land, Brazel led them on an alternate route around the site to water.

Shortly after his discovery, Brazel learned that several strange objects in the sky had been reported in the area. Thinking there might be a connection with the debris on the ranch, Brazel headed to the nearby town of Corona and informed Sheriff Wilcox of his discovery, and Wilcox notified Colonel William Blanchard, the base commander at Roswell Army Air Field. Blanchard dispatched intelligence officer Major Jesse Marcel and counterintelligence agent Captain Sheridan Cavitt to accompany the rancher and inspect the area in question.

Marcel and Cavitt followed Brazel in their own cars. Upon arrival, they saw firsthand the massive debris field and began to inspect the area, picking up samples and loading their cars with pieces of the mysterious material to take back to the base for examination. After collecting several pieces of the strange debris, it was agreed that Cavitt would return to the base with the first samples while Marcel stayed behind to collect further specimens. That's where it gets interesting. Before taking his load of debris to the base, Marcel decided to stop by his home first.

Overcome with the excitement of seeing something so extraordinary, and believing that it was a once-in-a-lifetime experience, he wanted to share the items with his wife and son. His decision was about to become the litmus test of the authenticity of the Roswell incident.

Jesse Marcel Jr., who was eleven years old at the time, recalled the event quite clearly. Like his father, he would go on to a distinguished military career as a flight surgeon, even doing a tour of duty in Iraq. However, in 1947 he was a sleepy-eyed boy trying to understand why his father had roused him from sleep in the middle of the night. Major Marcel's wife, who was already up, joined her husband and son in the kitchen, where they looked through a half-empty box of some type of material, much of what Marcel had laid out on the kitchen floor for closer examination. Jesse Jr. later recalled his father's excitement about the debris, which they all handled, inspecting each piece carefully for serial numbers or other markings that would indicate the material was man made. None were found. The foil-type metal would crinkle up in their hands and then spring back into shape when released, and the metal could not be cut or torn but apparently would shatter on impact. One strange piece looked like an I-beam section, with strange purple writing similar to hieroglyphics.

Major Marcel's bold move to share these fragments with his family signifies to me the unusual properties of the debris, which was real. Jesse held the smooth pieces in his hands, turning them over, feeling the rigidness of the structural pieces and the amazing light weight of the metallic skin. Major Marcel knew that debris was unusual, and if his thinking was correct, it didn't originate on Earth, as Jesse Jr. later recalled:

> The foil was similar to the aluminum kitchen wrap of today but appeared to be stronger, and it felt lighter than a feather in my hand ... The largest piece I saw was perhaps six or eight inches across, and the edges were irregular, with sharp tears covering the entire perimeter of the pieces. But even though I was curious, I did not try to bend or tear it. After all, this was some kind of very precious material, and as my father had told us, we were probably some of the first humans to see it.[74]

Perhaps we will never know the absolute truth about that incident, but we do know that the people who believed it *continued* to believe it until their dying day. The Army Air Corps wrote the craft off as a weather balloon.

The Roswell Army Airfield, part of the Strategic Air Command, was commissioned with housing an arsenal of nuclear weapons. It seems inconceivable to me that officers charged with the safety and security of nuclear weapons would be so excitedly confused over the debris of a weather balloon.

Looking back on that night in the kitchen with his parents, and the strange debris, Jesse Marcel Jr. said, "For me this was science reality, and it was more exciting reality than any of the science I had learned in School. It was an event that definitely changed me. From that evening on, my life took on a different meaning. I could never look at the night sky the same way again, because for all I knew, someone might be looking back."[75] And perhaps someone or *something* is looking back, because from that point on, things would get personal.

Evading or baiting? January 7, 1948. In the early afternoon something unusual was spotted by air traffic personnel in the control tower at Godman Field, Kentucky. A report was immediately dispatched to the base operations officer of a bright, disc-shaped object sighted in their airspace. When the object was still visible an hour and twenty minutes later, orders were given to a group of four P51 fighter planes, led by twenty-five-year-old Kentucky Air National Guard pilot Captain Thomas Mantell, to divert from their training mission to investigate. At fifteen thousand feet Mantell sighted the object and began climbing for a closer look. Two more pilots joined in the pursuit, while the fourth had to break off because of low fuel. Mantell radioed that he saw the object as metallic and of tremendous size and traveling at and estimated 180 miles per hour.

Now at sixteen thousand feet, the air was becoming thin. First Lieutenant Albert Clements put on his oxygen mask, but he was concerned that neither Mantell nor Second Lieutenant B. A. Hammond had oxygen on board, and breathing was becoming more difficult. At twenty thousand feet Mantell said, "Look, there it is, out there at 12 o'clock!" Right wingman Clements would later say that he was able to make out a small bright object but was not able to determine what it was. Now at 22,500 feet, Clements's oxygen was low, and Clements and Hammond notified Mantell that they were breaking. Mantell told them he was going to try to follow the object to twenty-five thousand feet. Mantell radioed to the tower at Godman, "The object is directly ahead of me and slightly above and is now moving about my speed or better. I am trying to close in for a better look." That was the last transmission Godman received from Captain Mantell. Within minutes, Mantell's plane was seen diving nose-first toward the ground and crashing onto the farm property of local resident Carrie Phillips.

Was a UFO ever a serious consideration? According to this account author Jerome Clark cites a local newspaper, the *Louisville Courier*, as covering the story with a headline that read "P-51 and Captain Mantell Destroyed Chasing Flying Saucer." [76]

It has never been proven that Captain Mantell was truly in pursuit of a UFO, but neither has it been proven that he was not. Was the object stationary, moving away as if to evade the P-51, or baiting it to follow? An ominous shadow was cast by whatever was up there, and it wouldn't end there. Whatever they were, they were becoming more aggressive. No longer evading, but engaging. This was to be a turning point.

Fargo, North Dakota. On the clear autumn evening of October 1, 1948, at approximately 9:00 p.m., Second Lieutenant George Gorman of the North Dakota Air National Guard, piloting his F-51 en route to Fargo, was on approach for landing. The tower radioed Gorman his landing instructions and advised him that a Piper Cub aircraft was nearby. Gorman confirmed that he had visual of the Piper Cub, which was about 500 feet below him. At the same time Gorman caught sight of a light that flashed by him on his right. Gorman immediately radioed the tower to confirm whether there was another aircraft in the area, and the tower replied that no other planes were in the area.

Gorman then saw the light again and decided to investigate. He sees the object which he describes as round, between six and eight inches in diameter, white in color with fuzzy edges. Suddenly the object made an abrupt turn and headed toward the control tower. Gorman immediately banked his F-51 and went into a steep dive toward the object, but he could not catch up with it. It was game on. The object began to rapidly gain altitude with Gorman in pursuit. At seven thousand feet the object made another sharp turn, putting it on a collision course with Gorman. Seeing the object coming straight toward him, Gorman pushed his F-51 into a dive, avoiding impact as the object streaked by overhead. Startled and a bit shaken, Gorman regained a visual on the object, which continued circling overhead, and resumed chase.

The tower had radioed that they too had a visual on the object. Gorman knew he was pushing the envelope in this pursuit, but he was determined to stay with it. He banked sharply toward the object, only to see it coming straight at him once again. Just before colliding with Gorman's plane, the object shot straight up. At one point, the diversions, climbs, and strenuous maneuvers caused Gorman to temporarily pass out. Regaining control, he continued into a steep climb and remained hot on the object's tail. Unfortunately, at fourteen thousand feet his engine stalled out and he was forced to break off the chase. Gorman watched as the object shot off into the northwest sky, as if thumbing its nose at him, and disappeared.

The dogfight between Gorman and the unidentified flying object lasted twenty-seven minutes. Official government findings would state that Gorman, an experienced World War II pilot, had engaged a weather balloon. One has to wonder why a well-trained pilot would have such difficulty identifying a weather balloon, let alone engaging in a dogfight with one. There are thoughts on both sides about what Gorman encountered, but John Spencer lets Gorman have the last word about it: "I am convinced there was thought behind these maneuvers. I had the distinct impression that its maneuvers were controlled by thought or reason. I am also certain that it was governed by the laws of inertia, because its acceleration was rapid, not immediate and although it was able to turn fairly tightly, at considerable speed, it still followed a natural curve."[77]

"A most remarkable balloon!" concludes Spencer.

The 1940s were ebbing, but lights and strange objects continued to appear over towns and provinces, including restricted areas. In April 1949, scientists at the White Sands Proving Grounds in New Mexico observed a white, egg-shaped object hover over the grounds of the facility and then shoot up out of sight. Similar events occurred, over and over again, as if to challenge national security and frustrate the powers that be. The challenge stateside proved to be a source of contention, but perhaps no more so than at strategic bases in Europe. According to Second Lieutenant and future astronaut Gordon Cooper, his squadron had more than they bargained for in policing these aerial unknowns: "I don't believe in fairy tales, but when I got into flying and military aviation, I heard other pilots describe too many unexplained examples of UFOs sighted around Earth to rule out the possibility that some forms of life exist beyond our own world. I had no evidence at the time that these examples conclusively proved anything, but the fact that so many experienced pilots reported strange sights that could not easily be explained only heightened my curiosity about space. And then—I had my own UFO sightings."[78]

In 1951, Cooper was a member of the 525th Fighter Bomber Squadron stationed in postwar Europe, where he was assigned patrol duty along the borders of Communist East Germany, Czechoslovakia, and Poland. It was a time of increased tensions between the East and West, and the animosities of the Cold War were in full swing. On more than one occasion, Cooper encountered less-than-friendly Soviet MIGs also on patrol and eager to egg on confrontation. But there was something else in the skies as well.

In *Leap of Faith*, Cooper recalls his first encounter with the *something other* that prowled about the skies above the base, perhaps looking for confrontation of their own. He recalls numerous occasions of being in the ready room with his squadron when an alert sounded, sending them all scrambling aloft in their F-86 fighter jets to intercept the *bogies*. "We reached our maximum ceiling of around forty-five thousand feet, and they were still way above us, and traveling much faster. I could see that they weren't balloons or MIGs or like any aircraft I had seen before. They were metallic silver and saucer-shaped. We couldn't get close enough to form any idea of their size; they were just too high."[79]

This same scenario played out on a regular basis. The saucer-shaped bogies continued to make themselves known by brazenly passing over the base, appearing in groups of four to sixteen at a time, as if enjoying the intercept chase. The saucers could speed up, slow down, or come to a complete stop while the jets shot past them, helplessly unable to copy their maneuvers. In time the military stopped trying to intercept them at all. The anomalous appearances happening in Europe was also happening over American soil, characterized by fruitless pursuits of objects too fast and too agile to catch. This wasn't Cooper's only encounter with the intergalactic rough riders; more was to come, and on his home turf.

On the morning of May 3, 1957, the now Captain Cooper was overseeing a crew assigned to the Askania-camera landing system at

Edwards Air Force Base in a desert region of California. The camera system was used to film and assess the landing characteristics of various aircraft. Later that morning, as Cooper recalled, two cameramen filming at the number four site came running over to him, quite "worked up and very excited." They told Cooper that they had just witnessed a "strange looking saucer" fly over them in complete silence. They described the saucer as having a metallic silver color and shaped like an inverted plate; furthermore, this inverted plate extended three landing gear and set down about fifty yards from where they were filming.[80]

Cooper remembered that he had heard insider reports, from people he trusted, about mysterious incidents involving strange saucer crafts—in particular, the Roswell crash report of 1947. Although the Roswell crash had been officially reported as a downed weather balloon, an air force major and friend of Cooper's had confided in him that he had actually seen some of the debris from the crash site and was certain that it did not come from a balloon. He also confirmed to Cooper that there had been a crash that day of some sort of aircraft and that they had recovered the bodies of the crew. The air force had countered this report by suggesting that the bodies that were reported as having been found were merely test dummies sent aboard the balloon for scientific studies—a weak explanation at best.

Cooper had also been privy to a report from an air force master sergeant that told of being dispatched to the crash site of a downed craft, which the master sergeant discovered was actually a crashed disc. To add to the intrigue, two human-looking beings in some type of flight suits had been sitting aloft the craft and waving. They had been taken away, and the master sergeant never found out who they were or what had happened to them. Cooper wasn't about to dismiss any report: "After my own UFO experiences in Europe, I was not about to discount any of these stories, especially coming from people I had served with and trusted."[81]

Now he was facing another situation regarding another UFO. What had the two cameramen seen? Was there any evidence? He asked a logical question: "Did you get any pictures?" Yes, the men told Cooper that they had been shooting stills and filming through the entire event. They described the saucer as silent, silver in color, approximately thirty feet across, and glowing. They told Cooper that they had tried to approach the saucer for a closer shot, but it had lifted up, retracted its landing gear, and shot out of sight at a terrific rate of speed.

Following protocol, Cooper contacted the Pentagon to report the incident. He was ordered not to "run any prints," but to send the developed film and negatives to Washington via the base commanding general's plane. Although no prints were to be made, Cooper did take the liberty of looking at the negatives before sending them to Washington. "I was amazed at what I saw," he later wrote. "The quality was excellent, everything in focus as one would expect from trained photographers. The object, shown close up, was a classic saucer, shiny silver and smooth—just as the cameramen had reported."[82]

After Cooper sent the film and negatives to Washington as ordered, nothing more was heard of them, much to the frustration of Cooper and the photographers. Cooper had earlier said that he was not the only military pilot to have encountered unidentified flying objects in the early 1950s. No doubt, he considered this incident in 1957 to be further proof of the bogies' existence—and he was not the only future astronaut to do so.

One astronaut of the Mercury 7 team, Donald Slayton, known as Deke to his fellow astronauts, had encountered an unidentified flying object in 1951:

> I was testing a P-51 fighter in Minneapolis when I spotted this object. I was at about 10,000 feet on a nice, bright, sunny afternoon. I thought the object was a kite, then I realized that no kite is gonna fly that high. As I got closer it looked like a weather balloon, gray and about three feet in diameter. But as soon as I got behind the darn thing it didn't look like a balloon anymore. It looked like a saucer, a disk. About the same time, I realized that it was suddenly going away from me—and there I was, running at about 300 miles per hour. I tracked it for a little ways, and then all of a sudden the damn thing just took off. It pulled about a 45 climbing turn and accelerated and just flat disappeared.[83]

The Mercury and Gemini space programs had their share of reported encounters. One documented event took place on April 8, 1964, with the first orbital launch of a Gemini spacecraft. During the spacecraft's first orbit around Earth, four objects were observed accompanying the craft. Once the orbit was complete, the objects broke formation and shot off into the dark void of space.[84]

These men of high caliber and training were going on record about unidentified flying objects, but other credible, respected professionals were chiming in as well. Although many news publications were keen on making sport of UFOs, the public was taking it quite seriously—and so was the air force. Around the world, UFOs were appearing over military bases, atomic test facilities, atomic power plants, missile silos, major cities, rural areas, and congested neighborhoods.

The air force was receiving numerous reports, not only from their own pilots, but also from commercial pilots, the general public, and other military personnel. Then as now, people from all walks of life—celebrities, politicians, presidents, royalty, scientists, and other people of high regard— were seeing unidentified flying objects of various shapes and sizes. Saucer-shaped craft, spheres, cigar-shaped objects, brightly colored orbs of light, and shape-shifting silhouettes were seen in the night sky. The objects were appearing at all hours of the day and night in all locations—deserts, mountains, valleys, rural farming regions, and cities large and small.

Although the air force continued to document and classify UFO reports within Project Blue Book, their findings provided no significant answers, other than chalking it up to the misidentifications of balloons.

What might come from all of this? What's the reason for all these encounters? I can think of one good reason—*validation*. Reports from government agencies, the military, and respected experts can offset any lunatic fringe reports and give serious consideration to the idea that humankind is not alone in the universe. We should not be surprised if someday extraterrestrials choose to land on Earth and introduce themselves to us. I believe they just might. There is a patent certainty in the minds of individuals who have either seen a UFO or weighed the evidence for themselves. "We all know that UFOs are real," declared Apollo 14 astronaut Edgar Mitchell. "All we need to ask is where do they come from?"[85]

From the tracking of the green fireballs of Project Sign, to unidentified flying objects reported to the air force's Project Grudge, to Project Blue Book, all of these investigative efforts have concluded that—Nope! UFOs don't exist! However, trained observers and professionals haven't bought the balloon theory, and neither should anyone else. "Nobody tried that weather balloon line on me," former astronaut Cooper would write. "If they had, I would have told them what I thought: *I've never seen a saucer-shaped balloon with three landing gear on it.*"[86]

"There ARE things out there! There absolutely is!"
—Major Robert White, X-15 Pilot, during a flight on
July 17, 1962[87]

CHAPTER SEVEN
Do You Want to Report?

"Ask them if they want to report officially."
"TWA 517, do you want to report a UFO? Over.
"TWA 517, do you want to report a UFO? Over."
"Negative. We don't want to report."
"Air East 31, do you want to report a UFO? Over."
"Negative. We don't want to report one of those either."[88]
—Close Encounters of the Third Kind

Department of Transportation, Federal Aviation Administration (FAA), Air Transportation Security, Form 1600-32-1, November 17, 1986:

As per telephonic request from FSDO-63, the following are the events which took place on November 17, 1986 and were taken from my personal notes during the interview: Responded to Japan Airlines station office as instructed by Manager (James S. Derry), AAL-700. Myself and Jim Derry interviewed the crew of JAL Flight 1628, which reported the sighting of unidentified air traffic. The flight crew consisted of the Captain, Kenju Terauchi, First Officer Takanori Tamefuji, and Flight Engineer Yoshio Tsukuda. Captain Terauchi stated the cargo only flight had departed Reykjavik, Iceland. Captain Terauchi stated he first sited (visually) the unidentified air piloting (B747) was at flight level 390, airspeed 0.84 Mach. Captain Terauchi indicated that the UAT was in front of his aircraft at a distance of approximately seven to eight nautical miles for approximately 12 minutes. The Captain stated the distance was indicated by the onboard Bendix color radar. Captain Terauchi stated that while he had a visual on the UAT, he spotted yellow, amber and green lights, and a rotating beacon, but no red lights. The Captain said there were two distinct sets of lights, but appeared to be joined together (as fixed to one object). Captain Terauchi ascertained through visual sighting and radar, that the UAT was equal in size to a B747, possibly larger.[89]

This is the opening statement from the report filed by FAA investigator Ronald E. Mickle regarding the sighting of an unidentified flying object reportedly keeping pace with Captain Terauchi's Boeing 747 cargo plane. The captain and crew were in flight from Iceland to Japan by way of Anchorage, Alaska. This reported sighting of a UFO garnered media coverage around the world, in part because the pilot's willingness to discuss it. It had caught the interest of newspaper journalists and was the starting point of my interest as well. Like so many other readers, I was captivated by the detailed report from such credible witnesses as Captain Terauchi and his crew, and the fact that the sighting was confirmed by both air and ground radar.

To understand the significance of this report, one must understand that the event itself was unusually complex. There wasn't just one object shadowing Captain Terauchi's aircraft that evening—there were three.

It all began around 5:30 on that clear November evening. The sun was setting in the west, leaving a soft amber glow of softly fading light on the western horizon as Japan Air Lines (JAL) Flight 1628 sited unidentified air traffic (UAT) near Alaska and the Air Defense Identification Zone (ADIZ). The aircraft turned and banked slowly into the dark expanse of the northern sky. One by one, shimmering stars appeared as the 747-cargo plane became totally engulfed by the darkness of the night sky. It had been by all accounts a routine flight, as they were returning from Paris to Narita International Airport in Tokyo with a cargo of fine French wine. After a quick stop in Iceland, they were now en route over eastern Alaska on the final leg of their trip home.

At approximately 5:11 p.m., Captain Terauchi had received a course correction and was completing his turn on a new flight path toward Talkeetna, Alaska, when he noticed two small craft about two thousand feet below his altitude. At first he thought they might have been military aircraft from a nearby US Air Force base, until something completely startling and unexpected happened. The two objects, which had been to his far left only seconds earlier, were now stacked one, over the other, directly in front of his aircraft. Terauchi was amazed at their incredible speed and the apparent immunity to gravity necessary to move such a distance within seconds. The objects then made what he described as a "reverse thrust," flaring up with a brilliant flash of light that filled the cabin with such brilliant intensity that Captain Terauchi could feel its heat. This lasted for three to five seconds, after which the objects began to fly side by side in an undulating motion, keeping pace with the aircraft. The cylindrical objects were able to match the speed and altitude of Terauchi's aircraft, and one of them was estimated to be the size of two football fields.

In the aftermath of the sightings and the subsequent report, which was being reviewed by both the FAA and Japanese authorities, Terauchi was placed on leave but would later be reinstated. The facts remain—the sighting was well documented and the event happened.

The FAA received much media attention because of the incident. Although the FAA could not substantiate what was seen, they speculated that it was unidentifiable, which boosted the incident's believability and resulted in broader acceptance by the general public. Was there really something to the *somethings* that were out there? If so, the air force was keeping it under wraps.

The JAL sighting is a classic example of why people, especially pilots, are so reticent to report having seen anything even remotely like a UFO—the ridicule and damage to their professional status, including being grounded for psychological evaluation. For aeronautic safety overseers, UFOs are an unacceptable topic. Pilots such as Captain Terauchi face a real threat of being grounded or even seeing their careers terminated. JAL grounded Terauchi and assigned him a desk job, and it was years before he was reinstated as a flight officer.

Only two months later, in January 1987, Alaska Airlines Flight 53, flying from Nome to Anchorage, picked up a fast-moving object on their onboard weather radar system. That same month, the pilot of an air force KC-135 en route from Anchorage to Fairbanks encountered a large, disc-shaped object flying a mere forty feet from his aircraft, and then it vanished. Since radar systems are affected by these unidentified flying objects, could they affect other systems as well? Apparently they can.

An article published as the Sturrock Panel Report gives an account of an incident that occurred in the skies somewhere between Buffalo and Albany, New York, on March 12, 1977. According to the article, the report was provided by Dr. Richard Haines, a former NASA scientist and aerial anomaly investigator. The report says that at approximately 21:05 EST, United Airlines Flight 94 out of San Francisco was on its flight path to Boston when something out of the ordinary occurred. The DC10 was cruising at 275 knots at thirty-seven thousand feet with the autopilot system engaged. The darkened skies were clear ahead and visibility was good. Then the unexpected happened:

> Suddenly and unexpectedly, the airplane began to turn to the left, making a 15 degree bank. Within a few seconds, the First Officer and Captain looked to the left side of their plane and saw an extremely bright white light at about their own altitude. Subsequently, the Flight Engineer also looked and saw the light source. It appeared to be perfectly round and its apparent diameter was 3 degrees of arc. However, the Captain estimated the object to be about 1,000 yards away and to be about 100 feet in size that corresponds to the angular size of 2 degrees. "Its intensity was remarkable—about the intensity of a flashbulb," he remarked.[90]

Of course, this sudden change of course did not go unnoticed by Boston ATC, and the controller was quick to radio in asking, "United 94, where are you going?" The captain replied, "Well, let me figure this out. I will let you know." To complicate matters more, the captain noticed that three cockpit compasses were all giving different readings. Noting the obvious discrepancies in the readings, the copilot immediately turned off the autopilot and took manual control of the aircraft. Although it must have seemed longer, the object was with the aircraft only four or five minutes before shooting off in a westerly direction. And as is often the case, when the captain inquired if ACT had radar traffic in that area, the reply was negative.

Although the objects appear to be able to avoid radar contact in their vicinity, they do not seem to want to avoid contact with aircraft. Besides questions of safety, this also raises questions of the UFOs' intentions, and yet pilots and other personnel are unable to express their concerns for fear of repercussion.

With the gravity of such questions looming, Haines and co-researcher Ted Roe have established an international database and reporting center called the National Aviation Reporting Center on Anomalous Phenomena (NARCAP). This organization provides a safe outlet for pilots, air traffic controllers, radar operators, and other aviation specialists to report these types of encounters.

And the need is real. Haines and Roe are quick to point out the real concerns that exist because of the actions of the UAPs (unidentified aerial phenomena)—close pacing or passes that result in near midair collisions, electromagnetic disturbance of avionic systems, the distraction of the crew, light intensity that affects pilot vision, and even injuries sustained by crew and passengers from dives or quick turns to avoid colliding with the UAP. Serious stuff, yet NARCAP notes that these incidences, which are sometimes validated by ground radar systems, crew, and passengers, often go unreported.

And data backs this up. The FAA, NTSB, and NASA all have incident/accident databases from which this information can be gathered. Another source, NASA's Aviation Safety Reporting System, which allows individuals to maintain anonymity in reporting, has amassed over 332,000 incident reports, according to Haines. In a data search in 2000, Dr. Haines was able to access this data, which revealed that there had been 5,053 cases of near misses with unknown/unidentified objects, 973 cases involving near misses possibly caused by crew inputs to avoid collisions, 125 in-flight system failures, 9 official reports of an unidentified object, 3 of unidentified traffic, and 1 UFO.

According to NARCAP, characteristics of UAPs include close pacing, erratic movements, interferences of avionic systems, high-speed passes, near or actual midair collisions, disruption of electrical systems, and downed or missing aircraft.

UAPs may appear as single or multiple lights, or as balls of white, blue, green, red, amber, or orange color. They may display stationary or flashing lights, spotlights, or beams. They can be in the shape of cones, triangles, cylinders, rectangles, spheres, discs, or doughnuts, and they reportedly range from a mere six inches to several hundred feet in size. They may hover or move erratically and exhibit great speed. They seem to have a penchant for the risky business of appearing over airport facilities, and they're able to divide into two or more objects and release and retrieve smaller objects.

Dramatic interference with aircraft flight instrumentation has been well documented, and the results can be devastating, as Haines suggests. One well-publicized example of a flight instrumentation failure comes from a report given by an Iranian fighter pilot in pursuit of an unknown aerial object on September 19, 1976.

An extremely bright light was spotted in the vicinity of Meharabd International Airport. The airport contacted the military, and F4 Captain Mohammad Reza Azizkhani scrambled from his base in Tehran at 00:30 hours to intercept the object, now on a bearing of 40 nautical miles north of Tehran. When the F4 got within 46 km of the object, all instrumentation and communication abilities ceased to function, and Captain Azizkhani had no choice but to break off the intercept and head back to base. Once he veered off course of the object, the systems began to function once again.

Another F4 was scrambled, piloted by Lieutenant Parviz Jafari and Lieutenant Jalal Damiria. At a range of 50 km, Jafari locked on to the object, which he reported gave a return the size of a 707 aircraft, but it was too intensely lit to make out any shape. He saw an array of rapidly flashing blue, green, red, and orange lights arranged in a square. Suddenly a second object separated from the first and quickly set out on a course directly toward the F4. Lieutenant Jafari, thinking he was under attack, tried to fire an AIM-9 sidewinder missile, but all instrumentation was lost, including weapons control and communications. He then tried to eject, but even the ejection system, which was mechanical, failed.

Now the object was directly behind him. Jafari was able to bank away from the main object, and as he did so, the systems resumed to function.

Another bright object dropped from the main target and shot straight down on a crash course to the ground, but it didn't crash. Instead, it softly set down, illuminating the ground around it with intense light. A search of the area the next day turned up nothing. It is important to remember the abilities these objects have, when assessing this later.

It goes without saying that reliable testimony from witnesses such as these should be taken seriously, from the standpoint of crew and passenger safety alone. But ignore it and it won't go away. If pilots find themselves in a precarious position regarding seeing a UFO, let alone reporting one, how much more so for a president? "I don't laugh at people any more when they say they've seen UFOs. I've seen one myself!" said President Jimmy Carter in a 1975 interview with the *Washington Post*. "It was the darndest thing I've ever seen," Carter added, recalling the evening of January 6, 1969, when he had been about to give a speech to attendees of a Lions Club gathering in Leary, Georgia.

At approximately 7:15 p.m., someone in the audience had called Carter's attention to a strange-looking object that had suddenly appeared just above the horizon and west of the podium where he was standing. "It was big, it was very bright, it changed colors and it was about the size of the moon. We watched it for ten minutes, but none of us could figure out what it was. One thing's for sure; I'll never make fun of people who say they've seen unidentified objects in the sky. If I become President, I'll make every piece of information this country has about UFO sightings available to the public and the scientists."[91]

Well, he did—and he didn't. UFOs remain an apparent hands-off topic for presidents and other high-ranking officials. Presumably any information obtained is disseminated on a need-to-know basis, and apparently the president has no need to know. Who or what agency or combined organizations are behind this cloak of secrecy has been long debated among UFO investigators, with the onus of responsibility resting on a mysterious government official called the MJ12. Why or why not disclosure would be coming from the government will be discussed further, but for now, suffice it to say that Carter had batted a thousand in the no-information-forthcoming league.

Early on, Presidents Truman and Eisenhower were briefed on sightings, and it was rumored that Eisenhower even met with some of the occupants during a landing in a California desert. Nothing official was released to the public, nor were there any confirmations by the presidents themselves. Carter was the exception, even filling out an official report form for Alan Hynek's Center for UFO Studies (CUFOS), but he was not the only president to approach the subject from the witness perspective.

Ronald Reagan, while serving as governor of California, had a dramatic sighting of his own. Reagan's personal pilot gave this account:

> I was the pilot of the plane when we saw the UFO. Also on board were Governor Reagan and a couple of his security people. We were flying a Cessna Citation. It was maybe 9 or 10 o'clock at night. We were near Bakersfield, California, when Governor Reagan and the others called my attention to a big light flying a bit behind my plane. It appeared to be several hundred yards away. It was a fairly steady light until it began to accelerate, then it appeared to elongate. Then the light took off. It went up at a 45-degree angle at a high rate of speed. Everyone on the plane was surprised. Governor Reagan expressed amazement. I told the others I didn't know what it was … The UFO went from a normal cruise speed to a fantastic speed instantly … If you give an airplane power it will accelerate—but not like a hot rod, and that's what this was like.[92]

Governor Reagan would later say of the incident, "I was in a plane last week when I looked out the window and saw this white light. It was zigzagging around. We followed it for several minutes. It was a bright white light. We followed it to Bakersfield, all of a sudden, to our amazement, it went straight up into the heavens."[93]

International chaos. It appears that these objects have been making deliberate, calculated efforts to be seen for some time, such as what took place in Eupen, Belgium, on November 29, 1989. Journalist and UFO investigator Leslie Keen has delved deeply into the events of what has been called the Belgium Wave due to multiple reports of triangular shaped craft with bottom lights observed from November of 1989 to April of 1990. Keen was able to obtain firsthand information from retired Belgium Air Force

Major Wilfred De Brouwer, who disclosed details from reports received of a silent, 120-foot, triangle-shaped craft. The large craft displayed a brightly lit trajectory of white beams and red balls of light from its underside. The balls appeared to probe the area below the craft and then return to the craft. On a couple of occasion two triangle crafts were observed. Keen reports that thirteen policemen witnessed the craft, seventy reports came in, and an estimated 1,500 people were confirmed as witnesses on the busy night of November 29th..[94] From the high volume of reported sightings there was no doubt that Belgium was witnessing large unidentified objects in their airspace. Then it was our turn.

Bringing it home. Phoenix, Arizona, March 13, 1997. One sighting of this magnitude would have been sufficient and newsworthy, but for Phoenix, on this evening, there would be two. The evening of March 13 found thousands of individuals, families, and astronomy buffs gazing into Arizona's night sky in search of the awe-inducing Hale-Bopp asteroid. However, they were actually about to see another kind of spectacle.

According to reports from several witnesses, shortly before 7:00 p.m., a large V-shaped object the size of a 747 jet was first observed in the skies over Henderson, Nevada. A witness saw lights on both bottom and nose portions of the V. At 8:15 p.m. it was spotted over Paulden, Arizona, where a report was made by a retired police officer who described seeing a cluster of red-orange lights in formation with a fifth light trailing behind. Two minutes later, witnesses in Prescott, Arizona, were calling in reports of a huge object in the sky that was blocking out the stars as it passed overhead. John Kaiser, of Prescott Valley, reported seeing a cluster of lights in a triangle formation, all red except for a white light at the nose of the object. Tim Ley and his family observed an inverted V-shaped object, with lights on both sides and at the point of the nose, slowly glide noiselessly down the street where they lived and then move in the direction of the Phoenix Sky Harbor International Airport.

At 10:30 p.m. the public's attention shifted to a brilliant display of round white lights in an arc formation, silently and ominously hovering over Phoenix. The lights would appear one by one and then go out one by one, as the object remained stationary in the dark sky overhead. The object hovered in the area for more than two hours and was covered by the local and national news authorities with video of the lights hanging in the sky.

Phoenix was abuzz with reports of the strange lights, and the police department was inundated with calls, as was nearby Luke Air Force Base, whose only response was to later announce to the public that the lights resulted from flares being dropped from a military aircraft as part of a training exercise. That wasn't even a *plausible denial*, because flares do not fly in formation. Needless to say, the public didn't buy it and the story went international.

In the days that followed, the nation looked to Arizona officials, including Governor Fife Symington, for some sort of explanation for the strange lights that had invaded Arizona airspace on the night of March 13. The Arizona governor assured the public that he would get to the bottom of the matter: "We're going to find out if it was a UFO." That investigation resulted in a press conference with a room full of anxious citizens and reporters waiting for the official explanation. At that event, the governor's chief of staff—in full alien attire and a bulbous rubber mask—was led handcuffed into the room by a few of Phoenix's finest. It was amusing to some people, but for the serious-minded public, it went over like a pregnant pole-vaulter. The stunt served only to fan the flames of discontent among those who had absorbed the seriousness of the unexplained aerial intrusion that had occurred over their city.

Councilwoman Frances Barwood was the only city official to launch a serious investigation, which involved speaking with hundreds of witness, including police officers, pilots, and former military personnel. The evidence was there, but apparently no one in the government was interested, and Barwood became fodder for the local press. She commented to Leslie Keen, "If you talk about this, you will get ridiculed, chastised, pummeled with everything you can imagine, and eventually lose credibility."[95] That's often the modus operandi for keeping the lid on things, but the lid would not stay on.

Years later, having completed his term as governor, Fife Symington was interviewed by film producer James Fox about the Phoenix sightings, for a new release of his UFO documentary film *Out of the Blue*. On the topic of the ridicule endured by former constituent Stacey Roads, who had actually seen the object on that evening years earlier, Symington was direct and surprisingly forthcoming. "I never felt the overall situation was a matter of ridicule, although we certainly took advantage of it, no question about it," he admitted. "But I don't consider it a matter of ridicule. It was a legitimate occurrence; a craft of unknown origin; who knows where from; inexplicable, and probably one of the major sightings in modern history in the country, because so many people saw it in Maricopa County—and I saw it too."[96]

It was a stunning revelation. Symington wanted to set the record straight, and Fox and Keen had the resources to help him do just that. The former governor disclosed that his office did indeed make inquiries to legitimate government agencies dealing with public safety, the National Guard and Luke Air Force Base. But they had received no replies, except for an unceremonious "No comment" from the military. Even governors bat zero in this information arena. Then there was Stephenville.

Stephenville, Texas. Was it a case of hiding in plain sight or not hiding at all? This case involved a large object of massive length and girth that could slowly hover or shoot off at unbelievable speed. The town of Stephenville, Texas, gained national notoriety from a series of reports about unidentified flying objects witnessed in the night sky on January 8, 2008. One witness, pilot Steve Allen, said the object was huge and traveling fast, reaching an estimated elevation of three thousand feet. He described the object as being "about a half a mile wide and about a mile long. It was humongous, whatever it was."[97] Allen at first noticed a group of flashing white lights above his home, with green, yellow, and red lights forming a rectangle shape. Multiple witnesses described the lights as brighter than a welder's torch and moving at an estimated five thousand miles per hour. Steve Allen also reported seeing two F-16 fighters, presumably from nearby Carswell Air Force Base, in hot pursuit. Other witnesses described the object as possibly a mother ship because of its gigantic size.

AP reporter Angela Brown covered that angle by checking with the 301st Fighter Wing, at the Naval Air Station Fort Worth Joint Reserve Base, about whether they had F-16s in the air on the evening of January 8. Major Karl Lewis, spokesman for the 301st, reported that no F-16s or any other aircraft from the base had been in the air that evening. That claim was retracted days later when officials at the base suddenly remembered that ten F-16s had been in the air that night on a training mission. Even the news media raised an eyebrow at that sudden admission. But there is little doubt that *something* strange was in the skies over Stephenville that evening, and things were about to get a lot stranger.

Another witness, Rich Sorrells, interviewed by UFO investigator Linda Mouton How, gave an account of the sighting from a different perspective. His account was quoted in an article by Jim Marr, published in *UFO Magazine* in March 2008 and retold by UFO hunter William J. Birnes in *UFO Hunters, Book One*: "For some reason, I don't know what, I looked up and looked back down," began Sorrells. "I don't know what made me look up, but then I realized what I had seen with my eyes and immediately looked back up." Carrying his hunting rifle, which had a high-powered scope, Sorrells had been headed to the woods to go deer hunting, but then he had found himself hunting something else:

> I immediately turned down my rifle scope power to 3X and I looked back up there at it, and I can see what I would call a "mirage" coming off of it. It wasn't steam. I don't know, really—I've seen it like on a hot highway how the heat waves come up. And this was coming down … It basically looked like a piece of sheet iron that had been pressed. I couldn't see any nuts; no bolts, no rivets, no welds, no seams. I was really studying the structure of this trying to get an idea about how it was built. It is huge![98]

Sorrells estimated that the object was longer than three football fields and so massive in width that he could not see the edge of it. Whatever it is, he hopes it belongs to our military, because if it does have weapons capabilities and it's not ours, "then we're in trouble." He says that he doesn't know its capabilities, but "if they can build this, I'd sure hate to see if they got mad at us! You know what I am saying?"[99]

Another explanation that surfaces is that the event was a military training operation in which jets were dropping flares of phosphorescent chaff as a countermeasure against heat-seeking missiles. "These were the same explanations advanced a decade earlier to account for the dramatic Phoenix lights that captured the world's media's attention in 1997," says Birnes. "But now, as then, the flare explanation couldn't account for the strict formation of lights, their ability to move independently with respect to each other, and their ability to move in one direction without descending to the ground."[100]

More speculation would suggest that it may have been a jet guarding President Bush's ranch at Crawford. Birnes said that would have made sense except that Crawford was a good seventy-five miles away and President Bush hadn't been at his ranch that night.

Flight or fight? One could hardly blame any pilot for not wishing to see, report, or engage an unknown object of this magnitude. It appears that some of these unknown objects have a dark side when challenged and, perhaps because of their superior technology, a deep sense of invincibility as well.

This was the case when two Kentucky police officers had a run-in—or rather, a dogfight—with a UFO on the evening of February 27, 1993. "Two Jefferson County air unit police officers—described by their lieutenant as 'solid guys'—swear they had a two minute dogfight with a UFO during a routine helicopter patrol Friday night."[101] The report that appeared in the Louisville *Courier-Journal* said that the officers described their assailant as a "glowing pear-shaped object about the size of a basketball." Even though the fliers reached almost 100 miles per hour, the object flew rings around them. A third officer on the ground witnessed the strange interplay. The pilots, officers Kenny Graham and Kenny Downs, soon found themselves on a collision course with the object. All of a sudden the UFO hurtled toward the officers, firing three basketball-sized fireballs, which fortunately fizzled into nothing. An intimidation tactic? Perhaps, but the officers were none too relieved when the object disappeared after launching its assault.

These types of air encounters are not as uncommon as one might think. Some UFOs don't seem the least bit intimidated when discovered, and calling out the armed forces has little effect, not even with our advanced technology.

Calling all ships at sea. November 14, 2004. Navy Commander David Fravor and three other pilots were on a training mission 140 miles southwest of San Diego, California. What they were about to witness would cause a sensation when information of their encounter was released to the public in 2017, some thirteen years later. A video taken from his F/A-18F Super Hornet jet, released with the Pentagon's permission, shows Commander Fravor in hot pursuit of an unidentified flying object he described as looking like a "giant Tic Tac breath mint." "We chased it. I went after it," he said. Commander Fravor, one of the navy's best Top Gun pilots with eighteen years of experience, was in charge of Strike Fighter Squadron 41 aboard the USS *Nimitz*.

As they set out on their training mission on that clear, blue-sky day above the Pacific Ocean, they received a communiqué from the cruiser USS *Princeton*. The communiqué said that the *Princeton* had been tracking up to a dozen unidentified flying objects for two weeks, objects that could drop from above eighty thousand feet straight down to a hard stop at twenty thousand feet. Commander Fravor was given orders to break off the training mission and proceed to the coordinates of the USS *Princeton*, which was nearby.

Once on site, Fravor saw something that absolutely stunned him—a huge object he estimated to be ten feet wide and forty feet long, hovering at fifty feet above the ocean. The object was described as "an oblong, all-white tubular device with no window and no wings." It was not like anything Fravor had ever seen during his entire navy career: "It was almost jaw-dropping. It was very strange." He decided to go down for a closer look, but when he got within a half mile of the object, it picked up speed, crossed over the nose of his jet, and disappeared at a speed "well above supersonic." It was gone within two seconds. Commander Fravor would later tell *Fox News* host Tucker Carlson, "I believe it was something not of this world."[102]

Our world has taken notice, and the evidence continues to mount globally, but what will be our response? And what might be the reason for their self-revealing presence? Perhaps President Ronald Reagan's speech to the United Nations, on September 21, 1987, might offer a clue: "In our obsession with antagonism of the moment, we often forget how much unites all the members of humanity. Perhaps we need some outside, universal threat to make us recognize this common bond. I occasionally think how quickly our differences worldwide would vanish if we were facing an alien threat from outside this world."[103]

And maybe we are.

CHAPTER EIGHT
Stop and Be Friendly

Their very appearance in our skies in friendship carries the cosmic message of brotherhood.

—George Adamski[104]

If one thing is clear from the teachings of Adamski coming from the Venusian Master, from my Master, and, you will find, from Maitreya, it is that the Space Brothers are absolutely harmless to the people of earth.

—Benjamin Creme[105]

Brazil, South America:

The UFO had been making a faint buzzing sound, but when the light turned off, the buzzing stopped, and Hermelindo then heard a hissing like the noise of a small gaslight. Then something hit his shoulder and knocked him to the ground. Now panic-stricken, he jumped up and started to race toward his house, but the light suddenly came on again about twenty-five feet above him. At this point something even stranger happened. "They dropped four steel cables down with hooks on them and tried to catch me with them," he said. "I was dodging the hooks, and then a little creature came sliding down one of the cables. He hit me on the shoulder and tried to grab me, but I hit him and fought with him."[106]

This account of an horrific UFO encounter in Brazil comes from Bob Pratt's *UFO Danger Zone*, a well-written and carefully documented account of terrifying South American UFO encounters, most prominently those occurring in Brazil. Pratt was a seasoned journalist with over forty years of experience working for several newspapers and magazines, and in 1975 he became a UFO investigator. He coauthored *Night Siege: The Hudson Valley UFO Sighting* with Dr. J. Allen Hynek and fellow researcher Philip Imbrogno, and he has served as an editor of the Mutual UFO Network's journal publication. Needless to say, Pratt was very knowledgeable about the subject of human and alien interactions, particularly abductions.

Hermelindo Da Silva's altercation with the small creature was a life-or-death wrestling match until, in the mist of the alien-versus-human tussle, the creature fell to the ground. However, it was far from over. The small creature regained composure enough to slip a hook around one of Hermelindo's ankles and hoist him upside down toward the bottom opening of the craft. But before Hermelindo could be yanked to his doom, his foot became free of the hook and he fell to the ground. At that point the UFO occupants gave up the battle and took off. Pratt reported that Hermelindo, after regaining his wits, made his way home—scratched, bruised, and bleeding in part because of a sharp yucca plant that broke his fall. Not a pleasant experience by any definition.

Hermelindo was not the only one to find himself on the wrong end of a UFO abduction. Another Brazilian in desperate peril was Francisco Henrique De Souza, better known by his nickname Januncio. According to Pratt's report, it was about eight o'clock in the evening when Januncio began his walk home from a friend's house where he had been visiting. Along the way he lit a cigarette, and as Pratt wrote, "that's when his nightmare began."

Januncio looked up to see a large, black, silo-looking object hovering silently over his head. A door opened at the bottom of the craft, and Januncio could see clearly a man and a woman sitting in what resembled automobile seats. He observed that the woman, oddly, was possibly wearing a dress. A beam of light then projected down from the craft, and it was game on.

Januncio described the light as being uncomfortably hot, and he could feel himself being pulled up. Beyond terrified, Januncio wrapped his arms and legs around a nearby palm tree in a desperate attempt to anchor himself, but he was still pulled toward the craft. Suddenly there was a release and he slid back down the tree trunk, only to have the pulling sensation start again. This happened five times, and Januncio, who by then was in tears and hysterical, was convinced that he was going to die: "Then when the man and woman saw that I wasn't going to let go, they dropped something like hot oil on me to make me let go of the tree. I felt like I was between two big fires. I couldn't move. It burned my arms and hurt very much, but I was too afraid to let go. I almost died I was so scared."[107]

Finally the occupants of the craft, no doubt frustrated by Januncio's countermeasures, gave up the hunt. The bottom door closed, the light turned off, and the craft shot out of sight. As if the initial trauma of this event wasn't enough, Januncio suffered from burns resembling cigarette burns on his arms and legs, a painfully scratched chest, and severe headaches.

Admittedly these are some of the most bizarre encounters documented, but bizarre or not, the fact remains that these people suffered incredible physical and mental pain from their encounters with space people. That should be addressed, especially if promoting the idea that the Brothers (and I suppose sisters) from space have allegedly come here to help us. This kind of help, we don't need. UFOs are a difficult subject, but the malevolent actions reported by victims of these UFO encounters suggest a large and ominous picture. It is not all science, as one would suspect. These reports are quite different.

Why did these poor village people experience such hostile treatment from space people? Some might think that reports of these encounters are few and far between, but the evidence is quite the contrary. Pratt was well acquainted with the people of Brazil, having made over ten visits in a fifteen-year time span from 1978 to 1993. What he learned from going directly to these remote villages, talking one-on-one with the villagers, hearing their stories, walking their paths, exploring the evidence, and weighing the facts gave him deep insight about the Brazilian UFO phenomenon, as well as deep concern not only for these remote villagers but for all people. Of this he wrote, "The terror comes from UFOs—unidentified flying objects—and the aliens that operate them. These aliens are not our space brothers coming here to help us, as so many people want to believe.

These are nonhuman creatures that for years have been tormenting and terrorizing human beings, hurting many and killing some."[108] This isn't what one would expect from benevolent beings on a mission to save our species and our world from destruction.

While it is more pleasant to think of them as benevolent space buddies, their actions in many cases indicate that they have a much different and aggressive attitude toward humans. Although some people would disagree, pointing to the experiences of Adamski and other contactees, in reality the evidence suggests something much more sinister. If the kindly Space Brothers of Adamski's alleged association are out there, they have been keeping their distance while ill-tempered humanoids and other creatures run amok among the earth's populace.

Brazil has experienced spacecraft and their occupants taking quite malevolent action. One such incident of grave concern had the Brazilian government petitioning the United States for assistance in the investigation.

Can't take the heat. On November 4, 1957, at approximately 2:00 a.m., two sentries on watch at Fort Itaipu were startled by a brilliant light that suddenly appeared above them. They thought at first it was a star flaring up, but then they realized the object was not stationary. In fact, it was descending at incredible speed directly toward the fort. Slowing as it approached, at about 150 feet overhead the object came to a stop. It was huge. The sentries described the object as round, roughly 100 feet in diameter, and emitting an orange glow.

As the object hung silently above them, it began to display odd behavior, and they could hear a humming noise coming from its interior. Then the unexpected happened when, without warning, the soldiers were hit with a blast of intense heat. In *Aliens From Space*, US Marine Corps Major Donald Keyhoe writes of the attack:

> "It was instantly at full force with no flame, no visible beam. To the terrified sentries it seemed they were actually on fire. One, overcome by the intense heat, fell to his knees and collapsed. The other soldier, screaming from pain and fear, threw himself under a cannon for shelter. His cries woke up the garrison troops, but before any of them could get outside all the lights went out. Only

a moderate heat penetrated the interior of the fort, but this coupled with the total darkness was enough to start a panic. After a minute the lights came back on. Some of the Brazilian soldiers running to their battle stations saw the glowing UFO as it streaked skyward."[109]

The burned sentries were rushed inside for medical treatment, and although in serious condition, they were able to make a brief report to their superiors about what had happened. The question then arises, why were these men attacked?

Although speculations were made about motive, no reasonable explanation could be found and the case remains unexplained to this day. However, the incident did serve to attract a lot of attention from the military in both countries. A classified report was sent to air force headquarters in Washington, where it was quickly passed off as having originated with incompetent witnesses. In like manner, a report by MPs of an object landing briefly at the White Sands rocket test site would be explained away as the infamous planet Venus and a return visit by the same object as the moon. And so it would go with the official word from the officials in charge.

However, Bob Pratt wanted to tell what was actually happening, though often going unreported, to the men, women, and children living in some of the most remote areas of Brazil. It was enough that they were experiencing multiple UFO sighting, but unlike most other UFO sightings, these people were getting hurt. Pratt wrote of the reality of the cases:

> Frequently, an encounter of the unhealthy kind peculiar to Brazil begins when a UFO appears without warning just above the head of someone at night, revealing itself in a burst of sudden daylight and then chasing the terrified man, woman, or child as he or she flees in terror. At times, the UFOs have tried to pull a victim up into their craft with some unseen force, and sometimes they've taken people away. They've also used grappling hooks to snag unfortunate souls, and dropped hot liquid on the arms and shoulders of others to make them let go of trees and bushes.[110]

Any of these incidents would unnerve and terrify most individuals, no matter where they lived. These poor victims suffered hours of torment from the less-than-honorable Space Brothers' repeated attempts to flush their victims out from hiding places behind trees and bushes, or from the intense heat from a brilliant light penetrating the rooftops of their homes. And just when the Brazilian citizens thought it couldn't get worse, it did.

One of the most bizarre and disturbing reports to make press was an official documented case of a *human mutilation* performed in the exact manner of an animal mutilation. This shocking report, complete with photographs, stunned the general public and especially UFO investigators. Of this abomination, UFO researcher G. Cope Shellhorn wrote, "If this case is authentically UFO-related—and at this time I have no reason to believe it is not—then all of us are going to have to reevaluate to one degree or another our tentative conclusions as to the possible specific intentions, moral perspectives and general agenda that some of our extraterrestrial visitors may have."[111]

But before the 1970s Brazil UFO attacks were documented, things had been breaking loose in the United States. In Hopkinsville, Kentucky, on August 21, 1955, Billy Ray Taylor and his wife, June, arrived for a get-together with friend Elmer Sutton and his family at the Sutton's farm. The gathering included eight adults and three children, who were all enjoying their time together.

At about 7:00 p.m., Billy Ray stepped out of the house to get water from a well in the front yard. That's when it all started. While drawing water, Billy Ray noticed a huge bright object descending into a gulch nearby. The object appeared to be emitting some type of exhaust that billowed and glowed with all the colors of the rainbow. Startled and confused by what he had just witnessed, Billy Ray returned to the house and told the family what he had seen. Astonishingly, no one bothered to go outside for a look.

Approximately one hour later, the Suttons' dog began to bark ferociously in the yard. Fearing an intruder, Billy Ray and Elmer grabbed a shotgun and a .22 rifle and headed for the kitchen door. No one could have predicted what happened next.

There in the dark, making its way across the yard was a skinny, dwarflike creature with a large head, wide mouth, large elephant-type ears, and yellow eyes—and it was *glowing*. The creature had long skinny arms with claw-like hands, which it appeared to be holding above its head as it advanced toward the house. Billy Ray and Elmer decided to shoot first and ask questions later. The creature was knocked to the ground and somersaulted backward, but immediately it got up, turned around, and disappeared into the dark.

Hearing a scurrying noise, the men looked up to see another creature on the roof of the house. The men again opened fire and hit the creature, which instead of being knocked off the roof, floated gently to the ground. Panic began to set in when the realized that gunfire had no effect on the creatures. They quickly retreated inside the house, where everyone stayed barricaded for most of the night, all the while observing the strange creatures milling around outside the house.

Tensions began to rise from repeated attempts by the creatures to gain access into the house. Around 11:00 p.m., the Taylors and Suttons tired and terrified, could take it no longer and decided to make a run for it. They dashed from the house, jumping into two separate cars, and floored it all the way to the police station. The police chief could see that the entire group was quite upset and fearful. Later they all returned with the police to the house, where they found no sign of the creatures or the craft that had settled into the nearby gulch. It wasn't over. The police left about 2:00 am, and the family went to bed. Then the creatures returned, surrounding the house, and began peering in the windows. Gunfire erupted once again. The strange creatures finally withdrew around 5:15 am.[112]

Although no conclusions could be reached about what the Suttons experienced that August evening, the harrowing event remains fresh in the minds of family members to this day. One could easily add the dwarflike creatures to the "high strangeness" categories of Bigfoot, the Cupacabra, Mothman, and the Jersey Devil. However, until someone bags one of these creatures, there is no way of knowing the truth of their existence.

Taking the law into *their* hands. It was 1:40 on the morning of August 2, 1979, in Stephen, Minnesota. Marshal County Deputy Sheriff Val Johnson, on patrol in his squad car, reached the intersection of Road 5 and State 220. Looking down 220, he saw something odd that appeared to be a brilliant light eight to twelve inches in diameter, three to four feet off the ground. Thinking that it might me an aircraft in trouble, he turned onto 220 to investigate. That's when the unthinkable happened. "From the point of intersection," Johnson recalled, "my Police vehicle proceeded south in a straight line 854 feet, at which point the brakes were engaged by forces unknown to myself, as I do not remember doing this, and I left about approximately 99 feet of black marks on the highway before coming to rest sideways in the road with the grille of my hood facing in an easterly direction." Upon first seeing the strange light, Johnson had been, in his words, "rendered unconscious, neutralized or unknowing for a period of approximately 39 minutes."

When he awoke, Johnson assessed his situation and noticed that both his vehicle's clock and his wristwatch were slow by fourteen minutes. He noticed other things as well—the windshield of his car was shattered, one headlight and red emergency light were damaged, and the radio antennas were bent. Johnson called for backup, and when the responding officer arrived, he found Johnson's squad car sideways in the road and Johnson shaken and complaining of eye pain. An ambulance was called and Johnson was taken to a hospital, where he received a diagnosis of burns to his eyes similar to what could be caused by a welder's torch. Johnson was treated and sent home. His eyes would later heal from the burns and his eyesight would return to normal, but his life would not.[113]

Although many news publications had a heyday spoofing UFOs, the public was taking it quite seriously—and so was the air force. UFOs were showing up over military bases, atomic testing facilities and power plants, missile silos, major cities, and rural regions. Still the questions remained: Who and what are they, and what are their capabilities? It might be frightening to know.

A close encounter of the intervention type took place at Vandenberg Air Force Base in Big Sur, California, in 1964. The account was given by former Air Force Lieutenant Robert Jacobs, who was in charge of filming the launch of a large Atlas missile, which had been built to carry a nuclear warhead. That particular launch, however, carried an unarmed dummy warhead:

> "They counted down the missile and we heard engine ignition lift-off so we knew the missile was underway," stated Jacobs. "We were looking down south, southwest,

and the missile popped up through the fog. It was just beautiful and I hollered, there it is. Our guys on our M45 tracking mount with a 180-inch lens on it filmed the missile. And the big BU telescope swung over and got it and we followed the thing. And sure enough we could see all three stages of powered flight boosters, they burned out and dropped away. And then of course, to our naked eye all we saw was a smoke trail going off into subspace as it headed off toward its target, which was an island in the Pacific. Well, that was our first filming of a launch and we got it."[114]

And they got something more. Jacobs and his crew had just finished the filming of the Atlas missile launch off the coast of California. Jacobs was the officer in charge of optical instrumentation, and he and his crew were assigned to film ballistic missile tests for the air force. The Atlas was designed to carry a nuclear payload, but the one they were filming that day carried a non-nuclear dummy. Engineers wanted to catch a frame-by-frame sequencing of the launch to look for problems that might jeopardize launches in the future. Some of the early ICBMs—intercontinental ballistic missiles—were exploding upon launch, but that day was different. The launch went off without a hitch, or so they thought.

Jacobs and the crew, satisfied that they had gotten good film of the launch, sent it to the base for review. One or two days later, as Jacobs recalls, he was summoned to Major Mansmann's office at the First Strategic Aerospace Division. The major was present, along with two men in gray suits, a projector and screen, and the roll of film Jacobs had taken. Jacobs was instructed to have a seat, and they rolled the film. At first Jacobs was impressed by the film quality and capture of the stages of launch; stages one, two, and three fell away, leaving the warhead streaking sixty miles upward at an estimated speed of 11,000 to 14,000 miles per hour.

Then unexpectedly another object flew into the frame—a saucer with a dome on top. Jacobs remembers the event clearly: "So this thing fires a beam of light at the warhead, hits it and then it moves to the other side and fires another beam of light, then moves again and fires another beam of light, then goes down and fires another beam of light, and then flies out the way it came in. And the warhead tumbles out of space."[115] The object had taken down a United States nuclear missile.

That event was not made public until eighteen years later when Jacobs, no longer in the air force, chose to speak of it—and at great cost. As a result of his disclosure, Jacobs, now a university professor, has become an object of public ridicule, been threatened, received ominous phone calls at all hours, and had someone blow up his mailbox.

It's been said that the truth is out there, but sometimes that truth is hard to find. This is especially true of events involving military facilities, when national security is a concern and thus information is not forthcoming, perhaps available only on a need-to-know basis, or it may be sanitized for public consumption before being released.

March 16, 1967. An ominous and disturbing event took place at Malmstrom AFB in Lewiston, Montana, where UFOs shut down vital missile targeting systems. Ten missiles at one site, plus ten missiles at another site thirty-five miles away, went to alert status, and panic set in. Published by MUFON, our account of this event comes from the incredible testimony given by retired Air Force Captain Robert Salas.

Captain Salas was on duty as a deputy missile combat crew commander at a Minuteman Launch Control Facility (LCF). He was underground in the missile silo that morning when he received a call from his NCO in charge of topside security. The NCO informed the captain that he and other guards had observed UFOs flying over the LCF, objects that the guard could only describe at the time as lights. Captain Salas advised the NCO to keep a watch and inform him if anything further developed, and it didn't take long. "Five or ten minutes later," testified Salas, "I received a second call from my security NCO. This time he was much more agitated and distraught. He stated that there was a UFO hovering just outside the front gate! He wanted to know what he should do. I don't recall what I said except to secure the fenced areas. As we were talking, he said he had to go because one of the guards had been injured."[116]

The captain contacted his commander to inform him of the calls received from the guard. Then it started to happen: "Within seconds our missiles began shutting down from 'Alert' status to 'No-Go' status. I recalled that most, if not all, of our missiles had shut down in rapid succession." Salas was surprised by this, because in most cases if a missile went off alert status, it caused a power outage. In that situation a generator would kick in, restore power, and the LF would come back online. "The problem was not a lack of power; some signal had been sent to the missiles which caused them to go off alert," he explained.[117]

After reporting the incident to the command post, Captain Salas checked the status of the injured guard. The guard on duty told him that the guard had been injured when he approached the UFO, but not seriously, and that he was being taken by helicopter to the base. A maintenance crew was working to restore power to the LF, but by the time they were relieved by a replacement crew later that morning, the missiles had still not been brought back online.

Captain Salas made a point of talking directly to the security guard about the UFOs for any additional information the guard could provide, but the only additional detail was that the UFO "had a red glow and appeared to be saucer-shaped." Salas testified, "I do not recall any other details about its appearance" except for what the guard had told him. "He repeated that it had been immediately outside the front gate, hovering silently."[118] We may presume that sightings at nuclear and military facilities continue to this day, but we may not hear about them.

So were the objects showing concern for the planet or flexing their superior muscles? If these reports are accurate, they have shown that they are able to do either or both. This is disturbing. Disturbing, too, is what appears to be their lack of satisfaction with just stretching their legs or collecting dirt samples. These space beings, humanoid or otherwise, appear to have another agenda.

Add to that the combined descriptions of these perpetrators from the people who claim to have encountered them, and an entire alien social structure emerges. Now we are seeing a variety of beings and a hierarchy of command. Some look human—tall, blond hair, distinct facial features, wearing gowns or space suits—and are usually referred to as Nordics. Small beings with large heads, ears, and black almond-shaped eyes, referred to as the grays, have long arms and wear tight silver suits. There are tall grays, often seen as the leaders or supervisors, and small elf-type creatures. They make grunting noises, gibberish, speaking fast and hard to understand, but they can communicate telepathically with humans. Some give off strange smells, and their skin reportedly is hot to the touch. They can float, skim across the ground, and leap great distances—and most importantly, they may be working with governments in exchange for technology.

Catch and release has become a commonly reported experience among people claiming to have been abducted by aliens. Also common is the idea that the aliens need human resources—DNA, eggs, sperm, and partial pregnancies—for what appears to be a hybrid program being conducted in an attempt to mix human and alien DNA. The result, when successful, is the production of a hybrid child, and those who claim to have seen one describe it as an odd-looking child with a mix of human and alien features. These children are often shown to their abducted mothers as if for approval. The common assumption is that the aliens are attempting to produce a new race of hybrid beings for an undisclosed purpose.

Human abductees are usually returned to Earth, shaken but overall physically unharmed, with little or no memory of what transpired. Less fortunate are the cattle and other livestock that have been found mutilated, often with blood and reproductive body parts taken for use by the aliens. Something evil this way comes, and the aftermath is tragic and grotesque. However, I believe there may be another consideration—*rogue elements.* Brad Steiger and Joan Whritenour noticed this trend early on:

> There are the cosmic positive thinkers who sincerely believe such contacts to be initiated by the benign "space brothers" in order to better prepare man for the glories of the "new age" of interplanetary brotherhood. Then there are those who feel that such privileged communication from the Organization is but an elaborate ploy to insure the silence of those who have witnessed certain saucer sightings. Those who hold this view also believe that there is at least one UFO group which is, at best, indifferent to the fate of homo sapiens and which may even be hostile to Earth's inhabitants. Researcher Robert A. Stiff recently advised: Check your past copies of Saucer Scoop and other UFO publications and see how many cases are reported that suggest outright hostility and attack by the UFOs, based on fact, and how many others report friendly contact

with our "space brothers." You will find that the former outweigh the latter by a wide margin.[119]

The late John Keel was even more forthright: "The UFOs don't want us to know where they are from. They have been lying to contactees since 1897!"[120]

Hostilities? *UFO Interplanetary Visitors*, by the late Raymond Fowler, focuses in part on the hostile intent of some space visitors. One entire chapter is dedicated to a wave of reports that were springing up across North America in late fall of 1973. Strange things were being seen in the sky, people were getting hurt, and none of it was making sense.

One such encounter, in October 1973, involved a Missouri truck driver and his wife. The couple spotted a UFO while driving, and the man stuck his head out the window to get a better look. That was a mistake. A large ball of fire struck his face with enough force to knock his glasses off. Although temporarily blinded, he managed to stop his rig. He was unable to regain his sight, so his wife drove him to a nearby hospital, where he was treated for burns and released. The encounter with the truck driver may have been accidental or circumstantial, and there is no way of knowing for sure. But there have been several well-documented UFO reports that indicate unprovoked acts of hostility.

According to Fowler, there are several examples of what appear to be unprovoked hostile acts by UFOs and their occupants. An Ohio event that took place in March 1968 shows that even children can and have become victims. According to Fowler's report,

> Young Gregory L. Wells, of Beallsville, Ohio, was returning from his grandmother's house to his own home next door when he saw an oval-shaped UFO hovering just over some trees. It was shortly after 8:30 p.m., March 19, 1968, when a large red object appeared that was so bright it illuminated the road beneath it. According to Mrs. James E. Wells, the boy's mother, the object had a band of dimmer red lights flashing around its center. Then the boy saw it. "I stopped," Gregory recalled. "I wanted to run or scream but suddenly a big tube came out of the bottom

which moved from side to side until it came to me and a beam of light shot out." Gregory turned away as the light beam hit the upper part of his arm, knocking him to the ground. His jacket caught fire, and the boy rolled around on the ground screaming with fright. Both his mother and grandmother responded.

Mrs. Wells also reported that after the attack, the UFO just "faded away."[121] During the encounter, it was noted that a large night-light on a nearby pole went out, electromagnetic interference affected the television set, and the grandmother's dog reacted violently.

Gregory was taken to Beallsville Hospital and treated for second-degree burns. The scars were still visible three months later. The boy's jacket was sent to a nearby town for analysis and no evidence of radiation was found, nor was any found at the scene, although Civil Defense Director Ward Strikling, who combed the area with a Geiger counter, said that some types of radioactive beams leave no detectable traces.

UFO investigator Dr. James E. McDonald would later interview several people in the Beallsville area. Some said that they had seen a long, cylindrical object moving at very low altitude in the vicinity of the Wells property that night. Conversations with people who knew the boy and his family suggested no reason to discount the story:

> "What are we to make of this and similar incidents?" Fowler asks. "My own opinion is that events such as this may possibly be analogous to human behavior. In this case, perhaps this really was an intentional act of unwarranted aggression. Our country's recent involvement in Vietnam has brought news of atrocities committed against innocent civilians by U.S. servicemen. Someone told me that he knew of cases where U.S. soldiers had shot at Vietnam civilians for the fun of it. We shudder at such stories and rightly so. Men have been brought to trial and justice because of such atrocities. However, we do not condemn the majority of U.S. servicemen for the wrong actions of a few."[122]

However, aggression did occur, and there should be no excusing that aggression regardless of necessity or lack of emotion especially attacks against defenseless children. Neither should we assume, according to Fowler, that all UFOs are hostile to the human race because of the actions of a few. Have some UFOs and their occupants gone rogue?

Was this the case in the attack that occurred in Oklahoma one evening in 1964? The account given by Brad Steiger and Mary Whritenour said that eleven-year-old Mary R. was at home with her parents on a farm on the outskirts of Oklahoma City. An argument had taken place between Mary and her parents that caused the girl to run outside. Before her mother could even get to the back door, she heard Mary scream in a high-pitched wail of terrible pain. "She ran into the blackness outside in time to see something that she later described as 'sort of like a flying ashtray' flying away from the house. Mary was lying on the ground, about thirty feet from the house. There was the sickening, acrid stench of burnt flesh in the air."[123] Horrified by her daughter's appearance, the mother asked her what had happened, but the girl was unable to speak because of the intense pain she was experiencing from the burns. The girl was taken to a local hospital but within hours was transferred to Tinker Air Force Base hospital for further treatment and observation by the air force. No official word was released concerning the case. Was this a random flyby attack? What sense does it make?

One case that did receive widespread news media coverage involved an eight-year-old boy who suffered first- and second-degree burns from an unidentified object that hovered above him. It happened in Hobbs, New Mexico, on June 2, 1964. According to an official report published by the Aerial Phenomena Research Organization, that afternoon the boy had been standing outside the back door of his grandmother's laundry. His grandmother, Mrs. Frank Smith, had been preparing lunch for the two of them, when she looked up to see "an elongated metal object swoop down out of the sky and hover above Charles." She was so frightened that she couldn't speak. There wasn't time anyway. The object, later described as looking somewhat like a top, shot black soot and fire down upon the boy, who could only stand there with eyes shut tight and hair standing on end. Within seconds, the object shot off into the sky. When Charles's grandmother rushed out to him, she saw that his face was swelling, his eyes were swollen shut, and the black soot embedded in his skin made his nose barely visible. She described one ear as looking like a piece of raw meat. The boy was sent to a local hospital, where he was treated for first- and second-degree burns.[124] As you might suspect, I have a particular animus against these kinds of reports.

If we were to sift through the variety of UFO reports received nationally over the years, we would find several documented cases of people being nearly run off the road by a UFO, people being harassed by repeated visits to their homes, and UFOs randomly attacking civilians, military personnel, and police. Such attacks do not fit the general descriptions of what people consider to be valid UFO encounters, or at least not what is commonly reported to the public.

Steiger and Whritenour wrote two books on the topic of hostile alien encounters involving documented harassment of civilians and military personnel. Even acclaimed rocket scientist Werner von Braun had his misgivings about these visitors. As early as January 1959, Dr. von Braun issued a statement to a representative from Neues Europa saying, "We find ourselves faced by powers which are far stronger than we had hitherto assumed, and whose base of operation is at present unknown to us. More I cannot say at present. We are now engaged in entering into closer contact with these powers and in six or nine months' time it may be possible to speak with more precision on the matter."[125] That "matter" had to include encounters involving civilians as well as the military and what did he mean by getting closer in contact with "these powers"? Are singular UFOs performing random strikes, or is it a group effort?

One report seemed somewhat reminiscent of the clusters of UFOs that were showing up in Washington, DC, in the 1950s. This report, dating back to November 1965, found air force planes and one navy reconnaissance plane in a game of tag with fifteen "glowing spheres." According to the report, "The glowing spheres were playing tag with the jets, letting them come close, then speeding up leaving the AF planes with their faces hanging in mid-air."[126]

Although the pilots had been taking the flak of indignation, Steiger and Whritenour were taking flak too: "After the release of *Flying Saucers Are Hostile*, the authors were subject to a great deal of abusive mail from those self-appointed spokesmen for offended 'space brothers.' Did we not know, some letters asked, that the UFOs brought benign Big Brothers who were transporting cancer cures and salvation from their celestial dwelling place?" Furthermore, it was pointed out that Steiger and Whritenour had severely irritated the galactic messengers of peace and goodwill, although one person begged to differ. "One letter-writer, however, identifying himself as the 'official spokesman' of the beneficent Brethren, wrote to tell us that 'they' had approved of *Hostile* because there were, indeed, evil, or negative, saucer crews and the world needed to be warned of their presence."[127] Add to that the more recent reports of abductees claiming to see all manner of atrocities, body parts floating in vats of water, mutilated cows, hybrid infants, and ill-tempered grays, and our concerns become quickly elevated.

Most people who believe in the reality of UFOs want to picture alien ships and their crews in a positive light, as caring overseers of humanity. They want "We are not alone" to evoke warm fuzzy feelings, but these negative accounts are part of the evidence of the existence of aliens as well. Is it intentional?

There appears to be an obvious attempt to paint some of the Space Brothers in a bad light, whereas other Brothers appear to be benevolent and nonintrusive. Why? Are we looking at a good guy versus bad guy scenario? However, diabolically minded ETs might pretend to be good, when in fact they're all bad guys.

In recent years, there have been claims ranging from three to four alien types up to hundreds of alien types, and in each case there are warring factions within the mix. It is enough to look out for warring factions on Earth, let alone among aliens. But then again, if aliens seeded humanity, then they must be our benevolent caretakers, right? Right?

Well, maybe not. But pushing all reservations aside, we still want to think of them as the good guys, which could be terribly wrong. If there is a conflict, what is it about? Is there anarchy within the ranks? Rebellion running amok? Rogue elements striking out on their own? In my mind, all this raises a very important question. Biblically speaking, if God experienced anarchy in His ranks, as we read in Revelation 12:7, is it possible—just possible—that Satan might have anarchy in his?

Could some have vindictive motives for their ultimate doom? Are they out to even the score? Does one Mr. Big among the principalities think he is more powerful than another Mr. Big, while lesser groups call upon alien brethren higher up the nasty scale? Why not? Demons do, according to

Matthew 12:45. Could some be breaking ranks and riding roughshod over anyone or anything, without care or concern, while others seek to create their own forces with the help of human DNA? There is any number of possible reasons why aliens do what they do, and these might be some.

Logically thinking, if our space buddies *are* butting heads, wouldn't that leave the door open for a rescue of Earth should some of these bad boys get out of control? Will it be a triumphant return of our ancient ancestors in the nick of time? After all, our entire existence might depend on them, and what we think we have learned of them from our past may impact our future, perhaps in more ways than we can imagine.

Although many people believe that aliens are here for our benefit, even going so far as believing they are our benefactors, a more serious look at this presumption is needed. Does our salvation lie with the aliens? Or are we blindly welcoming our own demise? Steiger and Whritenour present some sobering thoughts:

> Certain saucer cultists, who have been expecting space brethren to bring along some pie in the sky, continue to deliver saucer-inspired sermons on the theme that the saucers come to bring starry salvation to a troubled world. The self-appointed ministers who preach this extraordinary brand of evangelism ignore the fact that not ALL "saucers" can be considered friendly. Many give evidence of hostile actions. There is a wealth of well- documented evidence that UFOs have been responsible for murders, assaults, burning by direct-ray focus, radiation sickness, kidnappings, pursuits of automobiles, attacks on homes, disruption of power sources, paralysis, mysterious cremations, and destructions of aircraft. Dozens of reputable eyewitnesses claim to have seen alien personnel loading their space vehicles with specimens from earth, including animals, soil and rocks, water and struggling human beings.[128]

Do UFOs present a threat to humanity? Some who have studied their existence say yes. According to physicist James McDonald, "The world better wake up to flying saucers before it is too late."[129]

CHAPTER NINE
Something's Here

At my home, I have been visited by unseen entities whom I believe to be the pilots of these weird disks. They were invisible to me and made no attempt to communicate. But I was aware of their presence because I could see my rugs and furniture sink down under their weight, as they walked about the room, or sat on various objects in the room.

—Kenneth Arnold[130]

A ball of light suddenly appeared in their home. It started in one daughter's room and then made its way down to the parents' room. "My dad was so frightened he fell to his knees and started reciting the Lord's Prayer."

—Kim Arnold on her father, Kenneth Arnold[131]

Kenneth Arnold's report of the nine objects he witnessed during the summer of 1947 received widespread coverage in the public media. However, there was an after-story that was not publicly known.

Kim Arnold has recently come forward with additional information about her father. In an article that appeared in *AP Magazine*, editor Brent Raynes relays interesting and insightful information about Kenneth Arnold, as provided by his daughter Kim in an interview given to Mike Clelland of Eyewitness Radio. Kim said that not long after her father had his famed sighting of the saucers, strange things began to occur in their home. A ball of light suddenly materialized in their home, first appearing in her older sister's room and then traveling down the hall to her parents' room. It was a frightening and unwelcomed event: "My dad was so frightened he fell to his knees and started reciting the Lord's Prayer." Arnold began to exhibit other strange behavior and, after seeing unusual indentations left in chair cushions, came to believe that invisible entities were visiting his home.

This was not Arnold's first encounter with a ball of light. In an interview, Arnold said that at age seven, he saw a globe of light in the room where the body of his great-grandmother lay before the funeral. He was convinced, too, that balls of lights were often seen at accident sites where fatalities had occurred.[132]

Then Kim spoke of another sighting that her father had in 1952. Arnold had reported observing two flying saucers while he was flying over Susanville, California. One was solid in appearance, and the other was transparent enough for Arnold to clearly see pine trees through its center. This discrepancy caused him to believe that perhaps the objects could change in density and appearance, likening them to jellyfish. As a result, he came to believe that the objects were possibly living things, perhaps even having a connection to death and dying, as assuming such a shape (orb) would provide a means of travel.

Additionally, in research conducted by Jenny Randles and Peter Hough, Arnold revealed that he had experienced many sightings. But the 1952 sighting, reportedly his eighth, offered a different perspective—that something *other* than spaceships might be frequenting the skies above us, and that no matter what else they might be, they are intelligent. Reflecting on the encounter, Arnold later said, "I had the feeling with these things that they are aware of me, but they made no effort to come close."[133]

Kenneth Arnold was regarded by many people as an honest and respectable man, who over the years became bitterly opposed to defending himself against those who wished to peg him as a phony and a crank. Despite the fallout, he continued to investigate unidentified flying objects, all the while enduring the aftermath of public opinion. Arnold eventually became disillusioned with the whole subject, and his attitude changed to one of anger and resentment. Who could blame him? What evidence other than his testimony could he present? Nevertheless, most of the public at that time was not willing to hear or accept it. Arnold passed from this world in 1984. Still, the public was keen to hear about the paranormal, and it would seem that those involved in the early UFO community did not disappoint.

Betty Hill should be considered a charter member of the UFO Hall of Fame. She and her husband, Barney, were the first to claim actual contact—or rather, *abduction*—by gray, almond-eyed aliens. Much has been written about their encounter, most notably John Fuller's *The Interrupted Journey*, which goes into great detail about the encounter and its aftereffect on the Hills. The alleged abduction occurred on the evening of October 17, 1961. The Hills, returning from a vacation in Canada, were driving in a remote area of the White Mountains of New Hampshire when they spotted what they thought was a brilliant star. The star appeared to be following their car. The details become sketchy after that, and it was only after they returned home that they began to question why the drive took an additional two hours. The Hills could not account for the missing time.

The Hills' case was unique in that the only recall they had of the missing time came in the form of disjointed dream sequences that, upon waking, left them confused and anxious. Adding to the intrigue, physical evidence indicated that something out of the ordinary had occurred—strange marks on the car, a broken binocular strap, a mysterious stain and tear in Betty's dress, and unusual scuffmarks on the tops of Barney's shoes.

When they sought counseling to deal with the unusual dreams they were both having, the Hills were put in contact with Boston psychiatrist Benjamin Simon. After meeting with the Hills, Simon recommended hypnosis as a way to recall the events of that evening, and the Hills agreed. Thus Simon set a precedent for the use of hypnosis by other investigators and provided a template of sorts for alleged alien abductions going forward.

Through a series of hypnosis sessions, several details surrounding the missing time began to unfold, all ultimately pointing to a dramatic abduction by alien beings. During one session, Betty recalled that she and Barney were grabbed and escorted aboard a spacecraft by the odd-looking beings, then undressed and placed on an exam table. Their captors conducted examinations on their bodies, including at one point the painful insertion of a large needle into Betty's navel. After the examination, as she was led out of the exam room, Betty noticed a peculiar star map that she was able to draw from memory later. She believed the map depicted the star group around Zeta Reticuli.

Betty Hill, as it turned out, was no stranger to the subject of UFOs. Several years earlier, Betty's sister, Janet Miller, had her own alien encounter. According to Janet's daughter, Kathleen Marden, who is also a trained investigator for MUFON, Janet observed a "blimp-shaped craft" hovering over a field. Several small disc-shaped objects began to approach the craft from all directions and were seen going inside the craft. Once all were inside, the craft rose straight up and disappeared.[134]

Nor were the Millers strangers to the paranormal, for they believed that a ghost was haunting their home. Janet believed the ghost was that of a young girl named Hannah. Betty wasn't so sure it was the spirit of a young girl, but she did acknowledge the strange goings-on in the house. Hangers would fly out of a closet, strange orb lights the size of baseballs were seen floating throughout the house, and doors would open and close on their own.

Marden believed these paranormal events may have been related not only to the "UFO hunts" she and her family participated in, but also to her aunt Betty's "psychophysical" experiments. These experiments were orchestrated by a science writer, Robert Hohmann, and called for Betty to attempt to communicate telepathically with the ETs. This was done in the hope of her setting up an actual meeting with them and acquiring physical evidence as a result. The ETs were not manifesting themselves, but other things were.

Marden writes that in a letter to Hohmann, her aunt Betty complained that strange things had begun to happen to her, Barney, and family members. "These things are happening to Barney and me as well to most of my relatives, but they have been witnessed by other people who were present." She adds, "We do not believe in ghosts, but we do believe in space travel and life on other planets, so we wonder if these space travelers might have the ability to be unseen to us."[135]

It is difficult to imagine space travelers performing antics long associated with poltergeists, such as banging doors, audible footsteps, water and lights turning on, personal items disappearing and reappearing later, and so forth. Although these events are unconventional, they are not unbelievable. Marden has documented accounts of others who have shared similar paranormal experiences in relationship to UFOs, including a sighting that she had from the porch of her parents' home in the 1960s. She described what she saw as a disc-shaped object with a row of windows, which was hovering over her grandparents' barn. Later she would experience more sightings when she rode along with her mother and Betty on evening UFO hunts.

As an investigator for MUFON, Marden has been given the opportunity to talk to witnesses firsthand, and she has retained particular interest in claims of abduction. From these investigations, she noted some similarities among many of the abductees. In an interview with author and radio host Brent Raynes, Marden said that the results of a survey conducted among abductees showed that paranormal aspects occurring after abduction was a common occurrence. "The majority of abduction experiencers," she said, "reported that they witnessed paranormal activity in their homes for the first time after their first abduction experience. A small percentage reported to me that it was already occurring prior to their first abduction event."[136]

One female abductee testified about an unusual and no doubt terrifying nighttime encounter. She had awoken one evening to find a nonhuman entity sitting at the foot of her bed, and he was not alone. There also was a negative energy there that spoke to her in a gruff voice, and then she was suddenly swept up, feet-first, into the craft.

Some investigators dealing with abduction scenarios can suffer consequences as well, perhaps because they become so closely involved in the abductees' lives that they put themselves into the experiences. Is that empathy or recall? Such was the case with Raymond E. Fowler.

Fowler was well acquainted with the topic of UFOs and believed strongly in their existence. In the 1960s, Fowler was already a seasoned investigator with the National Investigations Committee on Aerial Phenomena and had investigated several UFO reports. In 1971, he was the Massachusetts state director for MUFON and also served as an investigator for J. Allen Hynek's Center for UFO Studies (CUFOS). In 1975, Fowler became MUFON's national director of investigations and was instrumental in putting in place set standards and procedures for the MUFON training manual, including the proper method for taking reports and processing evidence.

However, Fowler's interests were not merely scientific. Like so many people involved in researching this phenomena, he experienced a deepening interest and a sense of providence in becoming more aware of the possibility of his own past or future contact, which some believe is of the fourth kind or actual interaction.

Seconding this notion with a succession of paranormal events is another abductee of a different genre, Betty Andreasson. For several years, she claimed to be the victim of abductions by small, claylike-skinned grays and their leader—events that, in her mind, often bordered on spiritual rather than hostile. Fuller is perhaps best known for his widely publicized investigation of Andreasson's abduction case and authored five books on the alleged Andreasson encounters. Andreasson claimed to have been abducted by small gray aliens that would enter her home with the ability to pass through doors and put her family in some type of suspended animation. Then they and their leader, Quazgaa, would take Andreasson aboard their ship for the all-too-familiar physical examination. Later on, her daughter would follow suit, claiming abduction by these same entities. Andreasson asked them if they were of God, and they told her they were. Oddly, they would talk of God, but not about Jesus.

At some point during his investigation of Andreasson, Fowler came to ponder the possibility of having had his own abduction. Much to his family's disapproval, Fowler continued to pursue that possibility and began to relate to much of Andreasson's experiences as if claiming them as his own. Whether it was because of his association with Andreasson or simply his own willingness to entertain the idea of a personal abduction, Fowler suddenly began to recall events of his childhood that, after much contemplation, convinced him that he had been an abductee too, as verified by a scoop mark that one day appeared on his ankle.

One can see a generational connection from the fact that Fowler's family experienced a variety of paranormal experiences. Allegedly, Raymond Fowler Sr. was visited by three light beings. His mother as a teenager saw a large silent object with flashing lights that hovered over her and her friends one evening in 1945, followed by three more sightings over a ten-year period. His three brothers have seen UFOs, and one brother and his son had physical evidence of what they believed was a scoop mark as well. His sister-in-law also claimed to have seen small gray entities outside her bedroom window and had observed poltergeist activity in her mother's home.

Despite jests about little green men, during the 1950s and 1960s there were no reported grays. Instead, it was friendly blond-haired, blue-eyed Nordic types scolding Earthlings for the devastation and nuclear threat endangering our planet. Now it is the gray aliens, a term attributed to Whitley Strieber, who have taken center stage. When Strieber's book *Communion* hit the bookstores, it prominently featured the popular alien head with huge slanted dark eyes.

Characteristically evasive and generally up to no good, the grays have become prominent among what society and abductees have come to imagine as the aliens behind the curtain. The grays are deemed responsible for the belief that Earth has been and is being visited by them and that they have been abducting and conducting experiments on humans for reasons known only to them. In other words, it is for them to know and for us to find out. But if finding out revolves around abducting humans for ingestion and procreation of human/alien beings, the cat is already out of the bag. Frankly, the stealing of human fetuses, as some women have claimed, is hardly what anyone with any reason would condone. Who are they? What are they? And what gives them the right to genetically farm our planet?

It's interesting, if not alarming, that the idea is not a hard sell. Could aliens be hard at work perfecting our species and conditioning our society for acceptance of themselves and hybrids? Further, do they really exist? How far we have come from the flying saucer fifties to the precarious encounters of today but is the public buying it? Are they aliens, masters, or specters of the night? What are we dealing with, and who's along for the ride?

A *Huffington Post* news service poll from 2013, updated in 2017, focused on the question of whether UFOs have been seen and whether they are extraterrestrial in origin. Of the one thousand adult participants, 48 percent responded yes. Additionally, a previous *Huffington* poll on the subject of extraterrestrials showed that a quarter of Americans think that alien visitors have come to Earth, which is more than just speculation. For good measure, 61 percent of respondents believed in ghostly interactions.[137]

In line with the *Huffington* surveys, a 2018 *Fox News* study of two thousand people concluded that a whopping 60 percent of Americans claim to have seen a ghost. Additionally, 40 percent thought that their pet had seen one too.[138]

Perhaps most enlightening is the data collected by the *New York Post* news service in a survey conducted between December 2015 and February 2016, which found that half of humans believe in alien life and want to make contact. That survey was conducted in twenty-four countries and fifteen languages by the research group Glocalities. The results showed that 47 percent of the twenty-six thousand respondees believed "in the existence of intelligent alien civilizations in the universe." Of Americans surveyed, 47 percent believed in the existence of alien life. The highest percent of respondents were the Russians at 68 percent, followed closely by Mexico and China. According to Glocalities, the survey findings represent 62 percent of the earth's population and 80 percent of the global economy.[139] The pump is certainly primed.

UFOs, alien visitors, and ghostly entities—something is here and it's reaching out, literally. Alien or otherwise, it is *not* okay to take people against their will, especially defenseless children. It's called kidnapping. Rather than "We come in peace," the message is more like "We come to take you, with or without permission." For many investigators who have dealt with individuals claiming alien abduction—such as Bud Hopkins, David Jacobs, Kathleen Turner, and Kathleen Marden—the messages, methods, and means are not pleasant. These attacks are usually nonconsensual and often continue as lifelong experiences beginning at an early age.

Kathleen Marden's friend and coauthor Denise Stoner is a perfect example. In *Making Contact: Alien Abduction Case Studies*, Denise recalls under hypnosis that her first encounter with aliens occurred when she was only two and a half years old. Staying overnight at her grandparents' home, Denise had been put to bed and was thinking about a strange, bright egg that she had seen in the sky that day. Suddenly "a small, dark figure appeared as if it walked out of the wallpaper." She recalled that the "little creature" was wearing a hooded, long-sleeved robe that covered its face and revealed only the tips of its fingers at the bottom of the sleeves. It carried some sort of light or instrument, and although the creature didn't speak, instinctively she knew it to be male. "He approached my bed and although his face was not clear under the hood with many folds, I somehow 'heard' him say he was taking me with him for a ride, and not to worry."[140]

Kidnappings of children by advanced spacemen dressed as hooded creatures, like something out of a *Star Wars* movie, does not strike me as intelligent or even permissible. Somehow we are led to believe that we should give them free rein to commit a felony. If their species is advanced enough to engage in intergalactic travel, why do they need our species? I'm not saying that these people did not experience these events, but for me it just doesn't add up. Some abductees claim to have adjusted to having been taken, whereas others appear to suffer from periods of sheer terror for the rest of their lives. Dr. David Jacobs, who has written three books on alien abductions, believes that the aliens are up to no good and that we should take defensive measures against them.

Reportedly the United States leads the world in alien abductions. Are the alleged alien kidnappers using our citizens to produce super alien/human beings, as per the supposed indigo children who are thought to exhibit extreme intelligence and abilities? Are Americans helpless victims of a new super race? Should the Russians be worried?

It all comes down to who or *what* is behind it all. Some abductees believe they were taken physically, whereas others claim to have experienced abduction out of their bodies—not physically. But if these rendezvous are out of body, are the abductors spirits? Certainly there are reports of aliens coming through closed doors and walls, a fact not lost on author and investigator John Keel. After years of research and hundreds of cases, Keel ultimately came to the conclusion that these beings are what he called "ultraterrestrials," because they appear to come from another dimension and are capable of passing through walls and taking solid form to carry off their victims in like manner. Furthermore, Keel believed that they are dangerous and that any pursuit of the topic should be avoided.

Let's backtrack. The earliest reported contact with alien entities came from people claiming hauntings and dead relatives speaking through mediums. So even aliens appear to use psychic mediums as their voice on occasion, apparently opting out of sending SETI a response.

Taking a closer look, we can see that some experts in the field of UFO investigations and people claiming alien contact don't necessarily come at this from a strictly scientific approach. In fact, I found that to be the case more often than not. Science often takes a nosedive when it comes to the experiential, and often those experiences start at a very early age.

CHAPTER TEN
Teach Your Children

Recently, I marked over two years that I have been broadcasting my weekly show on the paranormal ... I feel as though I am on a different journey of discovery right now, but I cannot deny when someone else's experience has some of the same qualities as my own. Like many abductees, Paul Schroeder's experiences in adulthood have triggered memories reaching back into his childhood. Not unlike Paul, I have a childhood memory that has troubled me far into the current stages of my life ... I was no more than seven when my own stranger came calling.

—Ash Hamilton[141]

But what does this have to do with UFOs? Well, it seems that many people who have experienced the paranormal have also experienced UFOs, and in many cases these experiences began in childhood. Most people agree that there are two forms of spiritual reckoning on this earth: that which is good and honest, and that which is evil and deceitful. The challenge is in knowing which is which.

We know that demons can appear in many forms and to people of any age, but if deception is the key, then the earlier, the better. Unfortunately children make excellent targets because they think in simplistic terms and believe what they're told. Also, in some cases, they innocently overstep boundaries put in place for their own protection—as do some adults as well.

There is an apparent outreach from the spirit realm regarding children, and the approach starts very young. The devil has no regard for women and

STORM ON THE HORIZON

even less for children, as they are a gift of God. The devil was behind the execution of infants when Moses was born, and then again when Jesus was born. Add to that the historical evidence of the horrific infant sacrifices to the god Molech. (See also Moloch, Marduk, Merodach, Bel, Baal.) This ungodly practice was absolutely detested by God and strictly forbidden: "And you shall not let any of your descendants pass through the fire to Molech, nor shall you profane the name of your God: I am the Lord" (Leviticus 18:21). This is reiterated in Deuteronomy 18:10: "There shall not be found among you anyone who makes his son or his daughter pass through the fire, or one who practices witchcraft, or a soothsayer, or one who interprets omens, or a sorcerer." The paranormal is a slippery slope, and many innocent children slide down it.

Based on an interesting survey conducted by writers and researchers of the paranormal, Brad and Sherry Steiger showed that paranormal events involving children often first take place between the ages of five and twelve. Although the paranormal experiences themselves vary widely, the common denominator is that they occur when the children are very young.

One good example of this involved the man who was to become famous as the "sleeping prophet," Edgar Cayce. As a child, Cayce reportedly had the ability to play with the "little folk" and once even claimed to have seen his dead grandfather. At the age of ten, Cayce began reading the Bible on a regular basis, and by age twelve he had a deep desire to help people, perhaps even to become a missionary. That idea was fostered when shortly thereafter, he saw "a woman with wings" who told him his prayers had been answered—though not in the way he had imagined. As if right on cue, Cayce met Mr. Hart, a traveling hypnotist who introduced him to the practice of hypnosis and trance mediumship, skills that he would hone and use as an adult to perform psychic readings. Cayce often began his trance (sleep) sessions with, "We have the body," when seeking spirit assistance.

Following a fairly predictable course, Cayce was contacted by a voice that would direct all aspects of his work and daily life. As a result, Cayce began using crystals and started promoting reincarnation and the occult doctrine of the Akashic record. He delved deeper and deeper into occult and esoteric teachings, including Blavatsky's writings, all the while wrestling with his Christian convictions. Early on he began to wonder if his psychic abilities, such as hearing the voices of relatives who had passed on or even engaging in conversations with angels, "were delivered from the highest source,"[142] but that question did not curb their appeal for him.

Sadly, the lure of the limelight can be more enticing that the lure of the truth. Cayce believed too in the existence of aliens, the existence of Atlantis, and that "soul entities on Earth intermingled with animals to produce 'things': giants that were as much as twelve feet tall."[143]

A childhood revelation was also given to psychic Jeane Dixon. According to author and spiritualist Ruth Montgomery, "Through a curious chain of circumstances, it was a gypsy who awakened Jeane to the strange potential within herself."[144] This awakening began when Jeane's mother took the eight-year-old to see a Roma woman who was conducting fortune readings in the area. This woman told the mother that Jeane was going to be a famous prophet. This meeting with the fortune-teller, along with encouragement from her parents, laid the groundwork for Jeane to develop her psychic abilities and set into motion her life as a prophet, fortune-teller, and astrologer, complete with her own crystal ball. Regarding UFOs, Dixon would go on to predict that space aliens would land and make contact in August 1977.[145] It didn't happen, but that didn't diminish the belief of many people that someday aliens will.

It's not surprising that Space Brother contactee George Adamski had alien interest going back to his youth. Adamski claims his first contact with aliens occurred when a UFO landed in the desert in 1952, but UFO researcher Nick Redfern points out that records show Adamski's interests "preceded the 1952 date by at least two years." Noting author Timothy Good's research, Redfern asserts that Adamski had "otherworldly encounters as a child and had received instruction from these beings in Tibet."[146] Courtesy of Uncle Sid, no doubt.

The spoon-bending psychic Uri Geller tells of an experience that happened to him when he was a young child of three or four. Playing in a garden across from his home in Tel Aviv, he was deafened by a loud, high-pitched sound coming from the sky. He looked up and saw a silvery mass of light coming toward him. The light came closer, and Geller was knocked backward. "There was a sharp pain in my head. Then I was knocked out. I don't know how long I lay there, but when I woke I rushed home and told my mother. She was angry and worried. Deep down, I knew something important had happened."[147]

Later in life, Geller met with parapsychologist researcher Andrija Puharch and underwent a series of hypnosis sessions that included manifestations of poltergeist activities and disembodied voices.

Geller's later UFO experience came as the result of making contact with a spacecraft named Spectra. Through channeled sessions with Hindu scholar and sage D. G. Vinod, he learned the identities of the occupants of Spectra, who were called "the nine."[148]

UFO researcher and author Raymond E. Fowler revealed that at the age of six, he observed a bright ball of light in his bedroom. The size of a marble, the light quickly darted off when his mother came to check on him. At age seven, Fowler was visited in the night by a long-haired woman in a bright light, possibly wearing a robe, who abducted him by floating him out of his house. He remembers only returning to his home, where the "lady in the light" told him that he was going to do something important for mankind.[149]

Journalist, New Age enthusiast, psychic channeler, and UFO promoter Ruth Montgomery wrote about the experiences of psychologist and hypnotist Dr. Leo Sprinkle, who dedicated much of his professional life to the study of UFOs and abductees. Sprinkle had seen UFOs on two occasions and believed himself to be an abductee. According to Montgomery, Sprinkle confided in her that as far back as 1949, he and a friend had witnessed a flying saucer in broad daylight. In 1956 he observed a "brilliant red star" near the Rocky Mountain foothills. Sprinkle was hypnotically regressed to the fifth grade, which triggered a memory of being aboard a spaceship looking out at the stars.[150]

Montgomery was no stranger to the paranormal herself. She claimed to have become psychic and used automatic writing for much of her book materials, which included a belief in "walk-ins," ET beings that take over a person's body when their soul wishes to leave. Convenient.

Not surprisingly, many ufologists have experienced UFO sightings and paranormal encounters that began in their youth. Some cases, however, such as that of the late army veteran Sergeant Clifford Stone, are a bit bewildering. Stone claimed to have been part of military operations that included the recovery of UFO craft and their occupants. In *Eyes Only*, Stone writes that at the age of four, he was taken outside his home late at night by a woman, possibly his half-sister, to meet a boogeyman with red glowing eyes who was wearing a suit and hat—and riding a tractor, no less.

At the age of six or seven, Stone recalls observing bright round objects floating in the sky and white overall–clad creatures on a hillside near his home; one creature appeared to be metallic. This frightened him, so he ran home and hid behind a stove. He states "And there I felt something like bony fingers just running on the top of my head. I had the impression that this was showing me that I couldn't run and hide from this."[151] This incident was followed by dark shadows in his room, a disembodied voice, and footsteps of something unseen. In 1957, Stone saw a white opaque disc passing over a friend's house and paranormal events by the bucketfuls, including some little humanoid-looking creatures that he hid from everyone. The little beings warned him that if any of his playmates saw too much, "We will have to kill them." These events, Stone admits, continued throughout his childhood.

Okay, so how does this tie into UFO crash retrievals and dead ETs? Good question, yet it does go to show that quite often there is a history of paranormal events that progress into the ET experience. As an adult serving in the army, Stone said that he was part of a secret crash retrieval unit and privy to information of secret government programs regarding UFOs and aliens. So vast was his knowledge of the aliens (of which he believed there were fifty-seven types) that he claims that he was granted a one-on-one meeting with an ET captive at an air force base in Virginia. At that meeting, he decided to help the ET escape his confines by cutting a hole in the perimeter fence and allowing the creature to escape.

Although Stone stood by this story, I find his strange testimony bewildering, especially from a military standpoint. I do believe, however, that quite possibly the paranormal events that Stone reportedly experienced in his childhood carried over into his adult life with the entities and ETs being one and the same.

Another interesting perspective on ETs and the paranormal comes from the late Brad Steiger, an expert on the paranormal who authored or coauthored more than 170 books, many dealing with paranormal topics. By now, it should come as no surprise that his interests started in childhood. Steiger claimed to have suffered a near-death experience after being severely injured on his family's farm at the age of eleven. He recalled having an out-of-body experience in which he left his body, watched his body being carried by his father to get help, and freely flying to various places before returning to his physical self. That experience helped launch his interest in the paranormal.[152] His wife, Sherry Hanson Steiger, has also claimed out-of-body and near-death experiences.

It is not difficult to see the similarities between spirit and ET contacts. According to the Steigers, "Although most of the contactees claim an initial physical contact with a Space Being, the operable mechanics of the experience seem very reminiscent of what can be seen in Spiritualism when the medium works with a spirit guide or control from the 'Other Side.'"[153]

The Steigers did extensive research covering all aspects of the paranormal. As part of this research, they prepared an extensive questionnaire that was distributed worldwide to tally paranormal experiences from dreams to alien abductions. Naturally this data included the experiences of children. What the Steigers learned was quite interesting. According to the data, most young children have their first paranormal experience with an elf, angel, holy figure, or otherworldly being, and these encounters usually take place between the ages of five and seven. Traumatic experiences among youth ages eleven to sixteen, such as beatings, bullying, and molestations, seem to lay the groundwork for visitations from entities of all sorts, mainly in human form but also more nondescript entities such as glowing lights. For many children, these encounters continued throughout their lives.[154]

Most interesting to me was an experience that Francine, Brad Steiger's first wife, had at the age of five in her home. This incident highlights the question of what abilities these entities may physically possess:

> I remember all this very vividly, though I was only five. Perhaps *they* have seen to it that I have. To my right and above me, I became aware of a person coming slowly down right through the ceiling. He alighted so gently that he stood almost directly before me, and I wasn't certain if he ever touched the floor. His white robe was draped over one shoulder, and the wind made it flow in and out around his body. His hair was straw-colored and straight, and was styled in a pageboy cut coming down to the base of his neck. His eyes were light, wide-set. He had a large,

full jaw and fair skin. There appeared to be no beard-growth area. I remember because my dad sometimes had a five o'clock shadow-type growth. The entity's robe blew open, and he did not move to cover his body, which was nude beneath the robe. I saw that portion of the male body I had never before viewed ... Obviously, in his realm, he viewed his penis no differently from the nose on his face.[155]

This entity began to speak to her in a strange voice that rose and fell, from a high pitch to a low pitch, likening it to someone singing and talking at the same time.

Francine interrupted the entity to call for her dad, who—with his back to her—was hanging a framed license on the wall in that same room. She wanted him to see the angel, but he continued to pound the nail. Then she noticed something else. Another angel appeared in the upper corner of the room, above her father's head, but he never saw it. This angel was female, but only her face and hair could be seen. "She looked as if she were from a different place from the male angel, as she had darker skin, eyes, and hair. Her dark hair was quite wavy and hung past her small-featured face."[156] Before the episode was over another female angel's face would appear in another corner, and then another; four angels in total.

Wanting to fully share the experience, she called for her mother, and that's when it all changed. "Upon [my] doing so, the male angel totally changed his voice. No longer was it a gentle, high-pitched singing one, but a low, harsh monotone, mechanical-type voice. He said, 'Do not tell your parents.'"[157] Despite the ominous tone of this command, Francine continued contact with the male entity, who would become her spirit guide.

Not all angels are angelic. Psychic medium Amy Allan is the subject of the television series *The Dead Files*, in which she uses her psychic abilities to communicate with the dead. She claims to have had many dealings with spirits, who quite often are evil, in her investigations. The evil side of entities is something she became aware of at a young age. She has gone on record to say that some entities are not looking out for your best interests and can be in many ways deceitful. In one interview, she tells of such an encounter she had as a child.

The first memory I have of dealing with the paranormal was when I was four years old and had encountered shadow people. I really thought they were my friends. They came every night and I would see them on the walls. It was actually a male and female presence. They were really friendly and nice. We were friends over a long period of time, and eventually they asked me to go with them. They told me to bite the electrical cord on my humidifier, which I did and was electrocuted. After that I realized obviously that they weren't good, and that's kind of when they got scary. They would peel off of the wall and stare at me, or they would scream at me. It was a very traumatizing experience, not only because they were shadow people and they were negative and they tried to kill me, but also because I really thought that they were my friends. They betrayed me in the utmost manner by trying to inflict harm on me.[158]

Without a doubt, spirits have a sinister side that should not be brushed off as just negative energy or dark matter. These entities, whether spirit guide or alien, good or evil, in my opinion are of the same ilk.

Occurrences such as these are often the catalyst that launches people into researching the strange and paranormal, having first experienced it themselves. John Keel was an excellent journalist and Fortean researcher of the paranormal, much of which dealt with UFOs. He coined the terms *men in black* and *ultraterrestrials* from his experiences with both during the course of his investigations.

Keel once said that he was born with psychic abilities and that at age eleven, he carried on conversations with a poltergeist who would answer questions by rapping on a wall. However, as an adult his perspective on paranormal encounters dramatically changed. Keel would go on to write many insightful books on the paranormal, and much of his research was dedicated to the investigation of UFOs. In *Operation Trojan Horse*, Keel says the idea of intergalactic visitors should be consigned more to the realm of the paranormal, as having arrived from a multidimensional habitation and not from outer space.

Interestingly, Keel had many witnesses tell him that they thought the objects they sighted were actually *alive*, a view that was held by Kenneth Arnold and others. In one article dealing with this very subject, Andrew W. Griffin aptly emphasizes Keel's misgivings about ufology altogether. Keel said, "I have in my files hundred of cases, some of which have now been investigated by qualified psychiatrists, in which young men and women obsessed with the UFO phenomenon have suffered frightening visits from these apparitions, been followed by mysterious black Cadillacs which appeared and disappeared suddenly, and have been terrified into giving up their pursuits of UFOs. Many contactees report similar experiences."[159]

Keel felt that the phenomenon itself was reflective, meaning "the more frightened the victim becomes, the more the manifestations are escalated." And thus the phenomenon is ongoing.

A case in point is the situation with Betty Andreasson, who claims a long association with alien entities and multiple abductions from small grays who somehow convinced her that they acted on behalf of the Lord. Again, one can see another early childhood experience serving as a catalyst for perpetuating an interest in the paranormal within families.

In *The Andreasson Affair*, Raymond Fowler writes of an encounter involving Betty Andreasson's eight-year-old daughter Becky. According to Fowler, one evening Becky awoke to see a glowing yellow-orange ball hovering outside her bedroom window. The object shot a beam of light at the terrified child. Shortly after this incident, it was reported that Becky "developed the uncanny ability to automatically write page after page of strange symbols,"[160] describing a writing practice similar to that practiced by the Shakers, an early American religious sect.

Many UFO devotees advocate the belief that human-alien hybrids exist. Some believe that alien DNA transference has already taken place, resulting in extremely intelligent children who from an early age are identified as star children or indigo children. This preconceived specialness is due in part to claims of unusual psychic abilities and other paranormal talents such as out-of-body travel and the ability to communicate with orbs.[161]

It is believed that some children develop these abilities by their association with "star visitors" who become their mentors. Others have a star visitor who takes control of the child's body, a sort of "walk-in" enterprise mentioned earlier by Ruth Montgomery, the journalist turned spirit-guide channel. Some people believe that these alien hybrid children exist; unfortunately the children may actually be the result of an occult influence rather than anything from outer space.

We can see from these reports that something—whether robed beings, alien friends, or elusive balls of light—has been taking the liberty of making contact with children. Italian UFO investigator and journalist Paola Harris has given much thought to these balls of light. "Do Cybernetic Brains devoid of bodies exist?" Harris asks, believing that telepathy or nonverbal communication is a "valid form of human communication with cosmic cultures and dimensional beings." Further, she feels that there is a purpose in how the entities choose to present themselves, how they choose to make contact, and what their message might be. "They may be among us in the form of disembodied intelligences or spheres of light who want to communicate," she says, or, more philosophically, "They may be telling us something important as they dart around the room in Florence or atop a crop circle in England."[162]

Depending, of course, on what *they* are.

CHAPTER ELEVEN
Orbs, A Curious Form of Energy

Out of the dark they come—spheres, luminosities, light-forms; like angel messengers writing in symbols of light! Something is happening—just a glimmer; a twinkle, a flash of light! Something different—something other!
—*Beyond Photography*[163]

According to the United States Energy Information Administration, there are various forms of energy sources, such as heat (thermal), light (radiant), motion (kinetic), electrical, chemical, nuclear energy, and gravitational. To simplify what this means, all of these sources are composed of atoms, which are made up of protons, neutrons, and electrons. The atom is the smallest constituent unit of ordinary matter that has the properties of a chemical element. Every solid, liquid, gas, and plasma is composed of neutral or ionized atoms, and all living organisms contain oxygen, carbon, and nitrogen.

Most importantly, atoms make matter, which has four states: solid, liquid, gas, and plasma. Plasma is an important state to consider, because plasma is hot ionized gas containing positively charged ions and negatively charged electrons. Examples of plasma includes lightning, aurorae, neon and fluorescent light, solar wind, welding arcs, some flames, Earth's ionosphere, stars, the sun, the tail of a comet, interstellar gas clouds, and the fireball of a nuclear explosion.[164] It's not surprising that plasma has been associated with ghostly apparitions and UFOs, since it produces a chemical exchange that gives off the smell of rotten eggs or sulfa, smells often reported in hauntings.

Plasma can be created using a laser, microwave generator, or any strong electromagnetic field. Unlike gases, plasma reacts to electromagnetic fields and conducts electricity. An electrical change can produce a magnetic field. Furthermore, when plasma is exposed to a magnetic field, it may assume structures, which can include layers, filaments, and beams. That's a lot of scientific jargon for the energy needed to form a structure such as a plasma ball or light orb.

Light orbs or plasma orbs commonly appear in reports of hauntings and UFO encounters. Often there are orblike objects appearing in both cases. These mysterious orbs can be seen floating or stationary, passing through walls, hovering, and even shape-shifting. Radiant orbs can be captured on film, observed in videos, and even seen with the naked eye. They may be as large as a basketball or as tiny as a pea or small speck of light. They can have colors, but they're usually bright white. They are self-generating light sources and should not be confused with dust orbs that are often caught on camera.

Orbs have been observed taking on the shape of small disclike saucers, spiraling down into vortexes, and morphing into humanoidlike entities. They may flitter about, bounce, or remain perfectly motionless. Some have even been said to deliver telepathic messages or act as liaisons between humans and ETs. Many are caught on camera, but I'll discuss photographic anomalies in the next chapter. Orbs have been observed over the wheat fields in England, leading many people to think that they are responsible for the crop circles that have been occurring there. Their actions and varieties seem endless.

Although they can deliver an electrical charge, their attributes rule out ball lightning, because they leave no explosions or burning damage behind, as is often characteristic of lighting. Orbs, however, can display *personal* characteristics of their own.

Brad and Sherry Steiger's research has verified the existence and actions of *light orbs* firsthand. Brad had an encounter with one of these transient energy balls at age seventeen. While driving on a remote country road one evening, he was surprised to see a greenish-glowing orb, roughly the size of a basketball, strangely bobbing along in the middle of the road. As he continued to drive, the orb suddenly set a course directly for him. Without warning, it darted through his car windshield, hovered in front of his steering wheel, and then exited through an open back window. Brad noted that although the ball appeared to be solid, it passed with ease through the windshield, so was it solid or perhaps gaseous? It didn't stay around long enough for Brad to learn more, but neither did it leave the area.

The next day, having learned of an orb harassing some teenage girls walking home near that same country road, Brad encountered the orb again. That evening he saw the orb near some trees in that same area, and as if to taunt him, the orb remained in the area for two consecutive nights. Brad couldn't help but think that the brazen orb was proudly showing off its ability to pass through solid matter—and more.[165]

Here we have *conscious* matter in the form of shape-shifting, intelligent spheres of light that can apparently display premeditated signs of aggression. However, some researchers have come to believe that orbs are simply the means of transportation for angels, spirit guides, and other etheric beings. Perhaps a ball of energy is the means by which spirit entities come and go from one place to another, a theory recognized by the Steigers: "Indeed, the globes of light may be the form these benevolent beings assume before fully materializing in our dimension." But this comes with a warning: "As a word of caution, however, we must remind the reader that not-so-benevolent beings may utilize orbs for more nefarious purposes."[166]

In *The Complete Story of the Worldwide Invasion of the Orange Orbs*, MUFON investigator Terry Ray gives several accounts of orbs, commonly orange in color, that are often seen as UFOs. Ray reports that one witness got more than an eyeful when he observed two balls of light darting about the evening sky. The witness became suspicious that the odd balls of light were not twinkling stars, and he began to take pictures and videos with a cell phone and iPad. The results were shocking. "I could see other entities and lights in the sky that were invisible to the naked eye. One white sphere, star-like orb, appeared as a green ball that moved in many directions, zipping up, down, diagonally, and sometimes sort of hovered. While in motion, the green ball moved very quickly with abrupt stops and starts." Then the witness saw *it*—a humongous object, three stories in height and two stories in width—hovering in the sky, where it appeared to be the docking station or mother ship for the orbs.[167]

Orbs of light, however, are not limited to sky dwellings. These luminous objects also appear to be right at home in people's homes. Katie

116

Hall and John Pickering have jointly authored two books on the balls of light phenomena. In *Beyond Photography*, they present their extensive research into what these orbs of light might be. According to Hall and Pickering, their exposure to the balls of light came quite by accident. They had been reviewing some photos they had taken of their nature walk through a wooded area. In one photo they noticed a ball, pink and blue in color, on the trunk of a tree. They described the ball as "transparent, its colors similar to a gas fire flame, its structure resembling a plasma globe, about the size of a ten-pin bowling ball."[168] This was the first of several types of orbs that would later be captured in photos taken inside their home as well. The couple began to see small flashes of light, and they quickly discovered that these small luminous objects were intelligent and could respond to their moods and commands. The family cat could see them too. I've had similar experiences in my home and with my own cat as well.

Other paranormal events had begun to affect Hall and Pickering's home and their lives. In retrospect, they could reach no conclusion other than to note that it all began with the orbs. These small transient lights could be caught on film, displayed the telltale properties of a plasma concentration, could change shape at will, and displayed certain interactions and behaviors. Synchronicity, it seems, was a constant of the phenomena itself.

Soon Hall and Pickering's photographs would reveal a much more startling development with the appearances of wispy light forms and a "light being." Of this being they write, "Theorizing about alien or higher intelligence is one thing, when you are dealing with a phenomenon with no visual human attributes, but when it suddenly turns into a form that looks humanoid, that is something else entirely."[169]

In their research, Hall and Pickering note that these energy orbs appeared to cover large areas of both land and space. Reviewing NASA film footage of the STS-75 shuttle mission's orbit, for example, they could clearly see a large number of spheres gathering around the shuttle. They were particularly struck by the similarities between the form and behavior of the *space spheres* and those of the Earth-based orbs and luminosities they had been photographing. The space spheres not only moved rapidly, but also changed direction, indicating intelligence and perhaps an organic life form of some type. "They didn't look at all like flying saucers or nuts and bolts alien spacecraft; they behaved more like living entities!"[170]

After reviewing many evidentiary pictures, Hall and Pickering were still no closer to a conclusion about who or what these objects or beings were. Although they were quick to rule out angels, aliens, and the like, no assessment could be made other than to consider them spiritual messengers of sorts, something attempting to raise humanity to a higher level of consciousness, something *other*.[171]

However, contrary to New Age spirituality, all is not light and love concerning orb entities. In 1965 Elisabeth Haich wrote *Initiation*, an autobiographical account of her belief that her current reality was intertwined with recollections of a past life as an Egyptian priestess. It was intertwined with other things as well.

Haich recalls that one evening as she lay in bed, two shadow figures appeared carrying on a pole a greenish blob or mass, which she determined—to her horror—was a demon. The figures were headed straight for her sister's room, and Haich cried out to warn her. "Even as I screamed, the two shadowy figures disappeared instantaneously, while the demon shrank in size and rolled up into a greenish phosphorescent sphere about the size of a football, then rolled with gliding and jumping movements up the steps."[172]

Sometime after this event, Haich went with her family to see some Walt Disney films at a local cinema. One film revolved around three Disney characters—Mickey Mouse, Pluto, and Donald Duck—as ghostbusters on assignment to rid a haunted house of its resident spooks. The spooks decided to turn the tables on the characters and frighten them so that they would leave the house. At one point the lead spook gave a sign, and all the other spooks disappeared by rolling up into greenish phosphorescent balls that rolled away, gliding and hopping along in different directions. Haich was shocked to realize that the cartoon had depicted the exact actions that she had observed in the real-time experience with her own phosphorescent balls, and no humor was intended. Green fireballs have occasionally been reported in UFO sightings, but I am aware of none that ever rolled up and bounced away.

So are orbs spirits? Some people believe that they are, but how does that compare with the orbs seen around a mother ship or other alien craft? Orbs are made up of matter, sometimes even dark matter.

Several years ago, the History Channel ran a series titled *UFO Hunters*, starring William J. Birnes. In a segment called "Dark Presence," Birnes and his fellow UFO researchers investigated ongoing reports of orb sightings, primarily in Indiana and Arizona. These sightings were of a particular concern to local residents who were having frightening encounters with the strange anomalies.

In their investigation, the UFO hunters found that many of the orbs reported were orange in color and that the orbs appeared most commonly during the evening hours. These orange spheres seemed to generate an orange light that glowed internally. They could bounce around the night sky in zigzag patterns, remain motionless for long periods of time, and split into two or more orbs at will. Some were even observed morphing into triangle shapes. Witnesses who had observed these orange-lighted orbs said that the orbs would simply blink out and disappear.[173]

Then there are the daytime versions. Some daytime orb sightings have presented a much different persona from their nighttime counterparts, and at times a more sinister side. These orbs or spheres, ranging in size from a baseball to a basketball, have exhibited much exuberance, but in a threatening way. The silent orange orbs would seem to appear out of nowhere, chase people, menace animals, and in general intimidate anything with which they came in contact. Contact with these orbs left some people with feelings of fear and dread, nightmares, and a reluctance to venture outside at night.

Motives, too, come into question. One woman reportedly encountered one of these daytime orbs up close and personal, but when she started to reach out and touch it, she heard the orb say, "Don't touch or you will die." Was this a warning out of concern for her safety, or was it a threat?

Another witness, Jeff Willis, seems to have developed a copacetic relationship with some of the orb entities and provided video evidence to *UFO Hunters*. These videos showed that these orbs, some traveling in large numbers, could be captured on film in real time and during broad daylight, over both densely populated cities and suburban locations. Some orbs allegedly responded to the videographer's command to appear in the sky at a given time, thus indicating intelligence and ability to communicate.

Then there are orbs that are simply out of this world—literally. As mentioned above, NASA video footage has captured orbs in space. Some of these space orbs have been videoed moving and congregating around the International Space Station, and have been reported by the astronauts on board. Some have even been photographed near the surface of the moon.

Here on terra firma, encounters by military pilots appear to be on the rise. Recently released video taken on board military jets show orb-like objects careening across the sky, leaving the pilots in near disbelief of their speed and maneuverability. A recent video shows an F/A-18/F fighter jet in pursuit of what looked like a *Tic Tac* breath mint in color and shape. You can see the object from the pilot's viewpoint and hear the excitement in his voice, making it easy to believe that the object was exhibiting extremely high speed and could easily keep out of reach of the pursuing jet.

Reports of orb encounters are increasing. Thanks to advancements in camera lens technology and improved digital quality, more and more anomalies are being captured in photos, and more people are taking notice of them. Ruling out dust, pollen, or raindrops, photographic evidence indicates the presence of self-radiating orbs that are often unseen by the human eye.

What are these orbs, and what do they want? One researcher has gone to great lengths in studying some not-so-elusive orange orbs. MUFON investigator Terry Ray, who has written an entire book on commonly reported orange orbs, has reached some startling conclusions. His analysis of thousands of reports from the MUFON databank, in addition to his own personal cases, reveals that these orange orbs have been appearing from all points and locations, both at home and abroad, and they appear to have a real agenda. Ray has concluded that they exist and they are not from here, and he believes they possess intelligence, travel through space via wormholes, and are present in Earth's atmosphere. Orbs have been witnessed both on land and moving in and out of bodies of water. Although the orbs are typically orange in color, other colors—blue, green, red, and pink—have been reported. The orbs have the ability to cloak themselves from view, split or merge with each other, and easily pass through solid objects.[174]

Cloaking is not necessarily common. Many witnesses of crop circle formations have reported actually seeing balls of light over fields in England. These balls of light have become such a common occurrence that they are referred to simply as BOLs (balls of light). Although crop circles have been reported in other places around the world, most are found in the farming communities of England. Much has been written about these huge, matted-down images, which range from simple concentric rings to highly detailed geometrical shapes. Some circles appear mysteriously overnight, but others have occurred during daylight hours. Hundreds of photos have been taken of these huge formations, which seem to depict planets, galaxies, religious symbols, occult symbols, geometrical designs, and in one case an alien head. So far no one, outside of a few pranksters, has claimed ownership of the immensely detailed formations in the fields. And although no saucers have been sighted, or alien beings seen traipsing through the fields, balls of light have been spotted.

In *The Deepening Complexity of Crop Circles*, Eltjo H. Haselhoff presents a scientific overview of what takes place once a formation appears: how it affects the crops (mostly wheat), the electrical types of sounds sometimes heard, and eyewitness accounts of people who claim that "the balls of light did it."

One witness observed an orange ball coming down from the sky and disappearing into a wheat field. Another witness, who had ventured out into a crop circle at night, reported seeing a football-sized orange light hang in midair, descend slowly, and became invisible. In a similar report, a sixteen-year-old boy witnessed multiple BOLs bouncing around in a field and generating a crackling noise while forming a crop circle. These balls, seen "spinning very rapidly through the crop," resembled fluorescent discs. "Sometimes the balls had a white-bluish or white-pinkish color, or at other times more orange-like." Haselhoff surmises that the change in color may be caused by intense heat generated by the balls themselves, which is possible, but no one has gotten a positive read on their base temperature. And as is so often the case, the balls simply faded and disappeared. Haselhoff believes the large number of accounts and the photographic and video evidence "prove the existence of the BOLs, sometimes simply referred to as light orbs—for reasons unclear to me—plasma balls."[175] An in-depth analysis and array of scientific data can be gleaned from his book.

One might say that there is a deepening complexity to the orbs themselves. Balls of light, light orbs, and plasma balls all appear to be one and the same, working in conjunction with one another. Whether whipping through windshields, skipping over agricultural fields, slowly descending from a mother ship, bobbing around in space, or passing through walls of homes, they make no attempt to hide. They appear at will, whenever and wherever, as if motivated by an agenda all their own.

Orbs of light are not new phenomena, but many of their actions have become the basis for concern, past and present. Incidents of fly-alongs with aircraft have been equally met with fly-overs. As early as 1950, Nick Mariana, of Missoula, Montana, gained notoriety as one of the first people to produce video evidence, using 16 mm film, of bright circular points of light flying in unison across the sky. In 1951, another flap of ominous orbs—the Lubbock Lights—appeared in a V formation over Lubbock, Texas. Then in July 1952, Warrant Officer Delbert C. Newhouse, a navy photographer using 16 mm film, captured images of a cluster of brilliant round objects moving in various configurations in the sky outside Tremonton, Utah. From July 12 to 29, 1952, orblike objects were photographed over Washington, DC. In recent years, these small orb clusters have grown to the size of huge flotillas, such as was seen in 1992 in the daylight skies over Mexico.

But even the Washington and Mexico sightings pale in comparison to what transpired on the evening of March 13, 1997, when the world was captivated by the Phoenix Lights, a huge formation of orbs that hovered for hours over Phoenix, Arizona, and made their way across three states. According to news reports, the lights arrived en masse between 7:30 and 10:00 p.m., and thousands of people witnessed them passing over Nevada, Arizona, and Mexico. The appearance of the lights came in waves, with the first—a V-shaped formation similar in size to a commercial airliner—appearing over Henderson, Nevada. Approximately two hours later, the formation crossed over Prescott, Arizona, where one witness described it as being at least a mile wide, gliding silently over Granite Mountain and blocking out the stars as it continued on its course. When the V formation entered the skies over Phoenix, it hovered over the city for more than two hours before blinking out.

For one Phoenix resident, the Phoenix Lights were not a stand-alone event, but the culmination of smaller events leading up to the large-scale orb appearances of March 13. Dr. Lynne D. Kitei had been experiencing her own up-close-and-personal exposure to orbs of lights from her home in Phoenix. Her extraordinary experiences were later recounted in *The*

Phoenix Lights, in which Kitei, who had a near-death experience at the age of eight, reveals that her exposure to these mysterious orbs of light began much earlier.

In February 1995, two years before the mass appearance of the strange lights over the city, Kitei was having her own close encounters. On the evening of February 6, 1995, while enjoying a relaxing evening at her home in the hills overlooking Phoenix, she was suddenly alerted by her husband to something strange hovering just outside their bedroom window. What she saw was jaw dropping: "Less than a hundred yards away from our property, three objects hung in midair, about 50 to 75 feet above the ground."[176] She immediately began to try to take in the details of these objects—size, shape, colors, actions—while wondering what they were doing there. She described the objects as spheres or ovals, three to six feet in diameter, and glowing a soft amber color while hanging motionless in a triangle formation, one above and two beneath. Maintaining her presence of mind, she was able to take a picture of the visitors before they faded from view. It didn't end there.

Twenty-three months later, on the evening of January 22, 1997, the amber orbs were back. Looking out at the horizon over the city, Kitei saw three orbs in a straight line, looking similar to the ones she had seen up close previously. The following evening she saw a large "golden-orange" colored sphere in the sky, later followed by six more, three over three on the horizon, which made her wonder if perhaps she was seeing some kind of mother ship or a fleet of ships clustered together.

The pattern of nighttime appearances continued, allowing her to witness and photograph them, but providing no information about who or what they were. These photographs can be seen in *The Phoenix Lights*. The mystery continued, and 2004 and 2005 saw multiple reports of actual flotillas of spherical/orb-shaped objects appearing in broad daylight. Many of these flotillas were sighted south of the border in Mexico and witnessed by hundreds of people.

These brazen appearances by the orbs captivated many people's attention. Pastor Billy Crone, who has studied these spherical objects in detail, admits to having been amazed by the massive number of objects that seemed to appear out of nowhere. He notes one particular event and video that focused on a formation of seven white, luminous, spherical objects that had been seen flying in formation. Crone noticed that some objects would break formation and perform individual maneuvers in an obvious display of intellect and purpose. Within minutes, a small formation of spheres could form into a flotilla of hundreds. "Suddenly there appeared an enormous fleet of UFOs, 100 to 200 of them, flying in perfect formation, contrasting with the blue sky and white clouds."[177] It was an amazing sight, and one Pastor Crone believes could be used in an end-times deception—a theory not lost on other researchers, myself included.

This grand show of orb flotillas surfaces again and again, showing themselves in different locations around the world. It is undeniable that *things* of unknown origin are frequenting the skies above us, and that has caught the attention of the world's population, including clerics.

What are these radiant orbs or spheres of light that have the ability to change shape and size? What are these curious forms of energy that exhibit intelligence, can interact with humans, appear and disappear at will, form designs in wheat fields, appear in and outside of homes, respond with aggressive or passive behaviors, pass through solid objects, hang motionlessly in the air, shape-shift in size and appearance, and merge or split apart? We know of the Foo Fighter orbs that accompanied pilots during World War II; they appeared again in the Korean and Vietnam wars.

Are these sentient energy sources visitors from another planet? Or is it possible that they have been here all along?

I have made my own assessments.

CHAPTER TWELVE
I Want to Believe—and I Do

Many say that ignorance is bliss, but God says, "My people are destroyed for lack of knowledge" (Hosea 4:6). I am astonished by how many people (including Christians) are unaware that we do not inhabit, but we cohabit, this planet.[178]

—Pastor Kris Vallotton

"From childhood you have known the Holy Scriptures, which are able to make you wise for salvation through faith which is in Christ Jesus" (2 Timothy 3:15). This is true, and about the loving, redemptive sacrifice of Jesus on the cross. I learned about the ancient times and the supernatural abilities of angels and of God through the scriptures. And I knew about miracles of God as well when, at six years old, my life was saved when my dress accidentally caught fire from playing with a lighter. I have been told that I am lucky to be alive, but luck had nothing to do with it. God did.

I was raised in a Christian home, and we attended church regularly. My father was the Sunday school superintendent, so he saw to that. Like other families in the congregation, we had devotionals at home. And like most families, there was occasional talk about strange occurrences, psychic precognitions, ghosts and hauntings, and even UFO sightings that some relatives or friends had experienced. It seemed that Christians could talk among themselves regarding these topics, but there was nowhere to go within the church to discuss such experiences.

The topic of the paranormal is not often touched on in churches, if at all. But it should be, because in reality—and as the Bible says—we are not fighting against flesh-and-blood enemies. Do they affect Christians? We are the ones fighting, right? There is an unseen realm, but many pastors of conventional churches do not wish to address it.

Kris Vallotton, however, is one pastor who does. In *Spirit Wars*, he writes, "Although Christians typically acknowledge this unseen realm on some intellectual level, I personally do not think they really believe that the spirit world has an effect on their daily lives."[179] He laments that trying to teach some people the reality of the spirit world is like trying to convince someone in the 1800s that there really was such a thing as germs.

But some of us don't need convincing, for we have experienced strange, unusual, unexplainable, even miraculous events in our lives. We know there are good angels who are hard at work, and consequently there are bad angels hard at work as well. There are different ranks of demons or evil spirits, just as there are good angels and ministering spirits. There is an active spiritual realm portraying themselves as spirit energies, angels, or even spacemen. What's your preference?

Witnessing a paranormal event doesn't mean you're a closet Satan worshiper, as some might assume, or entertaining demons in your off hours. Instead, it means you're a target. "Most Christians, however, are completely unaware that the resistance they encounter as they step into God's promises is part of a spirit war,"[180] writes Pastor Vallotton. The inability of many people to even conceive of a spirit realm leaves them vulnerable to the influence of these unseen intruders. These covert entities can influence something as elementary as our thoughts, bringing to mind things that affect our minds and spirits. "The enemy and his cohorts also attack our imaginations by inspiring terrible visions or pictures that wrestle against our minds and can be deeply troubling, especially if we do not understand the source of these assaults," explains Pastor Vallotton. Sometimes it's only a matter of preying on *feelings*, making a person apprehensive or insecure, even encouraging thoughts of suicide. These are all spirit attacks, and evil thoughts are theirs—not yours.

We can all appreciate Pastor Vallotton's insight on this subject. This is a man of God who has been in the trenches where confronting the enemy is concerned. We can learn much from his example and be wise to the tactics the enemy employs. He's been there. At one point in his life, he was plagued with nightmares. He became gripped in fear, understandably, when one night he awoke to see two large glowing red eyes at the foot of his bed. This torment continued for months despite his numerous attempts to make the specter leave. "I rebuked the thing in Jesus' name," he writes. "I read Scriptures to it for hours. I worshiped God while it watched—nothing seemed to faze it." That is, until one day when he felt led by the Lord to read Philippians 1:28: "In no way be alarmed by your opponents, which is a sign of destruction for them, but of salvation for you" (NASB).[181] In other words, ignore them. Once he began to ignore the entity, the power it had to terrify him disappeared, and so did the entity.

I have added this chapter as evidence of what our eyes normally do not see. Just as Pastor Vallotton was harassed by an evil entity, I was harassed by photo-bombing spirits. For me, these intrusions began with the click of a camera. As I mentioned in the introduction, I've collected several pieces of photographic evidence over the years, not that I intended to do so. I want to stress that these photos were not the result of a stakeout with photography equipment in hopes of capturing something. Most of the objects caught on film were incidental to what I was photographing, and I never saw them at the time.

I concede that what was caught on camera, with the assistance of my cat, may have been the by-product of an investigation after which *something* followed me home. The pictures were taken using several different cameras, both 35 mm film and digital, with no camera straps attached. By the twentieth or thirtieth photographic anomaly, I was beginning to get suspicious. Seriously, though, I never stopped to examine many of the pictures until years later, when I happened to see a television show about misty vortexes that were showing up in photographs. Although the swirling masses have been mostly attributed to haunted locations, they can appear at any time, in any place, and on any occasion—weddings, funerals, birthday parties, and so on. It was usually after such an occasion that people first start noticing them, myself included.

The program set off a chain reaction of people who reported having vortexes in their photos, and they began to bombard ghost hunters with their finds. But for me, the vortexes were just the beginning. Vortexes led to orbs of light that led to more orbs, and streaks of light that led to more streaks, and eventually to full-on apparitions. Apparently these were just a preamble of what was to come.

There wasn't any rhyme or reason for why these anomalies were occurring, or so I thought. I would photograph a family member or even one of our pets, and a swirling white blotch would occasionally show up in the picture. I attributed it to a camera malfunction, but as I took photos with several other cameras, using both 35 mm film and digital and without straps, the swirls and orbs continued to appear. I could understand one camera, but all of them?

Nothing made a difference—the residence or location, outside or inside, at public events or family gatherings. We went to church nearly every Sunday, and no occult practices were ever taking place in our home. Yet these occasional *somethings* kept photo-bombing my photographs. I would later learn that these anomalies were also happening to other people, who either had the same type of defective camera, lousy film, or just the same ability to take terrible pictures. Soon I was capturing orbs and swirls and something that looked like ectoplasm. I hadn't caught on yet.

I began to notice my cat running through the house, as if chasing something unseen by me but obviously seen by the cat. I decided to take photos of my cat with a digital camera each time this occurred. I was surprised to see what appeared to be an orb near the cat each time a picture was taken, on both film and digitally. It was fascinating and disturbing at the same time, and it needed to be given serious consideration, as I would find out. What were they? No one likes to think the worst, but were they the worst? Demons? Hold that thought. Some people have reported small orbs of light that seem to innocently flitter about a room, but little lights can turn into big problems. Occult investigators Brad and Sherry Steiger gave this account from one experiencer:

> I became aware of a small but fairly bright light to my left … somewhat like a Christmas tree light. When I looked directly at the light (it would be about eye level had I been standing), it rather expanded downward as a column of cloud/smoke/frosty drift until it was almost touching the sidewalk. It never fell all the way to the sidewalk, which I did not find odd or surprising. It never formed into a "human" form. It was always a column of fog about the same dimensions, height and breadth, as an

adult human. I noticed that it was wavering and quivering rather like it was trying to catch up with our world. Then I realized with a jolt that it was trying to slow down so it could enter our world![182]

Does evidence of the supernatural exist? Many people, including some Christians, roll their eyes at the mere mention of the supernatural. But warnings against entertaining these entities are real and necessary, because often people do not respect the power that some of these entities can have over them. Once you enter the paranormal realm, you are on *their turf.*

Paranormal investigators, ghost hunters, and crytozoologists agree that spirits can manifest in the following ways: mist, cloudlike ectoplasm, light orbs, swirling energy or vortices, see-through ghostly images, partial manifestations, full-body apparitions, dark shadows, little people, fairies, animal forms, and alien-like creatures. Sounds heard can be chimes, whistles, grunts, growls, groans, crying, screams, yells, unknown language or gibberish, disembodied voices, rattles, booms, knocking, chains, footsteps, or stomping. Communication can occur through automatic writing, drawings, symbols, gestures, use of a Ouija board, tarot cards, pendulums, verbal, and mental telepathy.

Spirits' actions can be flashes of light, moving objects, physical harassments, scratch marks, angel-like visitations, bedside visitors, hovering orbs, pushing or shoving of an individual, whispers, out-of-body travel, possession, and other physical or spiritual anomalies. People who claim to have been abducted by aliens have reported some of these experiences.

The Bible mentions evil spirits as well as good ones, but the bottom line is that we just don't know what we are dealing with in the spirit realm, good or evil. The direction we are given as Christians is to "test the spirits" to see which is which. Those who belong to God will confess that Jesus came in the flesh as the Son of God. Those spirits who do not, cannot, or will not confess that Jesus is the true and only Son of God, or simply talk around it, are not of God, be they ghosts, extraterrestrials, or angelic watchers.

Robert C. Brenner, who has done extensive research into the supernatural and strange happenings in the Bible, has written an interesting observation about what he believes is another type of watcher, a *shadow being*: "In my research, I found another legend concerning a third type of Watcher, one who resides in dark places. These creatures have been described as shadow beings. They are purported to hide in the shadows watching your every move. They are very dark beings—black dark. Their purpose is to spy on, distract, harass, or physically harm humans. Theses beings are thought to be evil. They too are part of the unseen."[183]

Brenner goes on to say that you may see these dark shadows out of the corner of your eye, feel creepy sensations in various rooms of your house, experience a sense of evil or foreboding, or feel something brush up against you that you cannot see. "All these are manifestations of the unseen," he explains. "The unseen are real, and entities from other dimensions are coming into our world. They've been doing so for years. Some of them are good. Others are evil. That is why for each of us God has assigned a protecting angel. And if need be, your angel can instantly get legions of other angels to keep evil from reaching you."[184] Most of the time, he maintains, we never know about or see the battles that occur in the unseen dimension or in the heavens above.

Many people would argue that Christians shouldn't experience these things, but does our faith exempt us from such? We are told in the Bible that these spirits and devils exist, so why should we be surprised if we encounter them? After all, we're the targets, aren't we? The big difference is that through our faith in Jesus Christ and His sacrifice, we need not fear them—but we should not seek them out. We need to respect the power of these entities and avoid any association with them. Sometimes that's not as easy as it sounds, when so many people embrace the idea that angels and spirit guides are here to help us, and that we can meet with them in their spirit realm. "Let no one cheat you of your reward, taking delight in false humility and worship of angels, intruding into those things which he has not seen" (Colossians 2:18). *Intruding* is right. But what if the unseen intrudes into your life, or perhaps it claims some generational right? In any case, we often find ourselves dealing with things outside our human existence, either willfully or stupidly—and I'm no exception.

I need to provide some background before moving to my next topic. My mother, who was six or seven at the time, the second oldest of seven children, was living with her family in an old, two-story farmhouse in Tennessee. They got their water from a hand pump at the sink in the kitchen, which was just off the foyer, next to the staircase leading to the second floor. One afternoon when my mother and her siblings were lined up to wash their hands for lunch, an unusual and frightening event took place. The children who were gathered near the staircase noticed something odd standing at the top of the stairs. There was a woman in a long white gown, with long black hair and lovely facial features. She began to come down the stairs one step at a time until she had reached the bottom step, and then she suddenly disappeared.

Of course, the children all screamed and ran out of the house, frightened by what they had just seen. My mother, who was closest to the stairs and the woman, remembered that she could actually see the woman's bare feet and remembered how pink they had looked. It was a real event, and one that would later have significance for me as well. Several years later, I captured a phenomenal picture of a woman in a long white gown, with long black hair—not standing atop the staircase at my home, but actually suspended in midair. I had not sensed her presence at the time, as I enjoyed a mundane breakfast.

It was just before dawn on a weekend and I was having a quiet breakfast by myself in the kitchen. I was enjoying my coffee and surfing the Internet on my laptop, not thinking of anything in particular and just appreciating the calm of the morning. The house my husband and I were living in at the time had a reverse floor plan; meaning the kitchen and living room were on the second floor. Our house was at the end of the street in a small community that backed up to some hills. Getting up to place my dish in the sink, I looked out the window and noticed three deer making their way down the hillside. Thinking that would make a great picture, I left the kitchen and returned with a small digital camera. Directly in front of the window, a large crape myrtle tree had just begun to bud. Although it was just beginning to get light outside, I thought I would still try to get the picture using the flash. I snapped the picture, put the camera away, and went about my day.

That evening I sat down to upload the picture to my laptop. When I clicked on the picture, I was absolutely shocked at what I saw. Looking out through the window, I could see the branches of the budding tree, the three deer, and—reflected in the window—the rear of the kitchen where I had been sitting. I had not been alone in that room.

In the photo, there appeared to be a collage of faint faces and figures. The most distinct was a woman in a white gown with long black hair, suspended in the air as if descending from the ceiling. I could clearly see that she had one hand on the slat of the plantation shutters in the room, as if to steady herself, and next to her appeared other figures in white. I could clearly see, in one corner, a man with hair and a beard resembling an apostle from that era, and there were other images I couldn't quite make out.

I was as shocked as anyone could be. I had just been in that room eating breakfast, and I had felt and seen nothing. What was going on? It seems that once your eyes are open to these things, once it's not a secret anymore, the fight gets harder. Was this the result of truly gaining more insight? Had all the other abstracts of orbs, vortexes, and streaks led up to this grand photographic appearance? All along, I had proceeded in this research with prayer and precaution. I had met with my pastor, and we had prayed together about these things, but still they continued. I couldn't understand why these things were happening to someone of faith.

Like Pastor Vallotton, I tried countermeasures. I played religious music during the day, read my Bible, met with my pastor to share the photographs, prayed about it, and counseled to make sure I was not being spiritually affected. He assured me that I wasn't, but he also warned me that I had to do something about it. You always hope that these experiences might have something to do with God's angels or goodly messengers of some type, but I got a scripture also: "God is not the author of confusion"(1 Corinthians 14:33). I was going to have to meet these things head-on, so I pulled out the best weapon I had—prayer. With a contrite heart and an apology to God if I had offended Him by any thought, word, or deed from my research, I asked to be rid of any of these beings that were not from Him. I believe God honored that prayer. It's been very quiet, film and otherwise, but that doesn't mean the battle is over. Another pastor concurs.

For believers in Christ dealing with the paranormal is not always a simple passive resistance stance. Pastor Chip Ingram believes it often puts us in a position where we have to stand firm in our spiritual armor mentioned in the Bible in the book of Ephesians chapter 6. In his book *The Invisible War*, Pastor Ingram writes that sometimes we have to engage the enemy. Explaining that engaging the enemy takes place "when we're taking significant steps of faith for spiritual growth, when we're invading enemy territory (through evangelism, for example), when we're exposing him for who he really is, when we repent and make a clean break with the world, a long-held sin pattern, or an unholy relationship, when God is preparing us, individually or corporately, for a great work for his glory."[185]

The bottom line for me is that knowing about, experiencing, and having evidence of the unseen world proves that these beings exist. And if they exist, then God exists. And if God exists, then Jesus exists. Therefore the reality of Him truly having been on this Earth, and the sacrifice He made for us, resonates with His promise that He will return one day exactly as He said.

I can't help but wonder if what I have encountered, or at least some of what I have encountered, was a test of faith or loyalty. Was I allowed to see these beings to see what I would do? Would I seek to contact them, or delve further into that realm? By the grace of God, no. But on the other hand, was there something to learn from it? I believe there was. It finally dawned on me that it could have also been recruitment. Trying to rationalize the supernatural with what the Bible says can be a slippery slope, and if a person is led astray, the results can be damning.

We need to remember that many people who have come under the control of these dark forces started out as Christians. Edgar Cayce and even Alice A. Bailey, for example, were Christians at first, before giving themselves over to lying spirits and doctrines of devils. It is subtle and can happen to anyone, and sadly it has.

The late UFO investigator Raymond Fowler, who was perhaps best known for his books on the Betty Andreasson alien abductions, once said in an interview,

> At one time, I was a fundamentalist Christian but since have expanded my theology. I had dismissed anything paranormal experienced by myself or my family as being Satanic. In my early days as a UFO investigator, I rejected any UFO report that contained any type of psychic phenomena. I also felt that UFO witnesses who reported such were mentally unstable. However, it became apparent that credible persons were reporting incredible things that

were similar to what my family, especially my father, had and were experiencing. My mind and theology gradually broadened to accept the paranormal aspects of the UFO phenomena. I might add that when I did this, I began to experience such phenomena on a more regular basis.[186]

Learn from these pictures, and see the spirits for yourself. Put down the ghost detector equipment and stay clear of them. Truly, there is more than one way to play with fire.

Ghosts, orbs, swirling matter, and full-on apparitions are one aspect of deception; UFOs are another. The diversity that exists, the abilities they exhibit, the appearances they make, in my opinion, are all leading to something more sinister. And if an education was to be had by these close encounters, I have certainly received one—and UFOs have been part of it.

CHAPTER THIRTEEN

They Appeared Suddenly

On January 15, 1975, a squadron of UFO-like objects, resembling a celestial string of pearls, soared silently through the evening skies over half of Japan. As government officials, police and thousands of curious citizens stared at the sky in wonder, from fifteen to twenty glowing objects, cruising in a straight formation, flew over Japan inside a strange misty cloud. Further, they were sighted and reported in cities seven hundred miles apart in less than an hour.[187]

—Billy Graham, *Angels: God's Secret Agents*

"I looked at the sky, and there was something, like bubbles," he says. To me, it looked like a pearl necklace. While I was taping, I observed through the lens that it split apart.[188]

—Cuauhtemoc Alavarenga, Mexico City TV cameraman

Suddenly they appeared, cascading down from the sky like large pearls shining in the sun and grouped together like a cluster of grapes. Then, as if on cue, they pushed down and out, separating two by two, swaying smoothly, purposely back and forth in the wind like small pendulums in perfect sync with each other. I looked up at them and said, "My dear Lord, what are you?"

August 24, 2005. My husband, Kim, and I were returning from a trip to the mountain community of Oakhurst, California, where we had a second home. Oakhurst lies just south of Yosemite National Park in a beautiful mountainous region that provided a perfect getaway from the hectic pace of Silicon Valley, but the purpose of our trip had been twofold. As a MUFON investigator, I had been asked by our local director to check on a report regarding some strange lights in the sky in that area. Also, a couple had reported unusual activity involving black helicopters near their home in the woods near Oakhurst.

Although I had served as the MUFON state section director for Santa Clara County in Northern California, it was not unusual to take on extra regions when other investigators were not available, and the San Joaquin Valley and surrounding regions were areas I was familiar with. I had completed my high school years there in the valley, in what was once the very small town of Clovis, adjacent to Fresno. These cities were also of significance to me because that's where I had my first sighting. As I think back on it now, I realize how naïve I was about UFOs, much less ever thinking of seeing one. It was an eye opener for me, as well as my introduction to plausible denial.

It was about 10:00 p.m. on a warm, clear evening in mid-June 1969. I had just graduated from high school, and my best friend Connie and I were sitting outside my home and enjoying the dark sky and brilliantly shining stars. On a whim, we decided to go to a late-night market in Fresno, about five miles away, and buy some magazines to read. We got in my car and began driving south toward a shopping center near the Fresno airport. Along the way, we decided to take a shortcut on a small road that was adjacent to the airport and flanked by an open field. We turned right onto the small two-lane road and drove alongside the field, which was several hundred feet away from the fenced area near the end of the airport runway. We could see clearly the buildings and planes of the local Air National Guard unit on the backside of the airport. There were no streetlights, and the road was dark with no other traffic.

As we drove by, we could see that most airport activity had stopped for the evening, which was normal for a small airport. There would be no more flights in or out that night. We continued down the road, just talking and enjoying the evening. Then I noticed Connie leaning forward in the passenger seat and staring up at something in the sky. As she motioned for me to look out my driver's-side window, she asked, "What is that?" An intense white strobe light was hovering above and apparently keeping pace with my car. I slowed down, but it continued to follow at our pace. Since our windows were down, we most certainly would have heard an engine if it had been a plane, but it made no noise at all. Not knowing what we were seeing, I pulled over and stopped the car, and we both got out to take a better look.

The intense white light of the object, which now appeared diamond shaped, mesmerized us and was still strobing very quickly as it hovered above us. It was hard to estimate its altitude and size, but we guessed that it was about the size of a basketball. By then two other cars had come up behind us and pulled off the road to look as well. Within minutes, the object moved away from us and began to pick up speed. Then we heard the roar of jet engines and looked up to see two military jets lifting off the runway in hot pursuit of this object. The jets passed directly over us, so close that we could see their landing gear retract. We watched as the jets tried to close on the object. We were in a flat area of land, and we could clearly see the object and jets streaking away from us heading due west. When the jets began to close in on the object, it slowed and appeared to hover over them as if teasing them. Then it made an incredible 90-degree turn with several jerking, zigzag movements, and shot off at tremendous speed to the south directly over downtown Fresno. The jets were left in its wake.

Deciding to return home and call the airport, we were surprised when someone from the control tower answered the phone. We asked if a strange light was spotted near the airport, and whether they could confirm whether any jets had taken off. We were told that no planes had taken off, and upon asking if he was sure, we were told quite adamantly that *no planes had taken off.* Nevertheless, we knew what we had seen.

Having this history, I was not about to discount anything people had to say about any type of sighting, and I was looking forward to the interview. At a coffeehouse in Oakhurst, we met the couple who had issued the report to MUFON and listened to their account of strange lights people were seeing in the area and of a large black unmarked helicopter that had been flying over their property at night. Most everyone who lives in Oakhurst lives in forested areas near the national park and often on secluded roads. The couple appeared apprehensive and nervous talking about the unusual black helicopter; they felt that it must have been looking for something, and they wondered if they were being watched.

Knowing that the presence of black helicopters has been associated with UFO activities, however, they wanted to bring it to someone's attention. The couple was absolutely adamant about the constant buzzing of a black helicopter above the treetops around their home. But without photos or other tangible evidence, it was difficult to judge whether an unmarked black helicopter was, indeed, frequenting this remote area of the forest. I could do little except document their testimony and survey the area. No activity was present during our meeting with the couple, so I had little to go on except what I was told and my opinion regarding their sincerity and believability. I would submit my report, nonetheless, as unverified but documented.

It was pretty status quo, but dramatic sightings are few and far between. More often than not, a witness has mistaken the planet Venus or another light anomaly for a UFO. At that time, however, a rash of black, sometimes white, triangle-shaped objects were being reported in the Bay Area of Northern California. I investigated two other cases in which two different individuals witnessed a large silver disc at close range and in the same approximate area near the foothills.

Then there are the cases of actual contact. Although the topic of UFOs can be fertile ground for delusional people, most witnesses whom I have interviewed have been of sound mind, mature adults, and career professionals. However, people who work up the courage to talk about actual contact with extraterrestrials (in one case, grays) exhibit real emotions when speaking of it. I have seen people frightened by what they have experienced, but never such terror as on the faces of those claiming contact. It would appear the goodly Space Brothers have a mean side. One witness confided that they are ugly and frightening. Another witness, claiming to have been forcibly dragged from her car and into a ship, said that when she cried out to Jesus, the ETs (grays again) let go. But when the subject regained composure and began to swear at the ETs, they grabbed hold once again. Some have reported having been taken to facilities where body parts, both human and alien, were observed in cylinders of fluid. These are rare reports, but many people are very sincere about them. These cases are still open.

I couldn't help seeing the similarities in reports, among individuals with whom I spoke, from those who were involved in the New Age movement or outright dabbled in the occult. They often claimed to have made contact with a spirit guide or other being that seemed benevolent initially, but then the experience soured into harassment, poltergeist activities, shadow people, and things that appeared at their bedsides at night. The terror they felt, caused by these spirit beings, was similar to what some people have experienced with an ET.

At the time of this couple's report, the San Joaquin Valley had been experiencing a wave of sightings of unusual lights. Dark triangular objects and silent orb-like objects were being seen in broad daylight; one deaf person reported seeing a cluster of orbs by simply looking up. Sightings of all sorts were being reported from small towns in the area, and this was just one more. It was a typical report, but it was not to be a typical ride home.

I can remember distinctly our drive out of the mountains on that summer morning as we left our home in Oakhurst. We would take Highway 41 to Madera, and then 99 and 152 to San Jose. I remarked to my husband how absolutely clear the blue sky was and how great visibility was in all directions as we made our way down the winding mountain pass. It was a warm and beautiful summer morning, and I was drinking in the sheer beauty of it all.

By the time we reached the flatlands, the sun was nearly overhead and the temperature was rising. The valley gets very hot during the summer, and we were eager to avoid the worst heat of the day and get over the mountain pass to the cooler, more amiable temperatures of the Bay Area.

It was nearing 11:00 a.m. when we turned off Highway 99 onto 152 heading north. The valley is prime farmland with lots of orchards and ten-mile visibility in all directions. We had been talking and listening to the radio as we made our way toward Los Baños, where we would stop for lunch. Our two large standard poodles, comfortably sleeping on the back seat of our SUV, would no doubt enjoy a mini lunch and leg stretch themselves.

As we approached the outskirts of Los Baños, something caught my attention out of the corner of my eye. Glancing out the window of the passenger seat, I saw a shiny round object that appeared to vanish as I turned to take a closer look. At first I didn't think anything of it. That airspace was frequented by private airplanes landing at the small airport in Los Baños, and I thought I had perhaps caught a glint of sunlight off a small plane.

My husband was enjoying the drive—and the fact that traffic was still light for that time of day. That was the main artery leading into the valley, and traffic coming and going was constant. I leaned back in my seat and was looking straight ahead, but then I noticed something that looked like a cluster of white balloons in the sky off to my right. As we got closer, they appeared more like a bunch of grapes, cascading from the widest point and narrowing at the bottom, floating calmly in the sky straight ahead of us. As we drove closer, I could clearly see that these orblike objects were not balloons as they began to break off into pairs aligned with one another. I quickly told my husband to pull over, because they looked like the objects that had recently been seen en masse in the skies over Mexico City. He slammed on the brakes and pulled onto the side of the road next to a vacant field.

We both sat dumbfounded as the objects continued to break into pairs, which were stationary with a slight back-and-forth movement. Then they would rotate around each other in one full revolution with perfect precisian and begin the swaying motion once again. Their gentle movement was similar to the soft, fluid movement of seaweed gently swaying back and forth in the ocean's current. But this was not seaweed—and they, whatever *they* were, were perfectly aware of us. They seemed to sit idly in the sky, as if observing us just as we were observing them.

My husband ran behind our SUV for a better look. He was speaking in half sentences in his excitement, shouting "What is this? What is this?" I rolled down my window, keeping my eyes fixed on the objects while I fished around in my purse for my small camera. The sun was high in the sky and reflected off the view screen of my camera, but I began to shoot blindly in hopes that I would get at least one picture of them. It's strange that you plan for something like this, but when it truly happens, your body and mind are awash in pure adrenaline triggered by the fight-or-flight reflex. But we were definitely not leaving.

We estimated the large cluster of grayish-white orbs to be a thousand feet up. At first they appeared horizontally elliptical in shape, like a football, with small black areas on the ends, but then they appeared to rotate and became round. We counted twelve orbs, which appeared the size of aspirins from our distance. As we continued to watch, the grayish-white orbs flowed back and forth, up and down, and some continued to rotate around each other. They would come together in a tight group and then stretch out horizontally, evenly spacing themselves out as they continued to bob up and down. At times a group of five orbs would rotate upward while the others dropped down, and then they would come back together. They appeared to come closer to us and then back away, from a distance that we estimated was approximately two hundred to five hundred feet from our car.

As we continued to watch, with my husband still outside the car, I saw something quickly whip behind the cluster, and then a grayish-white cloud appeared to *puff* into sight. I watched this cloud emit a brilliant amber color in its center, which quickly faded into another cloudlike object that began to come directly at us. We estimated it was less than a thousand feet high and perhaps no more than 500 feet. The object moved very quickly and continued to come in a straight line toward us. I observed that it appeared almost flat and seemed to undulate in the wind as it moved. In a couple of seconds, it was right in front of us. It slowed, made three short stops almost like the movement of a hummingbird, until it stopped directly over us.

As I stared up at the object, which now looked like an elongated white cloud, I asked, "My dear Lord, what are you?" The object was somewhat transparent but had form, and I could see something that resembled a fine black grid or spine of some sort in its center. Although we could not determine the exact size of the objects, we estimated that whatever hovered over us was about ten feet in diameter. My husband thought it looked like an amoeba with a tail or a jellyfish. It seemed to be enclosed in a swirling plasma and generating a lot of energy, as I could see distortion, like heat waves, emanating all around it, though I felt no heat.

For the few seconds that it hovered above us, I couldn't help but wonder what it thought of us. Then it moved over us, accelerated, and sped at great speed out of sight. When we turned our attention back to the orb cluster, they were beginning to move north toward the hills. The objects had formed a straight line, resembling a string of pearls, with the ends turned up in the shape of a semicircle. We watched them until they disappeared into the horizon. The entire event had lasted less than five minutes.

We did not know if the objects made any sound, because the noise of Highway 52 traffic passing behind us was constant. Nor do we know if any other drivers saw the objects, but certainly no one else pulled over.

I was able to snap five pictures, two of which captured the objects. One picture was of the orbs and the second was of the cloudlike object coming toward us. Through the entire encounter, we felt no fear—only awe and amazement. Naturally we checked ourselves in the aftermath—our car and everything appeared normal, no missing time, and our dogs in the back seat were completely relaxed. We asked each other repeatedly, "That really happened, right?" And it had.

We drove into Los Baños, and all through lunch I wrote feverishly on every piece of paper at my disposal the details of the encounter. I wanted to remember everything. We had gone to take another couple's report, and now we would write one of own. But it wasn't over.

12:40 p.m.

We were in Los Baños for about an hour, and then we got back on Highway 152 going west toward San Jose. I was in the passenger seat once again, and my husband was driving. Highway 152 goes along one side of the San Luis Reservoir and through Pacheco Pass in the mountains. As we began to climb and go around the mountain curves, I again was looking out the right window. There they were again!

I caught sight of a cluster of the objects cresting a hill to our right and heading west. Once again my husband slammed on the brakes, and we pulled off the road just in time to see the cluster disappear over a hill. I scanned the horizon to see if they would resurface, but then we were in for another shock. A commercial plane was flying north over the pass, heading to San Jose International Airport, and I was amazed to see that the plane was not alone! Two large white orbs were keeping pace with the plane, one under the rear of the plane and the other above the tail section. We estimated the plane to be at approximately ten thousand feet, as it appeared to be on approach to the airport and was fairly easy to see. One orb stayed below the rear of the plane, while the other orb bobbed around behind the tail section. I don't believe the pilots or passengers were even aware of the objects as they were so far to the rear of the plane. We were able to observe the plane and objects for only a minute before they cleared the mountains and flew out of our sight.

I thought long and hard about these objects on the way home. What were they? Why did they behave the way they did? Where were they going? And why did they look like they were having, well, *fun* along the way? I have seen dolphins bow surfing off the side of a boat traveling through the water, and I wondered if the orb bobbing up and down in that plane's wake was perhaps surfing the jet stream. Furthermore, I definitely couldn't describe them as *craft*, because they did not have the form of a saucer or other object. Also, my husband had thought the object that came to us looked like an amoeba with a tail.

Whatever these are, they have the ability to change shape and move at great speeds. Was the brilliant amber burst of energy an indication of the object supercharging itself? Was it gearing up or down? If not machines were they biomechanical or something else altogether? Their actions, including those of the object that seemed to have a curious interest in us, didn't fit the standard UFO encounter. The only conclusion I could reach, from my observation of the object hovering over us, was that it was not a spaceship. I felt that I was reaching the same conclusion as Kenneth Arnold—the UFO appeared to be alive.

I know that whatever hovered above me was alive and cloaked within swirling clouds of a plasma-like substance. It didn't seem mechanical, although I witnessed a distortion like heat waves being produced all around it, indicating that it was generating a lot of energy. And yet it was silent and huge and I felt no heat coming off it. Why no heat from something that seemed to be producing quite a bit of energy, not to mention the speed it exhibited? That part bothered me for some time, but I found my answer. In *UFOlogy*, by James McCampbell, director of research for MUFON, the author writes that "UFOs are nearly always reported to be silent ... A loud explosion is rarely heard from a UFO but not accompanying the standard flyby of an intensely luminous object. It would appear that the blind light emitted by UFOs is not associated with extremely high temperatures. Otherwise, thermal expansion of gases would produce a horrendous racket, like continuous lightning."[189]

In numerous photographs, UFOs are depicted with luminous tails that heretofore have been inexplicable, and then there is the issue of colors. According to McCampbell, colors reveal the type of energy or gas being produced and its effect on the atmosphere. For example, a UFO glowing blue would indicate xenon, orange red means neon, a white glow accompanies a decay of metastable nitrogen, and a brilliant white indicates limited ionization of all gases augmented by the ball lightning mechanism. "The colors mentioned seem associated in some way with the speed, or more probably with the rate of acceleration. The silvery gray with an aureole of dark red is seen when the object is stationary or traveling very slowly. Then comes the vivid red. At high acceleration the white, green, blue and purple appear."[190]

McCampbell's analysis suggests that in some cases, the UFO is possibly able to generate colors from a reaction produced in the atmosphere and not necessarily from onboard light. That gives credence to the idea that some of these unidentified flying objects may indeed be living things. Bioluminescence, for example, is the production and emission of light by a living organism a form of chemiluminescence. Bioluminescence occurs widely in marine vertebrates and invertebrates, as well as in some fungi, microorganisms such as bioluminescent bacteria, and terrestrial invertebrates such as fireflies. These organisms need no electrical source to produce light.

The long tentacles and pulsating lights running up and down the long tentacles of comb jellyfish, for example, create a beautiful yet otherworldly appearance. The electric eel, which is actually a fish, can generate its own bioelectricity and deliver a shock of 860 volts and one ampere of current (860 watts) for two milliseconds. For humans, that's equivalent to being hit with a stun gun, which is also a reported effect of UFOs and their weaponry.

Then there is the consideration of lights as a form of communication. Ships at sea have long used lights to communicate with one another, and there's even the simple act of hanging a lantern in a window. It all means something. Could it be true of UFOs as well?

Many UFO reports involve two or more unidentified objects, and unusual pulsating patterns of different colored lights are often observed. Beyond gaseous chemical reactions, could these lights be a form of communication as well? One species that seems to have incorporated such signaling light sequences is the Humboldt squid, also known as the diablo rojo (red devil) because of its deep red color. Researchers have filmed Humboldt interactions, and one report on the activities of Humboldts notes the following:

> They travel in large numbers around 1,200 squid in one group. These squid are amazing hunters they all work together to initiate the attack, they are even thought of having a visual communication method, via flashing colors utilizing special cells known to scientists as the chromatophors. These chromatophors have recently been studied and a new discovery was astonishing—the color change takes place not just from red to white by open and close action, but rather various color changes may take place by actual movement of these specialized cells in an up and down motion. These cell are currently being investigated for further discovery.[191]

One has to wonder … If life forms such as amoebas and tardigrades were much larger, possessed a skeletal system, were highly intelligent, could fly, and knew how to attack or defend themselves, what would that actually look like? All are God's creation. Who has seen winged cherubim or seraphim, for instance?

How little we know about our planet, the oceans, and every creation that might be out there! We have such limited knowledge, especially of anything beyond what we see here on Earth. But every now and then, we get a glimpse of something not of this world, perhaps not even of this dimension. The best way that I can explain our position as humans on Earth comes from pastor Carl Gallops. In his wonderfully entertaining and informative book about the meaning of life, *The Magic Man in the Sky*. In one example he compares our existence to that of fish in a pond. The fish live in their own environment, just as we live in ours. A fish has no concept of what lies outside his pond. For the fish, *reality* is what he sees within his watery world, where he eats, sleeps, and dies. Occasionally he might break through the cloudy surface and catch a glimpse of something outside his world, but he doesn't understand what he sees and he is unable to live there. He has no concept of houses, highways, airplanes, space flights, science, or mathematics, because they don't exist in his world. In many ways, we are like that fish, trying to understand another realm or type of creation that just doesn't exist in our pond.

Why, then, could we not consider the possible existence of a creature just because we haven't seen it? Certainly it would not necessarily need to be humanoid in appearance. The Bible tells of several times when God used animals to carry out His will. In Noah's ark, animals of many species were saved by the grace of God (Genesis 8:6–12), Jonah spent three days and nights inside a whale or large fish (Jonah 1:17), plagues of frogs, locusts, and pestilence came against Egypt (Exodus 11), a donkey spoke to Balaam (Numbers 22:22–30), ravens brought food to Elijah to eat while he was in hiding (1 Kings 17:34), two bears were sent to kill young boys mocking Elisha (2 Kings 23:25), lions did not attack Daniel in their den (Daniel 6:22), and even Jesus rode on a colt, the foal of a donkey (Matthew 21:5). Remember, also, that Satan appeared as a serpent in the garden.

We use animals as well. For example, we ride on horses, donkeys, mules, elephants, and camels. We've trained dogs to be—in addition to our faithful companions—police dogs, drug-sniffing dogs, bomb-sniffing dogs, cadaver dogs, rescue dogs, guide dogs, and hearing-assist dogs. We have used oxen to plow our fields, pigeons to carry messages, canaries to warn us about unsafe mines, and birds of prey to help us hunt. Even dolphins, whales, and seals can be trained to perform various tasks, and dolphins have been known to save people from drowning. So it's not too far off base to think that there might be variations of other living things in service to God, just as there are reported variations of shapes, forms, and appearances of UFOs and aliens.

I am going way out on a limb here. This could well have been some type of being, and a thought popped into my head regarding armies and the variety of angels that serve God. Now, I am not saying these were God's soldiers, but could these things be otherwise in God's employ? What else might be up there? I thought about those battles at Basel, Switzerland, and Nuremberg, Germany, in the 1500s, when strange objects appeared to be fighting each other in the sky. They were never described as human-looking angels, or anything human or angelic at all. What was taking place during the battles fought by Michael and Gabriel? Who or *what* were they fighting, and who or *what* was fighting alongside them? An army has different regiments composed of soldiers of various ranks, with each assigned their own duties. You don't put a general on the front lines, for instance. We hear of angels and chariots, just as armies have various weapons and pieces of equipment.

When the Bible says that Satan was patrolling earth, does that mean *literally* patrolling? Who would *you* send to keep tabs on things—a reconnaissance division, a police force? All armies and police forces have patrols. Could this be some type of policing effort? Certainly these objects display intelligence, and if it's the same objects shooting a missile mid-launch, activating or deactivating missile silos, and outmaneuvering jets, then we would have to assume they are intelligent and powerful. At the same time, some of them seem curious and even playful. Are they a different kind of life form serving as a well-trained policing entity, armed and ready to act if necessary? Are the flotillas of orbs that have been seen around the world some show of force or display of military might? Often these objects have been seen grouped together, so does this suggest a hive mentality?

One need only think of the enormous variety of animal life God created on this planet. Could not such a variety exist elsewhere in His realm as well? If so, and if those life forms were more like animals than humans, perhaps they would be less inclined to buddy up with humans, like the fallen angels do, and more inclined to take care of business. We won't know unless we catch one—and because of their size, speed, and agility, I don't believe we ever will.

Like animals, you ask? How many times have ghost hunters reported hearing, and sometimes recording, growls from some unseen force? Why *growls*, and what is doing the growling? Why are so many of the ancient gods depicted as animals? This is certainly something to think about as we consider what could be *up there*, whether good or evil. The idea—of *something* nonhuman keeping tabs on us, maintaining the peace, keeping things in check—is an interesting one.

My husband and I know one thing for sure. What we saw wasn't a craft, a cloud, or a human.

Given the state of affairs on this planet, you'd think that something of superior intellect would be concerned for us. Are we some creation's AI, now left to our own devices? Do we need a role model to show us how to live peacefully and productively? Who or what would that role model be? Would we embrace an extraterrestrial that tried to help our world? Might we expect some superior creation to show up and correct our errors? In short, could something of extreme intelligence and concern come from off planet to save us?

One already did.

CHAPTER FOURTEEN
Who Do People Say?

I am not of this world.[192]

—Jesus

We have already had a close encounter of the highest kind, but many people choose not to believe it. So telescopes keep peering into space, radar units keep revolving twenty-four hours a day and seven days a week, transmissions keep pelting remote areas of the universe, and electronic ears keep listening, all in anticipation of someday making contact with something not from our world.

One would have to assume that any extraterrestrial winging its way into our galaxy and locked in on our coordinates would have the ability to successfully travel to this planet and then survive here. Would they breathe oxygen, look like us, be able to converse with us? What would they eat and drink? We presume so much about our intergalactic neighbors—that they would probably come in humanoid form, be able to converse with us at will, and eat what we eat (or at least bring their own provisions). Doesn't sound very *E.T.* to me, but that's the popular belief. Such an arrival would be front-page news and consume every news outlet globally.

But that would be old news. If the Bible is to be believed, then an extraterrestrial visitor has already been here, and it was a mission—not a social call. Born of a human woman, He became one of us, but He wasn't of us. He lived in a natural world but performed supernatural feats. He came to show humans Who created us, where we came from, and that there is something beyond us and others among us. He came to show us how to live in peace, heal our infirmities, and tell us about a heavenly dwelling for those who believe in Him. He came as a sacrificial lamb. It seems at times that all we humans know is bloodshed. Our blood was required of Holy God, but He took our place.

But true to human nature (aka sin), we just weren't getting it. You would think that someone who claimed to come from somewhere other than Earth would be lauded as "first contact" and welcomed with open arms and curious minds. But that didn't happen. Even though Jesus performed miraculous deeds, many locals and leaders wouldn't accept Him. Anything that threatens leadership and power is seen as a threat, and this was no different. As Jesus's followers and ministry continued to grow, so did the resentment among local church leaders. The mere fact that Jesus claimed to be a divine being, a king even, pushed them over the edge, and otherworldly status or not, they would have none of it.

The argument about who Jesus was, His status, and where He came from was ultimately debated by some of the highest-ranking Roman officials:

> Pilate ... asked him, "Are you the king of the Jews?"
>
> "Is that your own idea," Jesus asked, "or did others talk to you about me?"
>
> "Am I a Jew?" Pilate replied. "Your own people and chief priests handed you over to me. What is it you have done?"
>
> Jesus said, "My kingdom is not of this world. If it were, my servants would fight to prevent my arrest by the Jewish leaders. But now my kingdom is from another place."
>
> "You are a king, then!" said Pilate.
>
> Jesus answered, "You say that I am a king. In fact, the reason I was born and came into the world is to testify to the truth. Everyone on the side of truth listens to me."
>
> "What is truth?" retorted Pilate ... "I find no basis for a charge against him."[193]

This was the line drawn in the sand, the pivotal moment. Everything Jesus ever said about Himself was on the line. Would He admit His supernatural origins to the Roman court in the presence of the chief priests, scribes, and elders of the temple, who now stood in judgment of Him? Would He dare to say that His home and His Father were not on Earth? What would be the outcome? Would they believe that He had been assigned a mission by His heavenly Father?

This was the culmination of plotting by evil church leaders to remove Jesus from the public's eye. This Jesus—who claimed to come from somewhere other than Earth, performed miracles, healed the sick, raised the dead, taught peace, and changed lives—despite all the good He did by coming into our world, was on trial for His life. This close encounter of the ultimate kind, this Jesus, now finds Himself before the Roman governor, Pontus Pilate, defending who He is and His right to rule as a king, though a king not from Earth and a kingdom not of this world.

It may have sounded like insanity, but Jesus was dead serious. "If My kingdom were of this world, My servants would fight,"[194] Jesus told Pilate. But the Jewish leaders at the time would not hear of it. They saw Jesus as an earthly threat, not a heavenly king, and they wanted Him crucified. It was a kangaroo court, and time after time Jesus refused to speak, knowing that they were waiting for Him to say something they could use against Him. Pilate knew it as well, "For he knew that the chief priest had handed Him over because of envy."[195]

These church leaders became so enraged that the only way they could deal with this threat to their leadership was the age-old solution—kill Him. But His death was predestined not by them; it was part of what Jesus was sent to do.

On more than one occasion Jesus attempted to drive home the point to His disciples that He was not from this earth: "You are from beneath; I am from above. You are of this world; I am not of this world."[196] It was a matter of fact as far as Jesus was concerned, but it offered no real understanding to the disciples. After all, He was just another man, right? Well, what human could have performed the miracles that the Bible says He did? Not only was He not from here, but He arrived in a most unusual way, although a way necessary to allow Him to function in human form. His mission on Earth was designed by God Himself. Jesus was born of a virgin human woman who was impregnated by the Holy Spirit. Considering that God created humans from the ground up, providing the cellular makeup for a pregnancy would not have been difficult.

If one believes in the gods of antiquity and the fallen angels with their capacity to procreate with humans and create hybrid beings, then the idea of a being who is half human and half God is not such a reach. Jesus was on a mission to save the world and its people, which meant working with us on our level. As one minister explained it, if God had wanted to send a message to a bunch of ants, he would have sent another ant. So, too, we have received our messenger.

It made sense. Jesus would experience every human growth cycle, every human hardship, and every human emotion, in order to understand firsthand how we think, feel, and behave. It meant experiencing death as well. "I am going away," He told His disciples. "Where I go you cannot come."[197] Why? Because the place He was going was not of this world. "I know where I came from and where I am going," He told them, "but you do not know where I come from and where I am going."[198] It became obvious that this otherworldly being was speaking of things far above human understanding. Certainly living in our realm and trying to use human reasoning placed limits on what He could tell people. "If I have told you earthly things and you do not believe, how will you believe if I tell you heavenly things?"[199] To claim that you are God is one thing, but to prove it is another. Jesus proved it.

So much can be said about Jesus, His status as part of the Holy Trinity, His life, His mission here, His identity as the Savior of the world, His love for humankind, His sacrifice for the sins of humanity, the plan of salvation, and His ascension into heaven where He awaits His return. I want to highlight some significant events in this narrative that show the supernatural powers that set Him apart from mere mortal men.

Having been sent, Jesus was to complete His mission on earth and then return to His kingdom in heaven, perhaps even in another realm. It sounds like science fiction, but it was a predestined move on the part of the God for all creation, on and off this planet.

Time after time, Jesus proved his otherworldly abilities in astounding ways. He healed the sick, the blind, and the crippled; fed the hungry; calmed raging storms; walked on water (my favorite); and even raised the dead to life again—feats that no human on earth could accomplish. And Jesus performed one more incredible feat of the paranormal, when He cast out evil demons from human bodies and the demons knew who He was: "Let us alone! What have we to do with You, Jesus of Nazareth? Did You come to destroy us? I know who You are—the Holy One of God!"[200] These are the evil entities that plague this planet and are hostile to humans. Demons were absolutely real in Jesus's time, and they are absolutely real today. However, demons were not the focus of His mission here on earth: "I have come that they may have life, and that they may have it more abundantly."[201] In other words, this was not a simple reconnaissance mission. It was a mission to break the hold on humanity by another otherworldly being, the one referred to as Satan, and his fallen angel accomplices.

It was the ultimate close encounter. Jesus came from another place to give humans a way back to their Creator and a heavenly home, through Jesus, God's son, who is a king—but proving that wasn't easy. Despite the amazing miracles He performed, the sermons He delivered, His loving kindness, and the amazing feats He accomplished throughout His journey on this planet, He was rejected by many, even His own people. The unbridled animosity toward the Savior of humanity resulted in the trial of the century—and then the greatest event on earth.

"Are You the King of the Jews?" asked Pilate. "It is as you say," Jesus answered. This answer did not bode well with the chief priests and elders in attendance, who continued to level unremitting charges of heresy against Jesus and demand His death. Jesus said nothing, but Pilate had become quite frustrated with Jesus's silence. "Do you not hear how many things they testify against You?" he asked. Still Jesus said nothing. Pilate was astonished that Jesus would say nothing in His own defense. He knew the just trial was a mockery. There was an air about the whole proceedings that just stank. Although Pilate could not understand why Jesus would not speak up in His own defense, he understood the serious intentions of His accusers. Jesus's life was on the line.

There was a measurable uneasiness about the whole situation as far as Pilate was concerned, and the ominous message received from his wife during the proceedings didn't help. "Do not have anything to do with that innocent Man, for I have suffered a great deal today in a dream because of Him."[202]

The fever pitch of anger was nearing riot stage, and Pilate wanted an answer from the chief priests and elders. "What evil has He done?" Pilate demanded, believing that Jesus was innocent. The accusers cried, "Crucify Him, crucify Him! We have a law, and according to our law He ought to die because He made Himself the Son of God." That was not what Pilate wanted to hear, and no doubt the possibility of the prisoner being a divine being concerned him greatly. "Therefore, when Pilate heard that saying he was the more afraid, and went again into the Praetorium, and earnestly asked Jesus, 'Where are You from?' And again, Jesus gave him no answer."[203] The seething crowd was adamant. If Pilate would not condemn Jesus to death, then they would go to Caesar. Now fully under the pressure of the mob and despite the warning from his wife, Pilate washed his hands of the matter, literally, and ordered that Jesus be crucified. Things were about to get surreal. "Now it was the third hour and they crucified Him."[204]

"Now from the sixth hour until the ninth hour there was darkness over all the land." Jesus, the king, who was not from here, was dying on the cross, and incredible events were about to unfold: "And when Jesus had cried out again in a loud voice, he gave up his spirit." Then it happened. At that moment, the curtain of the temple was torn from top to bottom. The earth shook, rocks split, and tombs broke open. The bodies of many holy people who had died were raised to life. They came out of the tombs after Jesus's resurrection, went into the holy city, and appeared to many people. So strange was the spectacle that the Roman centurion and those with him who were guarding Jesus saw the earthquake and all that had happened, became terrified, and exclaimed, "Surely he was the Son of God!"[205]

Nothing that happened—sudden darkness, an earthquake, rocks splitting open, a huge veil in the temple ripped apart, dead people walking in the street—could be considered normal. It was far from over, however, and Jesus was about to give the greatest evidence ever that He was not from here.

After Jesus died, His body was placed inside a tomb provided by a rich man named Joseph, from the town of Arimathea. A large stone was rolled across the door and guards were posted at the entrance, in case someone tried to take the body. Jesus had said He was going to rise again on the third day, and the church leaders wanted to make sure no deception would be hatched on the part of His disciples.

Enter the men in white. The next day, Mary Magdalene and the other

Mary returned to the tomb where Jesus had been buried. This was not to be a peaceful solemn time. Matthew says,

> There was a violent earthquake, for an angel of the Lord came down from heaven and, going to the tomb, rolled back the stone and sat on it. His appearance was like lightning, and his clothes were white as snow. The guards were so afraid of him that they shook and became like dead men. The angel said to the women, "Do not be afraid, for I know that you are looking for Jesus, who was crucified. He is not here; he has risen, just as he said. Come and see the place where he lay. Then go quickly and tell his disciples: 'He has risen from the dead and is going ahead of you into Galilee. There you will see him.' Now I have told you."[206]

There are two additional accounts of angels wearing shining white garments or robes at the empty tomb. Luke 24:4 says, "Suddenly two men in clothes that gleamed like lightning stood by them in shining garments." And in Mark 16:5 we read, "And entering the tomb, they saw a young man clothed in a long white robe sitting on the right side." The men in white can appear at any time in any place that God chooses.

It is important to note also that when God sent angels to earth, they always appeared as men, never women, and never as ghosts, spirit guides, or extraterrestrials. So who is who? Apparently robes, even shining white ones, are not an indicator, for Satan's angels can appear as angels of light,[207] and even some extraterrestrials have been reported wearing them.

And who was this incredible being, this savior of humankind, the one who was not from here? Jesus made His presence known to the disciples and others for an extended period of forty days as evidence of His resurrection to life. However, one last display of His power and authority would leave everyone wondering—His ascension.

Having completed His mission, Jesus was soon to leave earth, rejoin His heavenly Father, and wait for the time when He will be sent to earth once again. For all of humanity, He had made the ultimate sacrifice of a painful death on a cross, and He showed us that death holds no finality for those not of this earth. His torture and death meant something then, and it should mean something today. All who believe in Him should gratefully acknowledge His death and rejoice in His resurrection. So who did people say He was? Jesus posed that question to the disciples who witnessed firsthand the many supernatural abilities He displayed. "Who do men say that I, the Son of Man, am?" They told Him that some thought he was John the Baptist, some thought Elijah, others Jeremiah or one of the prophets. Then Jesus asked His disciples point-blank, "But who do you say I am?" Convicted in his soul, Simon Peter said, "You are the Christ, the Son of the living God." Jesus was pleased with Simon's answer and said to him, "Blessed are you, Simon Bar-Jonah, for flesh and blood has not revealed this to you, but My Father who is in heaven."[208]

There was one more spectacular event to drive home confirmation of Jesus's Godhood. He was going home, but not in a fiery chariot or a landing craft. He would simply rise up to heaven. Knowing that He was at the point of departure, we can only imagine what was on His mind. Would the disciples and later generations believe what He had said to them? Believe the evidence of His majesty as displayed to them? Feel the love He showed to them, the concern, the heartache, the encouragement He felt for them? The sacrifice of His life that He made for them?

Now He was looking at His disciples' faces for one last time in this earthly realm. He knew He was leaving them—and us—with a momentous task of evangelism and a battle against a formidable foe. He did not want them—or us—to lose hope, as He had previously told them: "Let not your heart be troubled; you believe in God, believe also in Me. In My Father's house are many mansions; if it were not so, I would have told you. I go to prepare a place for you. And if I go and prepare a place for you, I will come again and receive you to Myself; that where I am, there you may be also." [209] A place off earth with many mansions (some Bible versions say *rooms*) was something that they probably had never considered, but now they would. It was a lot to think about.

After giving the disciples one last command, to go into the world and preach the gospel, Jesus rose into the sky. "Now when He had spoken these things, while they watched, He was taken up, and a cloud received Him out of their sight." They stood there looking up into the sky, dumbfounded, no doubt, from what they had just witnessed, when the men in white appeared once again. "And while they looked steadfastly toward heaven as He went up, two men stood by them in white apparel that said, 'Men of Galilee, why do you stand gazing up into heaven? This same Jesus, who was taken up from you into heaven, will so come in like manner as you saw Him go into heaven.'" Naturally, that could only mean from the clouds.[210]

And the clouds received Him. Was there something in the cloud? Jesus certainly didn't need help going up into the clouds, but from there, who knows? We may never be certain until the end. But one thing is certain— the second coming of Jesus will be from above. Therefore, any attempt to imitate the second coming as a means of gaining supreme leadership on earth, or to explain a massive disappearance of people, must have some association with something or someone very deceptive who comes from above. As Jesus displayed miraculous powers, even announcing He was not from earth, so too may be the one who would deceive the whole world. It's worth noting.

Do you believe in the powers of heaven? Who do *you* say Jesus is?

CHAPTER FIFTEEN
The Tall Ones

How many things they told us! That theirs was an
important mission, that they had been here for many
years, that he had been here three times, and that three
or four centuries ago he had been in Central America,
because in that area there were bases operated by other
aliens, which he helped to get hold of, and that there was
a war, unknown to us.

—Bruno Sammaciccia, "Conversation with the Tall
Alien"[211]

This quote comes from an account by Mr. Sammaciccia regarding a
meeting with his two human friends, one very tall man and one small
dwarf, that allegedly took place in Ascoli Piceno, a small town in Italy, in
1956. As strange as it sounds, the message reiterates that something is not
right in the universe. A war we know nothing about? No information was
conveyed about said war, but we can assume it was unseen on this planet,
off this planet, or in another plane of existence. It's interesting that this
alien would mention a war at all, although it has been alluded to before.

When alien abductee Betty Andreasson was asked during a hypnosis
session if the aliens had enemies as we have enemies, she replied, "There is
one planet that is an enemy, and also many men are enemies, only because
they don't understand."

"Men of this earth, you mean?" she was asked.

"Yes."[212]

We have met the enemy and they are us? However, it might just be the other way around. "And war broke out in heaven: Michael and his angels fought with the dragon; and the dragon and his angels fought" (Revelation 12:7). As a result, humans are waging a spiritual battle—not against flesh and blood, but against deceptive and sovereign principalities, powers of great magnitude, rulers of darkness, and spiritual hosts of wickedness that operate in heavenly places. Incidentally, the heavenly hosts referred to in the Bible are actually heavenly *armies*. This war, this conspiracy against humanity, began a long time ago.

Scripturally speaking, humans were created to occupy the earth, to be in fellowship with their Creator, and to be caretakers of the planet and all the life on it. It's easy to believe that some opposing force would want to mess with those plans, especially knowing that a Savior was to come from a totally human woman. The opposing forces undoubtedly had a game plan, early on, to contaminate human DNA.

Enter the sons of God. There are differing opinions among theologians about the identity of the sons of God. Some believe they were the fallen angels, while others believe they are the righteous offspring of the line of Seth, or perhaps even mighty rulers at the time, since spirit beings cannot reproduce. Well, not exactly. Angels can appear in physical bodies and have physical functions, like the angels who visited Abraham as men. Those angels were able to eat and drink, for they were in human bodies (Genesis 18:1–5). Using this example, one can assume other bodily functions may be possible as well.

In *Alien Intrusion*, Gary Bates presents a strong argument for this position by referencing the argument in Matthew 22 and Mark 12 regarding the question of who a widow would be married to in heaven. Jesus answered, "You are mistaken, not knowing the Scriptures the power of God" (Matthew 22:29–30). Furthering this argument Gary Bates writes as follows:

> Some use this passage to claim that angels are incapable of having sex or procreating, but this is not what the Scripture says. It does say specifically that the angels in heaven, or those angels who obey God, do not engage in this practice. In a parallel passage in Luke 20:34–36 the context is made clear: Jesus replied, "The people of

> this age marry and are given in marriage. But those who are considered worthy of taking part in that age and in the resurrection from the dead will neither marry nor be given in marriage, and they can no longer die; for they are like the angels. They are God's children, since they are children of the resurrection."[213]

The fact that spirits can and do materialize—usually in human form and as men—has been widely documented. Bates points out that every angel sent by God on assignment appeared in physical form as a man, therefore with gender (e.g., Gabriel and Michael). And without wings. Furthermore, "If masquerading angels are appearing as aliens," Bates continues, "then the experiences of abductees suggest that fallen angels, at least, can manifest as female, too."[214] It is well documented that abductees have witnessed humanlike entities, both male and female. (There is a reference to winged women in the book of Zechariah, chapter 5, but with ominous overtones).

Another minister supporting this view is C. Fred Dickason, who surmises that such an unusual relationship and cohabitation among humans and fallen angels is possible: "Matthew 22:30 does not exclude such cohabitation, but his point is that angels do not procreate among themselves." Yet in considering the possibility of becoming flesh and blood, angels have been recorded as engaging in very human activities. Furthermore, angels have taken human form and performed other human functions, such as eating, walking, talking, and sitting. Some angels were mistaken for men and sought for homosexual use by the men of Sodom (Genesis 18:1–19:5).[215]

Then we have the statement by Francine Steiger regarding her childhood experience with a white-robed male entity floating down from the ceiling with a revealing wardrobe malfunction. Certainly based on her testimony, there is room for argument that angels or spirit beings can manifest in full physical form with all the gender-specific equipment. Therefore, the idea of sexual relations with humans is quite plausible.

The unsanctioned union of fallen angels and human women, however, produced giants of tall stature and great strength. They were fearsome and enemies of God's people. The contamination of the human gene pool was well under way with the offspring these angels produced. "And there were giants on the earth in those days, and also afterward, when the sons of God came in to the daughters of men and they bore children to them" (Genesis 6:4).

Enter the tall ones. These hybrid beings, half-human and half-angel offspring of fallen angels, were known as the Nephilim, and they were ungodly, vicious, and well over nine feet tall. In *Judgment of the Nephilim*, Ray Pitterson documents that many discussions by the early clerics agreed that the intermingling of angel genetics with humans produced disastrous results. The French writer Sulpicius Severus (ca. 363–ca. 425 AD) agreed:

> When by this time the human race had increased to a great multitude, certain angels, whose habitation was in heaven, were captivated by the appearance of some beautiful virgins, and cherished illicit desires after them, so much so, that falling beneath their own proper nature and origin, they left the higher regions of which they were inhabitants, and allied themselves in earthly marriages. These angels gradually spreading wicked habits, corrupted the human family, and from their alliance giants are said to have sprung, for the mixture with them of beings of different nature, as a matter of course, gave birth to monsters.[216]

And what was in it for us? According to Pitterson, technology, noting that human talent and cultural advancement came from such an exchange, as in the case of Lamech, the first polygamist, and his family. "They then offered divine knowledge in exchange for the first human bride of an angel—an attenuated version of Satan's original offer of hidden divine secrets to Eve. It is no coincidence that during the time Lamech's marriage and childbearing humans made enormous technological advancements."[217]

From this association, Lamech's son Jabal introduced tent dwelling and cattle grazing, while his brother Jubal invented musical instruments. Tubal-Cain, another brother, became adept at working with metal and creating tools and weapons. Later God himself would share technology of His own with the righteous and non-giant descendant Noah by providing the building plans for the creation of an ultra-titanic-sized ark. There is little doubt then that Satan, by whatever means, wanted to create his own bloodline to destroy God's creation of humankind. I believe he still does.

The earth had been corrupted by the intrusion of fallen angel life forms. The DNA of humans was polluted with the DNA of the fallen celestial beings, which produced their wicked and feared offspring giants. And wicked they were. Some accounts speak of cannibalistic eating of human flesh by the Nephilim, and others mention tampering with animal DNA to further insult God, whom they mocked by the creation of their own gods and their own religions in an obvious effort to destroy the worship of the one true God. Nothing escaped them.

Perhaps connected to the contamination of animal DNA are reports of bigfoots being seen in conjunction with UFO sightings. Some researchers and Native Americans believe there is a bigfoot/UFO connection. Indians near the Humboldt Meridian in California, for example, named the large hairy creature Crazy Bear. The Indians believed that the creature had been brought to the forest "from the stars," and in fact, more than one had been brought to Earth. Investigator Nick Redfern wrote of one such account, "Nothing less than a 'small moon' had descended, ejecting both the creature and several others of its kind. The 'moon' was reportedly piloted by very human-looking entities that always waved at the Indians as they dumped the hairy beast on their land."[218] Genetics gone awry?

Hairy creatures or not, the ancient world was suffering from an infestation of the gigantic hybrid humans and all their evil deeds. Enter God's judgment and the flood.

We know from the Bible account that rain thundered down upon the earth, constantly and mercilessly, for forty days and forty nights. One can imagine the fear that people felt, watching in horror as large rivers overflowed their banks and great bodies of water rose to submerge the dry land. Mountains of earth gave way to unstoppable mudslides, as torrential rain continued washing away homes and cities and everything and everyone, until there was nothing left to do but tread water. Only horror and helplessness remained as the unabated force of rain continued to wreak havoc on earth, with giant swells and whirlpools of water pulling people down into a veritable pit of hell. The flood was meant to destroy the evil done by the fallen angels and their human cooperatives, except for

Noah, his family, and a high-tech ark full of animals saved to repopulate each species.

The gods continued to make their presence known, but little is known of them today. Archeologists dig through cavernous ruins in search of evidence of these illustrious beings. What then of the gods?

Recently, in Mexico, a massive number of golden spheres or orbs were found in a chamber deep below the ancient Temple of Quetzalcoatl, the Feathered Serpent, in the city Teotihuacan, which means "the place where men become gods." Two questions are often asked about these former great civilizations: What happened to them, and where did the people go? The Aztec city of Teotihuacan, with its gigantic pyramids for the moon, the sun, and Quetzalcoatl, the Feathered Serpent, lie in ruins. The Avenue of the Dead, except for tourism, has become dead itself. So many mega-structures and cities of the ancient past now sit deserted and silent, the abodes of gods long gone. The city center of the ancient Mayan city of El Mirador, in South America, covered ten square miles with thousands of structures ranging from 32 to 236 feet in height. Today El Mirador sits deep within a rain forest, its pyramids covered in dense jungle growth. How could such massive and glorious structures end up abandoned and disintegrating? What does this say about the gods those people worshiped? Who deserted whom, and why?

These lost cities exist all over the world, the only remains of diverse cultures that all embraced multiple gods. Telltale signs of their interior habitats have been left in their architecture carvings, and murals that remain depict the workmanship of the buildings, art, and religious drawing and sculptures. Many show explicit content such as can be found in the ancient cities of Pompeii and Herculaneum and among the Khajuraho Monuments of India.

Have our ancient alien predecessors left us architectural breadcrumbs to follow? Do artifacts of the ancient past acknowledge the former existence of these beings and their cohabitation with the mere mortals of Earth? Some ancient alien theorists point to carved artifacts strangely akin to modern aircraft, elongated heads of Egyptian pharaohs, towering statues, monuments of enormous size, skillfully drawn images in arid dirt, abandoned cities of perplexing construction and purpose—all in an attempt to propagate a popular theory that all of this resulted from those who came from the stars.

In the ancient Indus Valley, archeologists are scratching their heads over what happened to the ancient desert cities of Mohenjo Daro and Harappa, whose inhabitants appear to have been wiped out instantaneously. What happened? Modern science has been unable to come up with an answer, so the next logical step for the theorist is mythology. But does mythology have the answer? "The answer is yes. Mythology tells us that Mahenjo Daro and Harappa were both destroyed in a nuclear blast"[219] Ancient Sanskrit accounts attribute this incredible blast to the infighting going on between the gods, who apparently had nukes on board.

Yet it is far easier to believe that the ancient Sumerians had the inside track on humanity's interactions with the gods, even identifying some of the first space travelers as the Anunnaki, who, according to artist depictions, descended to Earth in a winged disc. In *Ancient Aliens: The Official Companion Book*, Jason Martell has a chapter titled "The Cradle of Alien Civilization" in which he cites the work of Zecharia Sitchin. A linguist and author of books on this subject, Sitchin has come by important information by interpreting Sumerian cuneiform writings. According to Sitchin, the Anunnaki made their way to Earth 450,000 years ago in search of gold and precious elements with which to repair the atmosphere on their own planet. The Anunnaki explained to the Sumerians, who obviously wrote it down, that the rise in technology in their society was the culprit that ruined the atmosphere. From global warming to simple smog, they determined that all could be repaired by spraying fine particulates of gold into the atmosphere, but apparently they had run through their own supply. According to the Sumerian text, the Anunnaki found it expedient to set up a way station on Mars to assist in shipments of gold from Earth to their home planet of Nibiru. Instead of planting a flag on Mars, the Niburuians (Anunnaki) built a large sculpture of one of their own faces— now the much debated *face on Mars*.

The plot thickens. One can look at all the marvelous and mysterious wonders of the world and wonder. Others don't do that, having come up theories that they act like are written in stone—which some have been. It is believed that the Anunnaki, who could appear humanoid, were actually spirit beings with the ability to change into human form, and that they hooked a ride through a wormhole (star gate) as a mode of interstellar travel.

But what did they give us in exchange for our gold? Culture? Art? It seems that every tool or carving found in ancient ruins is quickly jumped upon as possibly depicting some type of advanced technology or evidence of visitors from the sky.

But let's say that some advanced aliens shared their technology with Earth's ancients. Let's say the space beings used their technology to build intricately carved buildings and mega structures. Let's say they did it as a gift to humans and presented it themselves, perhaps, in the dress of the day, whether uniforms, spacesuits, or helmets. What if the aliens gifted mankind with scientific knowledge, like how to make crude batteries and electrical power? What if they increased mankind's understanding of astronomy, mathematics, tools, and agriculture? Just what if?

I ask, so what? Did these ancient cultures know what or who these beings truly were?

If we are to believe that these powerful Space Brothers are our parents from the sky, what then is our lineage? What did these spacefaring beings want in return? Worship, perhaps? Look at the cultures of these ancient sites, which many people believe offer clues to our alien heritage. What was the culture within these monumental cities of the gods? What were they taught, and how were the space gods worshiped in return? Was there regard for the special nature of *human life?* Apparently not. One would expect that highly advanced and sophisticated people would want a caring and nurturing environment for adults and children alike, but quite the opposite was true.

Historians have given us many accounts of what went on in these ancient_magnificent cultures. Looking at some of the highly touted people, cities, and regions presented as evidence of the star gods, we see an ominous shadow of things that were. As we look at the ancient Sumerians, Egyptians, Babylonians, Nazca, Aztec, Mayan, and those from the cities of Puma Punku, Easter Island, and lands occupied by the ancient Celtic people, a common denominator surfaces in their forms of worship— human sacrifice. If that's what those ancient gods required, do we really want them back?

The rule of the giants and the cultures of the gods of old have faded into antiquity. It had appeared that the visitors of old had chosen to keep their distance—that is, until something came crashing down.

Roswell, New Mexico, 1947. The reported crash of an alien UFO set in motion the belief that alien beings possessing real bodies were piloting it. Several books have been written about the Roswell incident, and the general consensus is that pieces of the craft and possibly alien bodies were secreted away by air force personnel and taken to Wright-Patterson Air Force base in Dayton, Ohio. This has never been officially confirmed by the military, but rumors persist about the existence of recovered alien bodies from the crash sight. If it's true, how could those alien bodies expand our knowledge of the universe and our place in it, and what technologies might be made available to us?

Recently, reports of alien bodies have surfaced again, this time thanks to physicist Robert Lazar who came forward in 1989 with claims of having worked at a secret military installation at Area 51 in Nevada. Lazar claimed firsthand knowledge of two things: (1) the military's involvement in the back engineering of recovered alien crafts that he claimed to have seen, and (2) the existence of alien bodies from official secret documents he had read.

Researcher Brenda Denzler has looked into Lazar's claims of crashed alien crafts, recovered alien bodies, and secretive military meetings with several extraterrestrial races. She writes, "Some of these races, as Lazar cites in the report, have been involved in human history for thousands of years as genetic manipulators of human physiology and shapers of human religious traditions."[220]

If this information is true, then we have more to consider than just ETs dropping by for tea. Are hybrids on the rise? Gene manipulation has been addressed by David Jacobs in *Sight Unseen*. Another group actively looking into the gene-splicing efforts of extraterrestrials is an organization called Hybrids Rising (HR). This group presents the theory that the repeated abductions of family members produce an entire lineage of a gene, which may explain why certain families or individuals are targeted for abduction. Therefore, the production of human-looking hybrids would be the forerunners of a new race of beings that could easily assimilate into society.

Based on HR's research, and using the testimony of an abductee named Angie, we may have insight to their intentions. "Angie was shown a 'clone' infant as well as nine 'hybrid tots' and was told they would be used 'to prepare [humans] for the changes."[221] The Hybrids Rising team believes that this preparation is not to get humans psychologically ready for the presence of blond-haired, blue-eyed extraterrestrials on earth, because "humans are being physically—genetically—altered." In their opinion, this refers to a change that is taking place within humanity itself. Where could this be happening?

Over the years, there have been numerous claims of underground facilities housing secret military operations where extraterrestrials and the US military have been working in tandem, but for what? Are they gifting us with advanced technology in exchange for human specimens? Such an agreement would validate the claims of some abductees allegedly being taken to such facilities, examined, and returned—not to mention their claims of having seen human body parts and alien-looking specimens floating in glass containers. Could this nightmare be real?

Some abductees believe that an underground base exists beneath Archuleta Mesa, in proximity to Dulce, New Mexico. Such claims have never been confirmed by anyone within the military, nor is the government talking. We can assume that unconfirmed reports like these can serve the purpose either of informing the public of such operations or preparing the public should such an announcement occur.

Meanwhile on the planet's surface, we have reports of tall extraterrestrials being seen in the company of much smaller ETs, such as the small, slender grays. Some of the tall beings have been seen wearing uniforms, robes, and capes, and they appear to be of various ranks and duties. Some abductees believe that the emotionless, almost robotic grays are themselves some kind of created beings.

If there is indeed a conspiracy, *why*? There appears to be a deliberate, ongoing conditioning of the public to accept the idea of the reality of aliens, and furthermore, to accept the idea that we need to rely solely on them for the betterment of our planet. I smell a rat—maybe two.

If *tall whites* are indeed working with the United States, we might be able to account for at least one of them. In an article written by exopolitical proponent Michael Salla, one ex-military source, Charles Hall, claims that tall whites were at Nellis Air Force Base in Nevada and that generals were salivating to get technology transfers from them. According to Hall, the generals would do anything—allow anything—to obtain the tall whites' technology.

Less amicable encounters with the seven-foot-plus tall whites have been reported over the years, but perhaps none so disturbing as what Charles Hall reported while serving as a duty weather observer at Nellis. The tall whites were less than accommodating to base personnel, and the generals did not interfere. According to Hall, "Generals would permit tall whites to kill service men if they were offended, threatened or harmed."[222]

In an article concerning the existence of these beings, Salla discloses information provided to him by an alleged space program whistleblower by the name of Corey Goode. Goode references a December 2016 report, which he claims discusses the possibility of the air force providing a partial disclosure about the "Tall White Extraterrestrials." Salla's article explains that these tall whites are believed to have been around for a very long time, and that a secretive cabal might be instrumental in introducing humankind to this group of tall aliens. The bonus would be a missionary effort to encourage people to follow a mystical religion offered by these beings. The tall whites' height can be intimidating; they seem to fulfill leadership roles among the alien forces, and that might hold true for ghosts and spirits as well. A photograph exists of a very tall entity in a long black robe standing near the altar at Newby Church in North Yorkshire, England, for example.[223]

Why then are these aliens seen as our only hope? Why would we want to be totally *alienated* from control of our own planet? This is a somber yet important consideration.

Seasoned researchers such as the late John Keel have spoken out against the extraterrestrials—or ultraterrestrials, as he called them—whom he believed are up to no good, well beyond their ability to manipulate objects in and out of our earthly realm. Brenda Denzler elaborates by referring to Keel's outspoken opinion of the aliens themselves. "Despite their new guise," Denzler writes, "these intelligences were something that humanity had always been aware of—indeed, had frequently worshiped as gods, or had revered and feared as angels or demons." Noting Keel's analogy, "He suspected that the changing forms by which UFOs had presented themselves were not just convenient devices for accomplishing some noble or even just useful task, but were instead deliberately false performances designed to mislead and to control us."[224]

It is not difficult to see how the conniving plot to use fallen angels to corrupt the DNA of early humans closely aligns itself with the efforts of these celestial alien visitors. Leery of the aliens' true intentions, UFO investigator Colin Wilson writes a sobering narrative about the abductions: "Many of them seem to make no sense; nothing much seems to be achieved. But, when Beth Collings asked a 'gray' why he was driving a needle into her navel, he replied, 'It is part of the change.' And she later realized that she had been abducted since childhood, and that so had her father and grandfather and probably her grandchildren. Why make an effort over several generations unless the purpose is to create a new kind of human being?"[225]

The tall aliens would have us believe that they are creating a human/alien hybrid race to help bring about a utopian world on planet Earth by their alien wisdom, knowledge, and intelligence. Or, perhaps not.

Psychiatrist David M. Jacobs has counseled many individuals claiming alien abductions, and he has come to the startling conclusion that the aliens are *not* here for *our* benefit. The altruistic vision of one scientific community meeting with another scientific community for the good of all has gone by the wayside. Jacobs concludes from his research that contact between the two races, ET and human, is not of equal benefit. He see it as one species exploiting another for personal gain, and he believes that it's time to give serious consideration to what might be going on—and what to do about it.[226]

The severe judgment against those fallen angels who were the perpetrators of this crime against humanity, and who remain now chained in a prison, is the reason that marriage and procreation between human and aliens doesn't occur today. Yet the idea of creating a hybrid human has not gone away, but maybe there is a workaround.

It is startling to realize that in today's world, the idea of human-alien hybrids has become almost a social norm among some people within the UFO community. The Hybrid Project has done their own in-depth analysis of what they believe is the ongoing splicing of alien and human DNA, resulting in hybrid beings and a new race of children sometimes called indigo children.

The Hybrids Rising (HR) team believes that many, but not all, hybrid beings are a biological combination of humans and extraterrestrials or advanced intelligences. And here is where it gets complicated, if not genetically corrupt. The HR team also believes that this type of new creation would not necessarily be limited to the combination of only two species of DNA. In other words, it's quite possible that a newly created being would have more than two parents. That process would involve transgenesis, the introduction of a specific transgenic gene into a living organism so that the organism will exhibit a new property and transmit that property to its offspring.[227] Although human DNA would be needed in the formulation of these beings, a human host might not be.

In something right out of an alien medical primer, humans are now making formulations of their own. DNA splicing is quickly becoming a proven science, and the manufacturing of a customized human being appears to be a manifest destiny. No sexual relations with humans necessary.

Scientists have already created what they call *biobags*, in which they have successfully *grown* baby sheep. An article titled "An Artificial Womb Successfully Grew Baby Sheep—and Humans Could Be Next," posted on the Verge website, explains how the fetus of a sheep was placed and grown to term in what looks like "oversized Ziploc bags strewn with tubes of blood and fluid." During this artificial birth process, the sheep continue to grow and develop the ability to breath on their own and function for all practical purposes as normal lambs.[228] I personally found the pictures of the bagged sheep difficult to look at. Can homegrown humans be far behind? Reports of abductees seeing fetuses and body parts floating in large containers on board alien spacecraft may not be the imagined horror that some have thought.

The science of creating a human being from the cell up, complete with customized DNA, is already under way. In this diabolical scheme, we humans will contaminate ourselves. Will *humans* destroy God's creation this time, and then strive to be as God? Can this be another attempt to thwart God's plan for His creation, and the promise of Jesus Christ's return to earth to claim His own from the body of believers? If these claims of hybrid infiltration among the human species are in any way true, what will be left of humankind to claim?

Following this rationale, a rapture of human Christians might be a necessary form of rescue to preserve the untainted seed of humans, similar to what Noah's ark accomplished. Aliens? Hybrids? Many people, including Christians, would scoff at the idea. But as unlikely as it may seem, it might be well to remember that "there were giants in those days," and that the predicted end times will be "as in the days of Noah."

CHAPTER SIXTEEN
The Shining Ones

> Many UFO reports, he said, seem to pertain more to accounts of "poltergeists" (cases where objects fly around the room and strange sounds are heard) and other types of "psychic" manifestations than to "actual solid items of nuts and bolts hardware. That is one of the reasons," added Dr. Hynek, "why I cannot accept the obvious explanation of UFOs as visitors from outer space."[229]
>
> —Allen Spraggett

As extraterrestrial and human hybrid stories continue to circulate, whether or not these beings openly emerge on earth, the very idea of such a possibility opens a door to a deception. Could such hybrid claims be legitimized by an *ancient ancestors* theory? Enter the shining ones.

In another book about the crop circles and their meanings, *The Cosmic Connection*, Michael Hesemann writes, "After a longish meditation, Isabelle received the first message. It originated, according to her, from 'an intelligence outside this planet' who called themselves 'the Watchers' … The Watchers told her that it had been they who, millennia ago, instigated the construction of Silbury Hill. The syllable 'Sil' had the meaning 'shining beings.'"[230]

In the introduction to Raymond Fowler's *The Andreasson Affair*, J. Alan Hynek focused on the more spiritual aspects of the Andreasson encounters. These spiritual aspects have to do with beings introducing themselves as benevolent and friendly aliens who have traveled from the heavens to be at our disposal (and us at theirs) in the hopes of creating an interspecies connection for the betterment of humankind. Metallic crafts landing in deserts or fields have given way to up-close-and-personal home visits and a recruitment program for assistance. Hynek says, "This present work will also challenge those who consider UFOs solely synonymous with physical craft that transport flesh-and-blood denizens from distant solar systems. A previous book by Mr. Fowler, *UFOs: Interplanetary Visitors*, upholds this more popular concept of UFOs and many of the cases he describes tend to give strong support to the hypothesis. But here we have 'creatures of light' who find no difficulty in exerting uncanny control over the witnesses' minds."[231]

In the occult world, mind control has long been established through telepathic communications to recipients eager to sign on for intergalactic communications, a point that Brad Steiger drives home in *Gods of Aquarius*:

> "At the Findhorn trust community in northern Scotland, there had been telepathic contact with alleged beings from outer space for many years, but in the summer of 1970, certain of the group began to receive a series of messages which dealt with the nature of new energies now unfolding and penetrating Earth. A message to begin the New Age. While in meditation, Findhorn operative, Dorothy Maclean made contact with beings living on a higher vibratory dimension from the physical which she call Devas; a Sanskrit word meaning "shining ones."[232]

Such appearances are not uncommon in UFO reports, including the type of ETs present. Linda Mouton Howe, in her appropriately titled *Glimpses of Other Realities*, mentions the varietal types of humanoid beings reported by abductees of a somewhat different caliber. She writes, "Other humanoid beings, tall and short, have been described by abductees as 'glowing' or 'surrounded by light.'"[233] But again one asks, who are these elusive shining ones? Maybe the government knows, or at least is trying to find out.

According to researcher Nick Redfern, information has surfaced regarding a secret Pentagon program through the Department of Defense in which attempts were made to contact non-human entities (aka extraterrestrials). They had some success—enough, that is, to need to consult a priest. Occult books flooded their operation, and they quickly set about to study demons, demonology, devils, and evil spirits.

Of particular interest was a book about devils and demons terrorizing the lives of the ancient Babylonian people, which made startling comparisons between incubus and succubus activities and those experienced by abductees. These evil entities could appear as male and female, and they were known to sexually assault their victims in their bedrooms in the dark of night. These actions have been compared to the sexual activities reported by abductees falling prey to their alien abductors. More books were obtained, including—for good measure—some by Christian authors.

In 2010, Redfern's interview with NASA safety specialist Joe Jordan shed even more light on the subject of the nonhuman entities program, and Jordan didn't pull any punches:

> The purpose of all this is to deny the reality of Christianity. And, they have probably the best propaganda machine I've ever seen or read about. I believe that's the purpose behind this whole experience. Look at the stories of old of gnomes, fairies, and elves; we wouldn't believe that today. So they come in the emperor's new clothes. And they come in a guise that we will accept. But their purpose is to defeat us and to delude us, so that we will take our focus off the one true God.[234]

Despite adverse and frightening experiences, the Pentagon's secret team continues to push the realms of darkness and the investigations continue. Well, they can't say they weren't warned.

The not-so-alien alien. If you were to ask someone today, even a child, what an alien looks like, you would most likely hear that they look like the bulbous-headed, large-eyed, spindly-bodied grays. The public has been programmed to accept this image. Next would be Nordics, blond-haired and blue-eyed humanoids, little elflike creatures with ray guns, or for the most studious, reptilian or insectoid beings. The point is that most people have an image in mind, but here's where it gets tricky.

Not all aliens are the same, and not all aliens look and act the same. Is this by providence or programming? Here's an interesting observation from John Spencer, who reasons that if all these highly advanced aliens of all different shapes and sizes have chosen to come from all points of the universe, "Then the Earth must be some kind of inter-galactic stopping point and probably the greatest tourist attraction in the Universe." However, if this same group of varietal alien species come from only a few locations and are basically the same, then they are often described differently by different witnesses because of one clever ability—they can change. Using the Beitbridge incident in Africa as an example, Spencer says that one alien "suggested that he could appear however the witness wanted; if he wanted the alien to look like a duck, he could look like a duck, or a monster, or whatever."[235]

Following this rationale, would it be unreasonable to believe that entities such as those encountered by ghost-hunting teams could also present themselves as whatever the history of the location offered—little girl or boy, man or woman, dog, horse, chicken, whatever? The entities appear to be willing to accommodate anyone, even using a person's name if it assists in their deception. Can preexisting lives be far behind in this charade? Reincarnation seems to be the fallback when all other explanations fail.

V is for Venusians, the talk of the town in the nineteenth century. Mystic and master contactee Helena Blavatsky (1831–1891), the highly publicized founder of Theosophy, put together an entire pantheon of ascended masters, some of whom made house calls to the faithful. By the twentieth century, Venusians had become somewhat passé, and Martians took center stage.

Then there is the curious case of Guy Ballard, whose trek to Mount Shasta in California garnered him a special meeting with an ascended master, one of Theosophy's favorites, Saint German, up on the mount. The abilities of these ascended beings appear to correspond directly to what the person is seeking, ergo displaying some of the same attributes as alien imposters. I think it's fair to say that if it looks like a duck and quacks like a duck, it must be an alien.

So are we seeded or created? Humanoids 2.0? Is this a random drive to seed with no understanding of who or what we are, let alone who *they* are? And what of the animals? Were they seeded too? Are there stables in space? It's difficult to believe in a Creator who has a specific plan for us, who wants us to *know* who He is, but simply leaves us to fend for ourselves, leading serendipitous lives with no real purpose. Then do we believe that our only hope for salvation comes from the kindness of intergalactic strangers? There must be something afoot, and there is—covert activity and an unknown war.

We go now to a meeting at a castle in 1956. Italian writer Stefano Breccia, in *Mass Contacts*, writes about an encounter he had with two beings from outer space. Contact was mostly telepathic, sometimes by automatic writing, and sometimes in person. These particular aliens said they were from Ummo, and over a short period of time, they arranged for a meeting with Breccia and two friends at a castle in Ascoli Piceno, Italy. Although much of Breccia's writing fits the same category as that of George Adamski and is equally difficult to verify, he still includes some interesting information—in particular, a reference to an *unknown war* about which we humans know nothing.

We know from multiple reports that there has been conflict between military jets and unidentified flying objects, some appearing nonconfrontational, whereas others engage. Perhaps we need only look at the peaceful night sky, which may not be peaceful after all.

A few years ago, one UFO researcher hit on something quite interesting. Using night-vision goggles, he was able to record objects streaking back and forth in the night sky, not only zigzagging in irregular patterns, but also actively engaging each other offensively and defensively. UFO researcher Ed Grimsley, using high-powered night-vision goggles, videoed several mysterious events involving these unknown objects in the night sky. Some objects were round or triangular in shape, and they spun, darted, and circled around each other in what appeared to be an ongoing battle.

Some leeway can be allowed regarding the validity of this report if you consider the aerial battles that allegedly took place in the skies over Nuremberg, Germany, on April 14, 1561. Local journalist Hans Glaser described that scene as a ferocious battle taking place between hundreds of "balls and cylinders," much to the alarm of the frightened local citizens.

So we have demons, devils, angels, and ETs. Who are the players in this cat-and-mouse game, and what do we have to fear? Is it the government's responsibility to inform us of the likelihood of an alien invasion? That would mean disclosure of any information the government has regarding the actual existence of these space beings and any perceived threats to earth's inhabitants, including any contact or association the government might have with aliens themselves.

Is our government in cahoots with alien entities? If so, why? Again, some theories suggest a trade of humans for technology. As outrageous as that might sound, one cannot ignore the reports by abductees claiming to have witnessed such a program of exchange. Linda Mouton Howe has dealt with that possibility in depth in *A Strange Harvest*. If the government is keeping secrets, this is a big one.

One active proponent of disclosure of government information regarding UFOs, should any exist, comes from Dr. Steven Greer's Exopolitically based Sirius Disclosure project. Retired physician and founder of the Center for the Study of Extraterrestrial Intelligence (CSETI), Greer considers himself an actual ambassador to the stars. Over the years, he has met with many notables in the science and space communities, as well as military personnel who, as part of his disclosure initiative, have decided to come forward with their testimony regarding evidence for UFOs, aliens, and what the military and government know about it. The problem is getting the government to admit what it knows. In an attempt to rattle information out of the government's secret alien files, Greer has lobbied for disclosure through press conferences and books he has written on the subject.

Along with collecting evidence of government cover-ups, Greer is helpful, through his organization, about instructing novices in a method by which they can contact aliens—a method that he claims to have used successfully himself. Greer claims that his group has called down UFOs through the methods that CSETI employs. Add to that the clamor for the government to come clean, and it makes for an interesting mix. I would think that Dr. Greer's association with aliens would have a stronger effect if he would disclose to the public what he knows, sans the government. Certainly he has connections in this regard, if what he claims is true.

I personally believe that a sort of preconditioning disclosure has been taking place for quite some time, with the unrestricted reports in which astronauts have talked openly about their UFO sightings. Add to that the movies, documentaries, TV specials, radio talk shows, government officials coming forward, high-ranking former military personnel giving testimonies, and so on—and you have quite a solid case for disclosure without dipping into government files.

But getting the government to cry uncle is another matter, because it would put them in a precarious position. After all, if these aliens are so elusive and UFOs are so uncatchable, what can the government say— *Yes, they're real, but we can't do a thing about them?* Not very reassuring, especially if they can't control these entities and don't really know their motives. Therefore I have to assume either that our government and military *do* know about them or that our intelligence is really subpar. But where it goes from there, we'll have to wait and see.

I wouldn't write off the possibility of some type of contact, especially if it involved a gifting of technology in exchange for who knows what, all for the chance to reverse engineer some alien craft. Unless we come up with a need to know, especially given the interest of national security, we will *not* know. Still, I would keep this in mind to avoid being caught off guard should something be revealed in the future. After that, all bets are off.

So ruling out covert activities on behalf of the world's governments, what is left? We have seen reports of unidentified objects in the sky going back to ancient times. We have had reports of actual physical crafts, humanoid aliens, grays, reptilians, dwarf types, and others; reports of amoeba-type creatures in the air; contacts with energy forms and space-suited aliens; contact with robed aliens and anything weird that says it's an alien—balls of light, discs, cigar-shaped mother ships, triangle-shaped crafts, wedge-shaped crafts, spheres flying in formation, flotillas of orbs, Foo Fighters, and flying shields.

Again, are these devils, demons, angels, or alien life forms from space? There has to be an explanation, and I believe it comes from Genesis, the first book of the Bible. Humans made it only to chapter 3 of Genesis before "the fall" into an imperfect state of sin, after disobeying God's command not to eat of the fruit of whatever tree was growing in the middle of the garden. Enter the serpent. In the very first verse of chapter 3, we read, "Now the serpent was more cunning than any beast of the field which the Lord God had made."

Looking at this verse in its original language, Hebrew, enables a deeper understanding. Dr. Michael Heiser, who has a PhD in Hebrew, makes an interesting observation about the serpent that was Eve's tempter in the

Garden of Eden. Heiser explains that the word for serpent in Hebrew is *nachash*, which can be translated as *serpent* or *snake* but has other meanings as well. "The Hebrew root is the basis for a noun, verb, and adjective. Of course as a noun it is usually the word for serpent. The verb form means deceiver or diviner with divine knowledge. The adjective version means bronze or brazen with a bright shine. Therefore, used as an adjective it should be translated as *'shining one.'*"

Shining or luminosity, according to Heiser, is "a quality that is characteristic of divine beings in the Hebrew Bible." It is Dr. Heiser's opinion that the *nachash* was not an animal and certainly not a talking snake, but "a member of the 'Divine Council' who choose to rebel against God's plan for humanity by causing humans to disobey God's command so they would be killed or removed from God's council and family.

"The Nachash is an angelic-type divine being perhaps masquerading as an animal, but not a member of the animal kingdom. It may have been in serpentine form or took a serpentine form."[236] Using this interpretation, Genesis 3:1 says, "Now the shining one was more cunning than any beast of the field which the Lord God had made."

CHAPTER SEVENTEEN
The New Old Age with a Twist

New Age World Server categories include: Telepathic
Communicators, Trained Observers, Magnetic Healers,
Educators of the New Age, Political Organizers, the
workers in the Field of Religion, The Scientific Servers,
Psychologists, Financiers, and Economists, and Creative
Workers.

—Sir John R. Sinclair[237]

Many feel that it is truly the end of the age spoken of in
the New Testament, and to those astrologically inclined,
the beginning, of the New Age—the Age of Aquarius—
means an age where mankind will live according to
ancient dictates of brotherly love, peace, and spiritual
prosperity. The space brothers, or whatever name one gives
the people from other dimensions of time and space, could
very well be the teachers that will see the fulfillment of
this better way. Many feel they are exactly that—teachers
and spiritual guides.[238]

—*The New UFO Sightings*

Journalist Ruth Montgomery had spent much of her professional expertise
covering the goings-on in Washington politics. Her style of reporting
granted her many sought-after interviews with presidents and others of
the Washington political scene—that is, until she stepped over into the
paranormal with her interests in the occult, spirit guides, walk-ins, and

past-life scenarios, of which she claimed many. In many of the channeled messages she received from spirits and aliens via automatic writing or conversations with her personal spirit guides, one topic seemed to rate high on the information scale: the idea of a coming New Age.

In one example that smacks of the old "Who's on first?" routine, Montgomery launched into a "Stop the presses!" scoop straight from the mouths of spirit guides regarding the pending dawning of an illustrious New Age. But is it really all that simple? In her book *Aliens Among Us,* Montgomery documented the case of the confusing, mistaken identity of David Paladin, who in reality, according to Montgomery's spirit guides, was a walk-in from Sirius.

As the story goes, Paladin was an American soldier and spy during World War II who had the misfortune of being in a German uniform without identification during an Allied offensive in which he was seriously wounded. When British troops arrived, they assumed he was dead and put him among the dead for burial—until they noticed him moving. Paladin was then sent to a British field hospital in Austria, where he remained in a coma although strangely mumbling in Russian from time to time. To add to the mystery, upon waking from his coma, Paladin informed the hospital personnel that his name was Vasili Kandinski, but Kandinski was a Russian artist who reportedly died in France in 1944.

Intrigued, Montgomery asked her spirit guides for confirmation of the man's story, and obligingly the guides confirmed that David Paladin was in fact the walk-in soul of the Russian artist Vasili Kandinski, and that the artist Kandinski had at some time been a walk-in from Sirius. The plot thickens. Paladin had his own story. After meeting with Montgomery, Paladin, who was also Kandinski, confided in her that he had recently had contact with space beings. Montgomery again sought guidance from the guides who, in their infinite wisdom, revealed to her that when the soul who was now David Paladin had not been able to keep Kandinski's body alive, he had returned to Sirius briefly and boomeranged back into the body of the soldier, whom he revived "for his work, which is concerned with the preparation of earthlings for the New Age."[239] It looks like the Space Brothers had been in on it since the beginning.

The subject of the New Age was tossed about in *Saucer Scoop*, an early-sixties publication that discussed the pros and cons of intergalactic fellowship, which found that opinions were split about 50/50. One group was definitely on board, the cosmic positive thinkers who believed that contact was being made by the Space Brothers in order to prepare everybody for the glories of the New Age of interplanetary brotherhood. Others were not so sure, thinking that it was all a ploy to silence those who had witnessed UFOs and felt that there was at least one UFO group that appeared to be indifferent to the fate of humans and might even be hostile to earthlings.[240]

The idea of intergalactic brotherhood has not disappeared over the years. Breathing new life into the concept is the idea that it's all in the timing. A New Age ought to do it.

More New Age thought for connecting the dots comes from the previously mentioned journalist and UFO researcher Paola Harris, an Italian-American photojournalist and freelance writer with a broad interest in UFOs. Harris has conducted interviews with many well-known authors and researchers in the UFO community. She says that after teaching science fiction at the high school level in 1977, her interests broadened into more avant-garde social issues, and in 1978 she became an avowed futurist, as noted in her book *Connecting the Dots*. "I even attended the World Future Conference in Vancouver, BC, in the 1980s," she writes, "where I was to read Marilyn Ferguson's work about shaping the future, and later I would hear Frijhof Capra speak about spirituality and quantum mechanics. I was hooked on the fact that there needed to be an open approach to this major philosophical shift in thinking, which later was coined as the New Age. I was fascinated!"[241] Harris is also the producer of Starworks, USA, which has done documentaries on the subject of UFOs and hosted symposiums on New Age and UFO subjects featuring many well-known speakers from both fields.

Many UFO and New Age conferences are held nationally and globally each year. There is a cohesiveness among New Agers and UFO contactees that often results in shared beliefs and experiences dealing with the occult. In some cases, people who did not have an interest in occult subjects before attending a conference established an interest shortly thereafter.

Lynne Kitei writes of a similar situation in *The Phoenix Lights*, about the aftermath of having the paranormal experience with the UFO orbs of light. Kitei is a sound and sensible person with a true concern for our planet's state of affairs and whether there is *something* out there that cares. Eliminating God from this scenario, which I have no knowledge that she does, we can only backfill with beings—no matter what form they're in or where they come from—to help fill the void of our understanding. Is that a good thing? In my opinion, no. Just having an encounter with something *other* does not mean that it offers the honest truth.

However, these experiences can often lead an individual to look at their life in a much more philosophical way. "And that's what happened to me," writes Kitei. "Because of the Phoenix Lights and my subsequent search for answers, I was slowly but surely looking at the world and myself differently. Topics I had considered gibberish, 'out there' New Age, were making more sense to me ... Are these entities aware of what may lie ahead for us, trying to warn us to change our violent, destructive ways before it is too late?"[242]

Altruistic visions of a kinder, gentler world are often sandwiched in between New Age and UFO ideologies. Feelings, emotions, senses of something outside oneself, drawing each individual to realize that we are all one family, that we should put away all aggression and conflicting philosophies and realize the god within, give rise to the *experiential* as the standard for truth. It is not difficult to see the progression of New Age beliefs and experiences, once they take hold, leaving many at the crossroads where life-altering paranormal experiences would impact their life going forward.

So if one were to buy in to this altruistic cause, perhaps with some not-so-innocent goading, what would be the logical next step? Dr. Kitei had a conversation with a friend who, along with her family, also had seen the Phoenix Lights on that night in March and shared an emotional insight to what she now felt as a result: "Well, the March 13th sighting totally reinforces what I'm saying. We should be citizens of the world. We shouldn't have boundaries. We need to be here to protect the planet."[243]

So the twist involving the heralding of a New Age, with its new political and economic systems, just might be brought about by the assistance and/or appearance of intergalactic beings from afar. Certainly the groundwork has been laid.

I think it is important to note that many people who embrace New Age teachings or even the teachings of the Space Brothers are not evil. In many cases they are truly convicted to try to better the world through these actions and beliefs. However, although their intentions are often good, they have innocently been misdirected away from the true source that could bring about change—God. Our responsibility is to respond in Christian fellowship and attempt to give them the gift of salvation through the One who is the Way, the Truth, and the Life—Jesus. Throw out the seed in peace and understand where they are coming from and where we can lead them, because the threat of what lies ahead is real.

Would such coming together politically bring us social globalism or global socialism? There appears to be a call for a kinder, simpler, authoritarian way. A question was presented to Maitreya, the Aquarian Age Christ, regarding what type of government the New Age would manifest. Without hesitation, his answer was that it would inevitably lead to a world government. That government would not be imposed on mankind, but it would result from manifested brotherhood. As Maitreya explained, "The sharing and the cooperation of all mankind, the redistribution of the produce of the world will result in world government. Any attempt to achieve or impose world government without the acceptance of sharing is doomed to failure."[244]

So much has been written about and said in speeches across all political persuasions regarding the advocating for a socialist platform, even in the United States. This is not the first time in our history that socialist ideologies have been tossed about in the political arena, but never before has it been done with such bravado. It would probably mean going from a sovereign people and nation to a borderless, socialist, globalist people and nation. Oddly, no socialist country has taken the lead in this. The idea of globally harmonious world citizens is being pushed to the forefront in such a manner that the desires and actions necessary to retain one's sovereign state would seem obscene to the global conglomerate of countries linking arms and enacting global mandates. It would be easy to presume that sovereignty then would lie with the United Nations as the go-to overlord for global issues and international law. Seriously.

As the members of United Nations have found themselves in near fisticuffs with allied nations, such fist pounding has accomplished little in bringing about an organized and united front willing to surrender the deed to the farm and become like the guys in the Euro-nations. Feeling the loss are those within the European community who have lost their single-nation status, their identity as unique and separate countries and cultures, reduced to cookie-cutter renditions of every other country on the map. Every nation on this planet is at risk.

If brute force won't work, how about kindness or progressive thinking when the old-school values of independent thinking still get in the way? It's the vision, the nice stuff that has to be the hard sell—planet sustainability, global warming, feeding the hungry, sharing the wealth or redistributing it, free education, or whatever comes first. They're all noble causes, but causes need oversight, rules, and enforcement.

Enter the world parliament. The mandates of the United Nations Parliamentary Assembly, or UNPA, are clearly laid out in *A World Parliament*[245] by German Jo Leinen, member of the European Parliament and former chair of the environmental committee and the committee on constitutional affairs, and South African Andreas Bummel, cofounder and director of Democracy Without Borders and Campaign for a United Nations Parliamentary Assembly. The book's endorsers represent a cross section of global democracy enthusiasts, with heavy representation by university professors worldwide. Concerns naturally include global economy issues, world currency, global taxation, and so forth, but also terrorism, nuclear weapons, and global food security—all addressed and supported by political leaders and high-profile financial backers from the United States and other nations.

Besides politics as usual, there are other considerations of a much more personal application for the world's citizens, which read remarkably like some of the alien initiatives such as genetic manipulation, or reprogenetics as it is sometimes referred to. The parliament sees genetic tampering as something that could have a profound effect in separating human beings into two classes: (1) nonmodified and (2) modified or genetically enhanced. Add to that transgender and transhuman (combining machine and computer intellect), issues that expedite the concerns even more for modified global citizens. But how could any organization monitor such *enhancements*, and what happens if some back-alley projects are conducted in secret? If humans morph into superbeings via gene customization, what happens then? Who regulates the regulators? These are valid concerns.

Then there are questions regarding the regulating of autonomous weapons, such as drones and robots, that would need oversight, presenting more serious considerations, and the same concern about how many nations would actually comply with global regulations. Add to the mix bioterrorism, nanobots, and new viruses, and a whole new drama emerges. Of course, these concerns have been expressed before, and all seem to come to the same conclusion. According to those who have adequately assessed the dangers involved, what appears to be the logical next step, as noted by Isaac Asimov, would be for the "world to get together and be sufficiently a unit to face the problems which attack us as a unit. What we need is some sort of federal world government."[246] I would assume an alien presence would fall into those considerations as well.

A world parliament to oversee the United Nations is necessary, according to Leinen and Bummel, in order to create a "world law and a supranational police authority."[247] Such authority would supersede individual nations' policing authorities. This is dangerous ground. Included too are regulations regarding population growth and global food supplies. Here's where it gets dicey: "From a broader perspective, what is needed is the establishment and institutionalization of a new global class compromise. The path to a fairer, a social world order will inevitably require reining in the dominance of the global elite … Otherwise, crisis is virtually inevitable." Only this way might it be possible to "avoid the fate of past elites that were brought down due to their overreaching greed, insensitivity and short-sightedness."[248] I couldn't help but flash back to the kid with the "Eat the Rich" button. Bolshevik Revolution, anyone?

One major problem, according to the parliament, is that humans are lacking in empathy for one another. Are we all to be seen as narcissists bent on destruction of the planet? They reference New Age staples Hazel Henderson, Jeremy Rifkin, Ken Wilber, and Alvin Toffler to show the significance of the inclusion of New Age ideologies into a new world platform. Thus from minds awash in progressive thinking comes the idea of a new global class of people to offset the overreaching powers of the global elites.

We need only to stare at Earth from space to realize that we are all people of One Earth propaganda. I think, however, that we have known this for a long time. In fact, wars have been fought to protect and liberate our fellow occupants of Earth, and in many cases, were it not for the philanthropic giving of many of the world's rich elite, we might be seeing more underprivileged people and more suffering. Of course, the rich elite on the side of global government are most welcome. Double standard.

New Age organizations such as Lucis Trust are not going to rest on their laurels in promoting global unity, especially if their efforts and their UN consultant status assist the emergence of their Maitraya. Lucis Trust and others have rolled up their sleeves and gone to work, promoting world goodwill and plunging headlong into global political activism again, through the activities of UNESCO, nongovernmental organizations, human rights proponents, and the UN's Sustainable Development Goals. Combine that with the sustainability backing of the new world teacher, assisted by the Space Brothers, and you have a very interesting global outreach program.

Programs of instruction such as Millennium Development Goals and those concerned with awakening the consciousness of the people of the world could serve only to assist in this global transformation. It all comes down to a new consciousness of being, plus help, of course, from politically persuasive ideologies such as socialism á la Karl Marx—and no wonder.

According to Benjamin Creme's spirit master, Karl Marx was a high-level initiate who worked for this hierarchy of occult masters. "Marx was indeed a member of the Hierarchy," wrote Creme, "of a certain degree, an initiate of some level: first, to have the vision and secondly to have the capacity to embody that vision so that the work could spread. He came into the world to release a certain teaching about new economic possibilities, new relationships, and new theory of social change, and he built it into a very structured dialect."[249] Unfortunately, it was a failed one. Marxism, as history as shown, has never worked to the benefit of the people in any country enacting it, yet Maitreya and the masters are all in. Then there was Creme's—and I have to assume Maitreya's—views on Joseph Stalin, who was allegedly a second-degree initiate. In their opinions, Stalin was not evil. He was sort of gray, but not black. Right.

Dave Hunt, however, clarified the socialist state with the Master's Plan: Marxism and the New Age movement share the common goal of socialistic world government. "Marxism is not just any kind of atheism, but the same apostasy predicted in the Bible that Darwin, Blavatsky, Besant, Freud, Wells, Bailey, Creme, and the New Age Movement represent."[250]

Some people today believe socialism and communism are viable forms of global governance, but both are controlling regimes sans personal ownership. Some educators describe socialism as an economic system that, on the surface, seeks to achieve equality among members of society. Communism, on the other hand, is both an economic system that seeks equality among members of society and a political ideology that advocates a classless, stateless society and rejects religion. Communism is commonly regarded as a more extreme form of socialism.[251]

Both -isms mandate absolute government control over its citizens. Both enact a form of totalitarianism and eliminate the right of the individual to choose in favor of all others' right to choose. Control is paramount if this form of government is to succeed. A warning here: history has shown that in many cases, control of the individual continues long after the policies themselves have failed. Some leader coming to the head of this state would have it all laid out for him or her.

But a controlling state is nothing new as far as the Space Brothers are concerned, as Nick Redfern points out in *Contactees*. The obvious political agenda of the Space Brothers goes all the way back to the 1950s and their association with contactee George Adamski. According to an FBI report that surfaced during that time, there was concern that space people's contactee Adamski was spreading Russian propaganda. Per Adamski, "The 'space people' are better people than those on Earth; that they have told him the Earth is in extreme danger from nuclear tests and that they must be stopped; that they have found peace under a system in which churches, schools, individual governments, money, and private property were abolished in favor of central governing council, and nationalism and patriotism have been done away with; that the 'space people' want nuclear tests stopped immediately and that never should people on earth fight; if attacked, they should lay down their arms and welcome their attackers."[252]

Governmentally speaking, Benjamin Creme, who unabashedly touted his involvement with the goals and objectives of both the Space Brothers and Maitreya the Christ, was once asked what form of government the new Christ would prefer to work within. Creme couldn't help but fawn over the idea of a pure socialist form of government with a greatly diminished form of capitalism. According to Creme's master, Maitreya, the government of the future should be a combination of 30 percent capitalism and 70 percent socialism—in other words, a stepping-stone to communism. No surprise here also. Apparently, even the masters want the ease of working within a socialist regime.

Then there's the new morality, the New Age vision of peace, service, and sharing, with an outright detestation of wanton materialism, greed, the lack of the sharing, the evil of borders, and the need for the redistribution of wealth. How is that accomplished?

Given these New Age ideologies, I believe a particular form of conditioning is taking shape in the form of guilt—guilt over possessions, guilt over not sharing, guilt over any success that does not include the whole of society. In short, guilt over capitalism. Thus capitalism must be bombarded with guilt complexes, in order to browbeat individuals into advocating for change of the democratic principles and freedoms that exist in our constitutionally based government and rule of law. And while we're at it, let's enact a new society, a non-offensive form of religion, an abridged form of history sans bigotry and offensive actions, and equal rights for all ideologies, which is basically the rights of individuals to have no rights at all.

Accolades for capitalism fall flat as far as the Space Brothers are concerned. In fact, they are dead set against it. Not bemoaning our overall economic structure, they observe passively, although doubtfully, our stumbling around in economic darkness, for which they have come to be of service. But as another of Brad Steiger's Aquarian revelations reveals, "We Space Brothers can only suggest; we cannot compel. Let go of materialism, for you are weighing yourself down and making it harder for you, and for us to raise yourself up."[253] Admonishing our childish behavior further, they say, "Material objects are still of the third dimension, and you are evolving into the fourth dimension." In other words, "Surrender, Dorothy." They are missing the point. It's the material things that we humans love. Capitalism will not go down easily.

However, if the ETs cannot guilt us, then perhaps they can draw us a picture—a message, if you will—in a field of crops. The aliens have not skipped a beat. For example, one book dealing with the existence of crop circles combines references to Alice A. Bailey and the Master D. K., teachings that are intermeshed in the messages and meanings of the crop circles in the fields of England. *Crop Circles: Harbingers of World Change* gives the "esoteric teachings of the ages" a big thumbs-up and furthers the concept of a New Age that will transform the world, through these large etchings by ETs, and turn popular opinion against the evils of a capitalist state. Alick Bartholomew, with the help of some redefined Bible passages, makes the following argument against a new world order of capitalism: "The New World Order is not new. It was predicted long ago as the time of the Beast. That would be worshipped in every land. The beast is the material Economy. Its number is 666, without which you shall not trade. The battle of Armageddon is not of angels and demons, but the duality of good and evil in the mind of man. It is not a place, but a time."[254]

With all due respect, the Bible clearly says that 666 is the number of a man. Here's wisdom: "Let him who has understanding calculate the number of the beast, for it is the number of a man: His number is 666" (Revelation 13:18). It will be the "mark of the beast" that one must have to buy and sell. The battle of Armageddon will be very real indeed. No message in a field can prove otherwise.

Shame on you, America! When the spokesman for the Christ was making his rounds at speaking venues in the United States, he seemed to have a propensity for attacking American values and patriotic leanings. Why that should bother an English citizen, I'm not sure, but it certainly seems to bother the world teacher, Maitreya. Lambasting traditional American values in *The World Teacher for All Humanity*, Creme takes off the gloves regarding America's values and our support for each other as American citizens, and he throws a few jabs at the Jews for good measure: "9/11 seems to have had an extraordinary psychological impact on the people of America, and this has been worked up, magnified out of all proportion, by the present administration. So you have not been allowed to forget it, just as Israelis make the Holocaust—an unbelievably terrible happening—something which humanity must on no account never forget."

Naturally Christians and Jews are targets. But the esoteric and New Age propagandist didn't stop there, but continued to take swipes at America, our democracy, our faith, our patriotism, and supposedly our complacency. Patriotism will be forbidden in the new world order, as nations and borders must disappear in the ultimate act of brotherhood on the planet. And so it begins: "You in America are born and brought up in a country which is so materialistic in its outlook that complacency is the inevitable result. You are so educated at school and by the media that

America becomes the limit of your seeing, your imagination, your sense of the world. "At school in America you are brought up to salute the flag everyday. This does not happen everywhere. You would not get the national flag saluted by many school children. They would think you were daft."[255] And on and on it goes, devaluing America's traditions, American pride, our belief in "one nation under God," and doggone it, even our flag. All these values are being chipped away at today.

Therefore, to be blindsided by the political posturing of Marxist doctrine, whether it comes from the round lips of humans or the slit lips of aliens, one cannot have a New Age without a cause, and the idea of a redistribution of the world's wealth, plus freebies for all, makes for good press. But in reality, it doesn't work. Former prime minister of England Margaret Thatcher hit the nail on the head: "The trouble with Socialism," she said, "is that eventually you run out of other people's money." Socialism has never worked. Someone needs to tell the ETs.

Smokescreens or not, the New Age vision of peace, property, and equality for all continues, no matter how mindless. And such thinking is shockingly real. It would not be difficult for a global governing authority to take effect, should certain triggers occur to change the mind-set of the world's populace. Advocates of the world parliament point to various scenarios that could play into the need for a global governing structure: a limited nuclear war, global pandemic, widespread natural disasters, escalating terrorism, and so on. Certainly people would be shocked by any of these threatening events and would probably endorse anyone coming on the scene who could offer valid solutions to a global disaster.

A political-spiritual platform will not gain this entity much acceptance, however. Humankind is too critical of anything or anyone challenging the status quo of our existence. Just another leader will not impress anyone, and actually would probably cause confrontation with other world leaders. So how could this planned agenda be carried off? What would make all nations and their leaders kowtow to a rival leader? What could cease an arms race and hostilities between diverse governments? What would create unity in diversity within the globalist community and launch a New Age—or rather, new world order—with all the political trappings that go with it?

Some see technocracy as an answer. Technocracy has been described as a science of social engineering, in short a government run by experts in their fields, i.e., science, banking, environment, economics, and so forth. Patrick M. Wood, who has studied and written about technocracy, reveals that the system is known under other names today, such as Sustainable Development, Green Economy, Global Warming/Climate Change, Cap and Trade, Agenda 21, Common Core State Standards and Conservation Easements for example. Serious questions arise when one considers what oversight would be granted to such organizations. Wood sees a real danger in this. "In America, the power grab of Technocracy is seen in the castration of the Legislative Branch by the Executive Branch, by replacing laws and lawmakers with Reflexive Law and regulations, and establishing regional Councils of Governments in every state to usurp sovereignty from cities, counties and states."[256]

Consequently, we stroll through the Internet of things, program our lives and our homes with the latest technology, and take our place among the monitored masses. Of course, tracking people to obtain information about them is not new, but in earlier times it was covertly cumbersome. For example, Beate Wilder-Smith, while a schoolgirl in the 1930s in Nazi Germany, had to keep a close eye on the motives of her own teachers and the tactics they employed. Of her particular challenge, she wrote, "One or two of the teachers were fanatic Nazis and tried to climb up the ladder in their career by spying through their pupils of various families, especially those who did not keep to the party line. Our family belonged to that category. So our parents instructed us to be very cautious and suspicious toward everything we were asked. One of these teachers had the habit of letting us write essays on special topics—such as 'What do you think about racism?'—and thereby extracting all wanted information about our parents' opinions and doings."[257] In our time, only a click of the keyboard is needed.

Who, then, could head up a united world? Certainly the spokesman for the cosmic Christ had an idea:

> Important events are taking place in many parts of the world. People everywhere will be astonished by the reports. These will include sightings in unprecedented numbers, of spacecraft from our neighboring planets ... Those who

have steadfastly refused to take seriously the reality of this phenomenon will find it difficult to deny ... Miraculous happenings of all kinds will continue and multiply in number and variety. The minds of men will be baffled and amazed by these wonders, and this will cause them to ponder deeply. Into this wonder-filled, wondering world Maitreya will quietly enter and begin his open work.[258]

Whether this man or another, someone unique will arrive on the world's stage, and as Christians, we are told to watch. According to scripture, there will indeed come a being with "all power, signs and lying wonders" (2 Thessalonians 2:9). The world might then ask, "Who is like the beast? Who is able to make war with him?" (Revelation 13:4).

CHAPTER EIGHTEEN
SETI or Not, Here They Come

Many scientists would now argue that the detection of extraterrestrial life is more a question of when, not if.[259]
— Brandon Ambrosino, *BBC News*

The world's largest radio telescope, in southwestern Guizhou province, is joining an international search for extraterrestrial intelligence focused on a strange, flickering star that has sparked unprecedented curiosity in recent months … FAST—short for five-hundred-meter aperture spherical telescope—has a dish bigger than 30 soccer fields and a diameter almost 200 meters greater that the world's second-biggest radio telescope, operated by the United States at Arecibo in Puerto Rico.[260]
— *South China Morning Post*, December 21, 2017

In a joint effort between the Berkeley SETI Research Center and their colleagues in China, the hunt is on for "evidence of advanced civilization in space," and they couldn't be more serious. FAST has become part of the Breakthrough Listen project funded by millionaire investor Yuri Milner as part of a ten-year search for intelligent life in space. This is such a serious endeavor that China's Communist government evicted 9,110 of its own citizens living in the region designated for the construction of the FAST telescope. They believe that the construction of such a large scope will make the search for signs of extraterrestrial life easier.

The giant scope with the ability to listen in to remote areas of the universe is in contrast with SETI's program of placing a call in hopes of receiving an answer. Conflicting opinions exist within the scientific community regarding whether we should be taking such aggressive action as sending radio signals to the far reaches of space. SETI, of course, is an effort to alert any space voyagers to the fact that life exists on our planet, in the hope that such effort will bring *them* to us.

The SETI Institute has been a longtime participant in this search. Listening through an array of radio telescopes is being done in tandem with other joint efforts, in the hope of receiving that *one definitive signal* from an intelligent life source in the universe. However, in recent years, the Search for Extraterrestrial Intelligence (SETI) has become even more active and more diverse. Active SETI, also known as Messaging to Extraterrestrial Intelligence (METI), is another approach being used by Permanent SETI to scan regions of space, this time by *sending* signals into space from our planet. Assisting in the hunt is Laser SETI, an instrument capable of scanning the sky 24/7 in search of pulsed light signals that have been hitherto unnoticed, therefore creating a dragnet of the entire sky.

For a long time, the Hubble Telescope has been sending back to Earth high-resolution photographs of the immensity of space, with its breathtaking views of star nurseries, galaxies, nebulas, supernovas, and much more. The infinity of space can be overwhelming to the onlooker, and one cannot help but wonder if we are not alone in this massive expanse. The romantic vision of the returning probe or a repacked "golden record" sent by return mail would be obvious confirmation of an alien existence. Less dramatic, yet an equally important validation, would be the one most astronomers and scientists support, a sound or signal picked up by one of Earth's gigantic radio telescopes. Scientists such as Shostak, Hawking, and Kaku have all predicted from the beginning that alien contact will come through radio wave frequencies, which have long been used for long-distance communications. Weighing the odds, China is not losing time or ground on that assumption.

A news article by reporter Michael Hawthorne, published in February 2016,[261] described the rush by China's astronomers to build the world's largest radio telescope, named FAST, and they wanted to be fast about it. The Chinese government plans to use the telescope to study the origins of the universe, look for signs of extraterrestrial life, and possibly be the first to make contact. Imagine the scientific leverage gained by the country that does that, not to mention whatever technological benefits might come as a result.

Another reporter, Ross Anderson, wrote an article a year later, in 2017, about the completed FAST apparatus, with the headline "China could make first contact with aliens. Would Beijing tell the world? Might it spell doom for the human race?" Anderson had gone to China to see the gigantic dish for himself and found himself in a completely different social environment. He reports that a government-imposed social transformation program appeared to be under way. Signs implored people not to spit indoors. Loudspeakers nagged passengers to keep an atmosphere of good manners, and when an older man cut in the cab line, a security guard dressed him down in front of a crowd of hundreds. No getting out of line, literally. However, mandated manners aside, China's quest to achieve a scientific edge was evident with this very impressive project. According to Ross,

> Almost twice as wide as the dish at America's Arecibo Observatory, in the Puerto Rican jungle, the Chinese dish, named FAST (the Five-hundred-meter Aperture Spherical Telescope), is the largest in the world, if not the universe. Though it is sensitive enough to detect spy satellites even when they're not broadcasting, its main uses will be scientific, including an unusual one: the dish is Earth's first flagship observatory custom-built to listen for a message from an extraterrestrial intelligence. If such a sign comes down from the heavens during the next decade, China may well hear it first.[262]

In an atmosphere of near-religious fervor within organizations such as SETI, the longing, the desire, the belief in something outside of us would most likely be from outer space. Anderson sees it that way: "SETI does share some traits with religion. It is motivated by deep human desires for connection and transcendence." Would we question *any* contact made from any mysterious sources, no matter how much was to be gained? Anderson pointed to China's other recent accomplishments, the world's fastest supercomputer, medical research, and a future atom smasher. But most impressive of all would be what China might accomplish, "In the technopoetic idiom of the 21st century, nothing would symbolize China's rise like a high-definition shot of a Chinese astronaut setting foot on the red planet. Nothing except, perhaps, first contact."[263]

Almost weekly come reports of the discovery of a planet or planets that could sustain life or that appear amazingly similar to our own. The Goldilocks Zone, where many candidate planets for sustaining life are mapped, raises the anticipation that life will be found in the universe. To assist in this effort, NASA's TESS (Transiting Exoplanet Survey Satellite), a probe that has already found eight new alien worlds, continues its search for planets less gassy than Neptune or Uranus, for example, and similar to Earth in its density. With the assistance of instruments such as Chili's High Accuracy Radial velocity Planet Searcher (HARPS), which finds new planets by their tiny wobbles, the search continues in all earnest and optimism continues to rise—as do concerns and suspicions.

According to a recent article in *Tech Times*, ex-NASA scientist Kevin Knuth is calling for a serious study of the evidence for UFOs. Knuth, a physics professor at the State University of New York, Albany, developed his interest in this subject from hearing other people in his professional community commenting on them. "You have no idea what's out there!" exclaimed one participant at a NASA conference in 2002. Consequently, as a graduate student, Knuth recalled a statement made by his physics professor, as far back as 1988, that UFOs were shooting down air force missiles, a claim that was validated when viewing a recorded interview with air force officials confirmed such actions.[264]

Something ET this way comes? A recent photograph showing a long, black, skinny meteorite-looking object is evidence, according to Harvard University's astronomy department chair Avi Loeb, of an "alien lightsail" hurtling toward Earth. Originally seen by astronomers in Hawaii in 2017 and dubbed Oumuamua, Hawaiian for "messenger sent from the distant past," the object generated speculation that it could be from a distant civilization. The object, which could be an alien ship, defunct or active, according to Loeb, has been highly scrutinized by other agencies (SETI heard nothing) but for now remains an unknown.[265] However, Loeb is not backing down on his claims, and this remains a wait-and-see.

The point here is that a growing number of astronomers and scientists absolutely expect to encounter an alien source, and thoughts of little green men from space have graduated to more sophisticated, technologically advanced alien visitors. The expectation is becoming intense. They *have* to be out there, because all our scopes and sensors tell us they are. Or at least they might be, and we are using all technology available on Earth to make it so.

The late British astrophysicist Stephen Hawking took umbrage at the idea that we should all embrace with open arms any advanced civilization that may perchance set foot on this planet. Hawking saw it as a dangerous proposition, similar to the Inca civilization succumbing to the more advanced Spanish conquistadors. It didn't work out well for the Incas, and a more advanced alien civilization coming here might not work well for us either. Hawking urged that caution be taken, but the SETI Institute's Seth Shostak doesn't see it that way, arguing that for years we've been generating broadcasts all over the planet that an advanced alien civilization could easily pick up.

However, concerns about aggressive actions and unknown space hardware heading our way raise questions about whether we are ready to deal with covert operations by extraterrestrials, such as the downing of missiles or other aggressive moves. Equally disconcerting is the revelation that there exists no protocol for use should actual contact be made with said extraterrestrials, friendly or otherwise, a concern that has been unreservedly expressed by SETI's lead scientist, Seth Shostak. Shostak explains that to his knowledge, there is no government-level plan of action to put in place should contact be made. In statements made to *Live Science* in 2016, Shostak reiterated his belief that contact would most likely be made by radio telescopes or by "spaceships from technologically superior extraterrestrial civilizations." However, the protocols that SETI has put in place encourage all countries, particularly the United States, Russia, and now China, to share information. "If you pick up a signal, check it out … tell everybody … and don't broadcast any replies without international consultation."[266] Sure.

The United Nations Office for Outer Space Affairs and its Space Law division have not published any specific protocols regarding alien contact. Instead, the agency is focused on space use, i.e., rescue of astronauts, preservation of space and Earth environments, and arbitrating disputes over damage caused by space objects. Damage by extraterrestrials would be another consideration altogether. Could this agency find itself arbitrating the rights of humans on the earth?

Fears have arisen over the idea that sending signals into space may indeed result in contact, but what would contact involve? Again, Hawking realistically pointed out that we would be unable to assess whether any response received from extraterrestrials would be of benevolent or malevolent intent. Reporter John Traphagan, writing in the *Huffington Post*, weighed in on that idea: "Perhaps a more important question is not about the risks of transmitting, but the dangers in receiving. Many in the SETI community have shown commitment to the belief that a technologically advanced civilization will be altruistic, despite the lack of evidence to support that assumption."[267]

Even less altruistic is the idea of the benefits of first contact. Any country that makes contact, invites a landing, and interacts with extraterrestrials would have an advantage unlike anything the world has experienced. High technology aside, having extraterrestrial fellowship would carry a lot of weight in the administration of global affairs. Would it cause an upheaval and a destabilizing of our civilization? "Will there be panic, infighting, conflict?" Traphagan asks. Like others who have studied this scenario, he points to some very real dangers: "Imagine if the Chinese intercept the first message from aliens and want to keep the information they gain to themselves. How will the American and other governments respond if they think the Chinese might have super weapons? How will religious zealots, who are suddenly confronted with the idea that humans may not be so special after all, cope with the news that we are not alone? Imagine if ET send us an encyclopedia of information about themselves in which we learn that they are a civilization of card-carrying atheists."[268]

Obviously, our society might do poorly in the shadow of a more advanced civilization. No doubt the governments of the world would be put on alert and appropriate defensive measures would be taken, just in case. But on a local level, everyone will need to fend for themselves.

In the United States, local fire departments have put in place contingency plans as part of their disaster preparedness training, in case a spaceship landing occurs. In the official *Fire Officers Guide to Disaster*

Control, chapter 13 is dedicated to that very possibility. "Enemy Attack and UFO Potential" (p. 458) describes strict guidelines and procedures addressing the dangers present and actions to take in dealing with a UFO.

Beginning with a brief overall history of UFOs, investigations and findings, chapter 13 moves into main areas of concern that firefighters might face: UFO hazards, force field impact, communications disruption, regional power blackouts, the panic hazard, personal physiological hazards, and emergency action. Any of these could involve total chaos locally and nationally, impacted by communications failures and energy blackouts, both of which have been at times associated with UFO sightings. This was done because of claims by UFOlogists that UFO landings could become a reality in the near future. Not knowing whether the visitors would be friendly or hostile, it would be to a fire department's benefit to know how to react if a UFO set down in their community, so directives have been put in place.

Some of these directives deal with an actual UFO crash scenario and cover such procedures as securing the crash site, looking for hazards such as fuel or oil leakage, rescuing occupants from a crashed UFO, triaging the dead and wounded, treatment of alien survivors, and what agencies to contact. Of course, there is also concern for the firefighters themselves. Because near approaches of UFOs could harm humans, nobody should stand under a UFO hovering at a low altitude. Likewise, do not touch or attempt to touch a UFO that has landed. "In either case," the manual says, "the safe thing to do is get away from there and let the military take over." Because of the potential danger of radiation emanating from a craft, it is best to keep your distance. "Don't take chances with UFOs!"

With all the seriousness given to the instruction and preparation of emergency response teams, it would almost seem that an arrival is anticipated. If the aliens don't show up soon, a whole lot of people are going to be disappointed—or relieved.

Some people, however, have already made contact and are less than enthusiastic. Others believe that extraterrestrials have already made their presence—and their intention— known through their hostile actions and human abductions. It appears, however, that the vision of uniformity and compliance is more important than the reality of any negative encounter.

Secularly speaking, what would be the impact of actual contact with extraterrestrials? Some scientists, such as Carl Sagan, believe that such discovery and contact would undoubtedly lead to religious and philosophical questions. Sagan asked this question early on: if we do make contact, will our religions accommodate these beings, or will it totally shake up our religious beliefs? He envisioned the creation of *astro-theologians* in response to issues of religion where ET is concerned.

Reporter Ross Anderson addressed the religious and cultural consequences of making ET contact and a transformation of humanity's religious beliefs. "Buddhists would get off easy," he says. "Their faith already assumes an infinite universe of untold antiquity, its every corner alive with the vibrating energies of living beings. The Hindu cosmos is similarly grand and teeming." The Koran, Ross points out, references Allah's creation of the heavens and of the earth and all the living creatures placed there by him. The Jews of course believe that God's power is without limits. But there is a snag. "Christianity might have it tougher," Ross says. "There is debate in contemporary Christian theology as to whether Christ's salvation extends to every soul that exists in the wider universe, or whether the sin-tainted inhabitants of distant planets require their own divine interventions."[269] Also, secular humanists would crumple under the realization that humans are not the apex of nature's achievement.

Such an analysis is not without merit. Reporter Ariun Walla wrote that in 2014, NASA brought a select group of scientists and theologians together to "prepare the world for extraterrestrial contact."[270] According to Walla's article, a group of respected astronomers appeared before Congress to inform them that without question, extraterrestrial life exists. SETI astronomer Seth Shostak emphasized that it's because of the sheer number of habitable worlds in our galaxy.

Exploring that possibility, NASA and the Library of Congress teamed up to bring together various scientists, theologians, philosophers, and historians from around the world to participate in a two-day symposium. The focus was how to prepare the world for extraterrestrial contact, whether microbial or living beings.

The multiplicity of planets has become a sounding board for some scientists to question how humans can consider themselves a unique creation of God on a planet nestled among billions. Will this lead people to question their faith? How would Christianity view the discovery of life on other planets, and in particular, when Jesus died for the sins of humankind, was that for living creatures on other planets too? Some clergy within the Catholic Church for example, have said that they would baptize aliens if they so wished.

What would happen if some intellectual aliens arrive with no knowledge of religion at all? Some scientists believe this would be the end of all religion on this planet. Although others believe that they could evangelize the aliens, it leaves the door wide open for reinterpretation of human spirituality in relationship with God within a new context. The question could also be asked, what if intellectual aliens arrive *with* religious beliefs of their own? Would it be just as easy to accept that it's all part of the whole of everyone's belief in God? Would we evangelize them, or would they evangelize us?

Whether through radio messages or some other method, the philosophy of SETI is that sooner or later we will detect a "civilization roughly equal to our own—for better or worse." One reviewer writes, "So if Sagan is correct, detecting an alien civilization at this point in our history would likely be a good thing. In addition to fostering science and technological development, it would motivate us to explore and colonize space. And who knows, it could even instigate significant cultural and political changes (including the advent of political parties both in support of and in opposition to all this). It could even lead to new religions, or eliminate them altogether."[271]

That is assuming that extraterrestrials come here at all, and it appears they might.

In a recent exposé, "Secret Pentagon Projects Reveal Gov't Looked Into UFOs, Wormholes and Other Bizarre Anomalies," reporter Chris Ciaccia wrote that newly declassified documents from the Pentagon reveal that the Department of Defense funded projects that are often the topic of conspiracy theorists. Funding was from the Department of Defense, through its Advanced Aerospace Threat Identification Program (AATIP). Some of the nonconventional projects included invisibility cloaking, traversable wormholes, star gates, negative energy, warp drive, dark energy, the manipulation of extra dimensions, and an introduction to the statistical Drake equation, an argument used for estimating the number of civilizations that might be present in the universe.[272]

According to an article that appeared in Space.com, the AATIP program was originated by Senate Majority Leader Harry Reid (D-Nevada). The former senator, who believes that "the truth is out there," allocated taxpayers monies to fund the program in 2007. The program was also supported by the late senators Daniel Inouye (D-Hawaii) and Ted Stevens (R-Alaska). Part of this funding was granted to Robert Bigelow, a constituent of Reid's, to participate in the research. Also involved in the program was former intelligence officer Luis Elizondo, who was in charge of AATIP and became convinced that we may not be alone, as evidenced by the recent fighter jet encounter with the "Tic Tac" UFO. Elizondo told a CNN reporter that craft being studied were "displaying characteristics that are not currently within the U.S. Inventory nor in any foreign inventory that we are aware of."[273]

The Mutual UFO Network, MUFON, was not slow to react to this admission. Director Jan Harzan pointed out the truth of what has been researched for decades, namely that UFOs are real and that they represent extremely advanced technology. He believes that incredible breakthroughs will happen if we give our scientists and engineers the ability to study this phenomenon unimpeded. Such breakthroughs, it is believed, could involve the fields of propulsion, energy, communication, biology, and consciousness.

For obvious reasons, "threat identification" is a serious reason for the program, but threat from *what*? "It is complicated, and I am still trying to make sense of things," said Mark Rodeghier, director of the J. Allen Hynek Center for UFO Studies (CUFOS) in Chicago, Illinois. He believes the AATIP program only confirms what has been reported for decades, but the public wasn't hearing about them. The public *is* hearing now. Why?

Danger lurks? Clint Rainey, a writer for *New York* magazine, recently wrote an article referencing UFO investigator Nick Pope's opinion on what might be happening. "Know that there are people who watch our skies to protect the sleeping masses," said Pope, a former UK minister of defense. "But also know that not all potential intruders into our airspace have two wings, a fuselage, and a tail, and not all show up on radar." Pope originally took the job as defense minister, Rainey explains, because he felt that the thousands of paranormal events, from crop circles to abductions, "only happened to weirdos," but then "unexplainable sightings soon convinced him that there is a war going on" with aliens. Worse, Rainey continues, the

UK defense minister cut his old UFO desk's funding in 2009, so whatever's out there he believed, could attack at any time. Earthlings' diminished odds have made him more fatalistic lately, too. After scientists suggested that Oumuamua, a bizarre-shaped asteroid that's the first interstellar object to pass through our solar system, might be an alien spaceship, he argued, "We probably wouldn't survive an alien invasion anyway, because if *they* find *us*, it's clear who has the upper hand."[274]

CHAPTER NINETEEN

The Cosmic Christ

Regarding the former United Nations Secretary General: "Robert Muller believes in the divinity of humanity and 'was deeply influenced' by Pierre Teilhard de Chardin, a Jesuit priest who taught that all of humanity would eventually meld into one super-being through the coming of the Cosmic Christ."[275]

—Walter J. Veith

Could an alien deception be part of the end times? We know that the events surrounding the end times, as described in the Bible, will include a powerful deception (Matthew 24:24). Recently interest has been rising in the theory that this deception will include alien beings from another planet. Odd as it may see, this theory is entirely plausible from a Christian perspective.[276]

—GotQuestions.org

Got Questions Ministries gets it: "Although the Bible gives us no word about whether or not aliens exist—there is no inclusion of them in the creation account in Genesis, and no mention of them elsewhere—the Bible does tell us about visitors from another world—the spiritual world." Knowing that this realm exists, and it does, what might we expect to see as we move closer to the end times? Deception.

Much has been written about fallen angels breeding with earth women and producing unusual offspring, but what would a return trip look like today? Knowing that these giants were wiped out, the originators of the hybrid beings might have to come themselves. After all, this might all be part of our heritage if we believe that beings from another world came to Earth bearing gifts for humankind in the form of advanced knowledge—a knowledge that in the past, some believe, allowed ancient civilizations to create amazing structures and inventions.

But we are a rational people. We have long progressed past trying to appease the gods by dancing around ceremonial fires and offering golden trinkets. We have stood upon Earth as rulers of all that is on it, within in, or above it. The likelihood of humankind willingly bowing to an outside force is slim at best. We are fighters, intellects, mercenaries, missionaries, scientists, theorists, atheists, believers in God, creators of destinies, destroyers of nations, deliverers of the oppressed, marauders of the innocent. We are armed and dangerous, and we can save life or destroy it. We are the advanced species on this planet. Who is greater than us? Any outside force who endeavors to control this planet will need to have the credentials and the means by which to do it.

But if our own pilots cannot catch them, our bases contain them, our radar detect them, or our missiles destroy them, then where is our superiority? Are we actually inferior to them? Are they truly the gods from the stars, the benefactors of humanity?

Ancient alien theorists and others look to the ruins of ancient cities and artifacts to somehow prove that the founders of our society were indeed extraterrestrial. People who look for evidence in early civilizations want to know who those spacemen were, where they came from, where they went, and if they will be coming back. However, it is quite possible that they never left.

Could an alien deception actually occur? Got Questions has an answer: "The Bible doesn't directly address the issue, but it is certainly plausible, for a variety of reasons. First, the Bible tells us that the world will unite under the power of the Antichrist. In order to achieve an agreement between all the world's religions, it would make sense for the 'uniter' to come from an entirely new source—an extraterrestrial source."[277] Certainly it's difficult to imagine that one religion would become the head of all others, unless "new unearthly knowledge" became the source of the appeal and power of a new religion, Got Questions rationalizes, noting that this would undoubtedly be an effective way of deceiving a large number of people.

An alien deception could provide science with a simple, plausible answer to Earth's origins, although it would negate the big bang theory. If alien beings arrived, presented themselves as our predecessors, and provided an extraterrestrial explanation for life on Earth, the origins of the world's religions, and even the origins of our planet, it could all be very convincing. Add to that a substitute Christ to satisfy religious prophecies, and we're in for a very good show. I would have to assume that our extraterrestrial creators, however, would be strongly in favor of *their* origins of man and oppose any Christian Christ. Cue the Antichrist.

The *Antichrist* is usually understood as the one who will be against Christ, but in Greek it also means a pseudo Christ, an imposter in place of Christ. Who or *what* might claim that title? In our world of rapidly advancing technology, this Antichrist will need to be able to impress the leaders of today's high-tech world. Could someone of unusual congeniality and powers of persuasion become a global head of state? That is certainly possible, especially if that man possessed an unusually high degree of technological knowledge.

Just exactly who might this man of impressive credentials be? Ron Rhodes, in *Unmasking the Antichrist*, points to scriptures that indicate there will be something very unusual about this person: "Passages such as Daniel 2, Daniel 7, 2 Thessalonians 2, and the book of Revelation point to the emergence of a unique person who is ultimately unlike any other person who has ever lived."[278]

Certainly down through the ages there has been much speculation about what kind of global leader would have the ability to command respect and hold the reins of global government without dissension. Would he do so through fear or fascination? What would compel our nations' leaders to elevate someone to this prestigious and powerful position? Does such a man exist today? History has shown that leaders come and go, while others jockey for high positions in a time-proven method of networking among leaders and politicians worldwide. So what would be different? Who among the status quo of government leaders would be able to demand worldwide disarmament, command total loyalty, be openly accepted by the world's population, and enforce a mandate for equal sharing of all money and resources, for example? What would make Earth's superpowers put down their weapons and cease all warfare? Would this be the result of a skilled negotiator or a dominating dictator? Perhaps there is one other possibility, something that would be literally out of this world: an extraterrestrial.

It has been suggested by many members of the scientific community that such contact would ultimately expose the ETs as being greatly superior, intellectually and technologically, to humans, which means they could present themselves as the teachers and protectors of humankind. Of course, such an alliance would have requirements from both sides. Superior technology, health, and longevity, for example, might be required in exchange for rule and oversight of the world, and perhaps even worship.

The belief that a superior force *could* take control of the planet does not exist exclusively in the secular realm. Christian authors Chuck Missler and Mark Eastman, in their excellent book *Alien Encounters*, explain: "Surprisingly, a number of prominent Bible teachers—Hal Lindsey and Dave Hunt as examples—have publicly stated their view that this leader will either be an alien or boast of alien connections! Remarkably, in addition to Daniel 2:43 there are many startling clues in the Bible that seem to connect the Coming World Leader to Satan and his 'alien' forces."[279]

Dave Hunt, along with friend and coauthor T. A. McMahon, took a serious look at the ET scenario. Realizing that there is substance to the claims of alien visitations, including claims of abductions by aliens, one needs to step back and take a closer look at the implications of such claims. The people making these claims are very serious, come from all walks of life, and include well-educated and powerful people such as scientists, physicists, military personnel, politicians, and even presidents.

Dave Hunt, who has traded his earthly home for a heavenly one, once commented that a mainstream UFO conference he attended included representatives from the government and the military, a Harvard psychiatrist, and more. Crackpots? Not according to Dave. He emphasized that they were serious-minded people who believe these types of encounters really happen.

Based on the UFO conferences that I have attended, I concur. In many cases, the speakers are sober-minded professionals who have witnessed or been exposed to UFOs and possess a wheelhouse of information about them. Regardless of whether any of the UFO evidence can be proved authentic, and much of it can, there is no question that people are being conditioned to accept an alien presence in our world.

The possibility of an alien Antichrist is a view shared by Christian writer Jeff Gerke, who has spent a considerable amount of time researching all things UFO—sightings, abductions, crop circles, mutilations, and so on—from a Christian perspective. Gerke sees the possibility of an end-times extraterrestrial deception: "If I'm right, then the End Times will have an unexpected flavor to them. Perhaps the Antichrist will be an alien—or an alien/human hybrid. It makes sense that the devil's false Christ would also be sired by a spirit but borne by a human woman."[280]

Certainly, those of no religious persuasion and many New Agers would not object to an alien leader; in fact, many would welcome it! After all, the Space Brothers must have a leader, and even a three-fingered handshake by aliens would have world leaders heralding the event as the next evolutionary step with our benevolent ancient forbearers.

The idea of a New Age is not lost on the space travelers. It has been relayed to contactees and abductees alike, and many tow the New Age party line. Missler and Eastman agree: "Finally when we examine the message given to alien contactees, we find they promote globalism, ecumenism, personal immortality (reincarnation), pantheism, ('you will be like god' Genesis 3:15), moral relativism, and the notion that the Bible is not the word of God. These are the beliefs that Satan himself, through the ministry of the Antichrist, will promote during the coming global confederacy."[281]

But the idea of an alien Antichrist is intriguing, if not ominous, to say the least. One could assume that this diabolical world leader, the Antichrist, might well be under the control of Satan in either affirming the existence of an alien brotherhood or being part of it. There's more to consider. The fact that a global leader of such magnitude would have a special air about him leads one to consider other possibilities. This person could be fully human and indwelt by Satan, fully extraterrestrial, or a human-alien hybrid. Regardless, he would influenced and directed by Satan, the "god of this world" and "lord of the sky." It would fit. So probably this person would have to be influenced in some way by the ETs, whether being in contact with them, sharing their DNA, or actually being one of them.

The extraterrestrial visitor hype over the years, combined with the fact that the public is slowly being conditioned to accept these aliens if and when they land here, raises the issue of *disclosure*. Any world leader would need to disclose that the aliens are real, that some are here, and that the ancient Alien Brothers of long ago are coming back to Earth.

What does that mean for us? Will we be convinced of their authenticity? Now, should the Antichrist choose to displayed supernatural abilities as evidence of his god status, how would *he* explain *himself* and his abilities to do paranormal wonders? This question presents a bit of a quandary. Again, Missler and Eastman:

> When we think about the supernatural characteristics of the Antichrist, an interesting question arises. What will he tell the world about the source of this power and knowledge? If he were to state that his power came from God, he would likely be rejected by those in the secular, scientific community. If he were to boast that his power was from the forces of darkness, he would most likely not be well received by the masses. We believe that it is very likely that the Coming World Leader will boast of a connection with the power-full, god-like alien entities who have, it is believed, overcome the problems of poverty, famine, disease, war, and the pain of cultural and religious division.[282]

This is vital, for if one claims to be associated with extraterrestrials or—even worse—to be one of them, this would call the aliens' bluff and force them to show themselves. Otherwise the ET theory becomes null and void in the eyes of the world's citizens.

Certainly a show of alien power in support of a global leader could cause considerable consternation among people not willing to accept them, who then would become a threat to global unity. Questions of faith would become questions of religion. For individuals not strong in their faith, a falling away could occur, if not a total disappearance of interest in religion altogether. It's got to be a good show, to present a deception so diabolical that it would "deceive if possible, even the elect" (Matthew 24:24).

At that point, everything might turn into a CYA (cover your assumptions) maneuver, especially if it is noticed that for some reason, a whole lot of people have gone missing. Enter the *rapture* of Christians from all around the world.

To spin this Christian fable, assurances would be made that the Space Brothers have intervened by moving masses of people off the planet in order to (pick a scenario) save the human species and human DNA from extinction, save the world from malcontents opposed to the new world order, or reeducate them and then return them at a later date. Pick one or come up with a scenario of your own.

In reality, what effect would the disappearance of 100 million people have on the rest of the world? People would want to know what happened. Undoubtedly any lack of explanation from the world's authorities would leave people anxious and fearful, even wondering if they might be next. Would people from around the world unite to prevent the extinction of our species? Whatever grievances between nations would become moot in the face of threatened annihilation by a superior species.

New Age writers like Tuella and the Ashtar Command's "Project Evacuation" have covered the bases, should things on Earth get really out of hand by people hooking up with aliens who have promised their evacuation and a welcoming party on board a UFO.[283] However, I fear the space masters may be lying out of both sides of their mouths. If indeed a crisis occurs, the space beings will snatch up a segment of the faithful for their own protection, who will be returned at a later date, just in case anyone wonders.

An Earth-based Antichrist would have to appear as a truly unique individual, a brilliant intellectual leader who will come quietly upon the world's stage. Perhaps tall in stature and striking in appearance, he'll be extremely impressive to world leaders and the general population alike and be a bit different in abilities as well. He will do wondrous deeds—political, social, and paranormal—and amaze people everywhere, even calling down fire from heaven. Biblically, calling down fire from heaven has been one of God's demonstrated abilities, as in the showdown with the prophets of Baal (1 Kings 18:38) and the incredible destruction of the cities of Sodom and Gomorrah (Genesis 19). However, we must remember that Satan, too, has mighty powers and was able to send down fire to destroy Job's sheep and servants (Job 1:16). Most importantly, this Antichrist will have wondrous abilities because he will be filled with the power of Satan himself.

How would the world receive an individual capable of performing such wondrous deeds? Who is going to buy into the idea that a super-intelligent man, perhaps a Harvard graduate, would be able to perform such miracles? Certainly the assistance of a superior force would be needed for a man of flesh and blood to accomplish these things. A display of paranormal abilities would be more easily accepted from a technologically advanced extraterrestrial or hybrid than from a human, because we would naturally assume that *they* have such powers.

Likewise, the False Prophet will be an exceptional religious leader who, besides uniting the religions of the world to worship the Antichrist, will be able to perform miraculous works by the powers given him by the human/alien/hybrid Antichrist. Displays of miraculous abilities will no doubt be a game changer in global management, which will be functioning as a single global entity in charge of all other global entities, such as the UN, and all nations.

Cue the aliens. We have acknowledged the legitimacy of seeking contact with other life-forms that may exist in the universe, from the SETI project to the gigantic dish in Puerto Rico and China's FAST radio telescope, and hundreds of observatories and scopes around the world are looking out into the vast distances of space. There is one rudimentary, yet impressive, piece of equipment out there still looking—Voyager 1.

Many years from now, what would happen if a UFO did land—let's say on the lawn of the White House—and a metallic piece of equipment resembling an antiquated space probe were ejected from a bay door? In this scene, NASA and the Space Force are rushed to the scene and make an immediate identification—Voyager 1! Then a door on the craft opens and out steps a tall being, humanoid in appearance with a gold record in hand. The world would be stunned and amazed.

Equally dramatic, what might happen if a transmission *is* received from space and communication *is* at last achieved between them and us? Will they follow the transmissions to our planet? Will they simply land, step out of an amazing spacecraft, and extend a hand (or claw, or whatever) in friendship? Again, the world would be stunned and amazed—but maybe not surprised. All the hype and speculation about the cosmic origins of humans, books and movies about outer space, and ancient astronaut theories have left a large segment of the world's population anticipating, if not longing for, such an arrival.

What would happen next? Would ETs claiming to be the *watchers* of humanity offer solutions to problems that have plagued us throughout the ages? Would they offer technology that would provide unlimited energy, cure disease, and provide us with a workable (albeit enforced) world system, after which no one will be in want or need? Could such manifestations of power and supernatural ability cause us to simply hand over the reins and put them in charge? If so, would we be heaping upon ourselves our own bondage?

Without question, such an advanced powerful being could handle any human military opposition or political coup attempt. That would be especially true if the world's leaders and nations are dealt with equally and reap significant financial gain. A display of loyalty would seem a natural progression of this new world order, which could easily result in a mandate that all humans take a mark of allegiance (666) on their hand or forehead in order to buy or sell.

Whether one accepts the possibility of an alien invasion or satanic ploy to promote an alien or hybrid Antichrist, it would behoove us to consider all possibilities. If we are watching, then we need to be looking in *all* directions. I know there are *things* in the sky above us and on the earth, because I have seen them.

Would an alien leader actually be accepted? Quite possibly, yes. Already the United Nations and Expolitical groups are hard at work putting together a sort of "Robert's Rules of the New World Order," in preparation for the possibility of an alien visitation or incursion. Procedures would include identification of the extraterrestrial species and a decision about which government, if any, would serve as liaison.

Michael Salla, who holds a PhD in government affairs from Queensland University, has already taken the initiative to write a primer regarding the steps to be taken, globally, when contact is made with ETs. In *Galactic Diplomacy: Getting to Yes with ET*, he outlines the steps that would be needed to orchestrate a workable system by which we can easily welcome ETs into our earthly realm, what diplomacy would be enacted, and what organization would serve as Earth's representative. In this regard, he sees the United Nations as the frontrunner to serve as Earth's ambassador. Again, no surprises.

But will we be getting to "yes" with the world leader? Pastor Ron Rhodes refers to Bible prophecy scholar Herman Hoyt's take on the matter: "The greatest person ever to appear on the earth, save One—the Lord Jesus Christ—is yet to come. This man will rise head and shoulders above men in general, calculated to earn him the designation of superman, in fact, the worship that belongs to a deity. His appearance on the scene, his rise to power, his genius as a military leader, and his exploits will be nothing short of spectacular, colossal, and supernatural."[284]

Suffice it to say that this spectacular leader will be a god unto himself. As the Bible says, "He shall exalt and magnify himself above every god, shall speak blasphemies against the God of gods ... He shall regard neither the God of his fathers nor the desire of women, nor regard any god; for he shall exalt himself above them all ... But in their place he shall honor a god of fortresses, and a god, which his fathers did not know" (Daniel 11:36–38). A god of "fortresses" and a god whom his fathers did not know—something unique. Prophecy says the temple will be rebuilt in Jerusalem and that which is called the "abomination of desolation" will transpire (Daniel 11:31).

It is prophesied as some point the Antichrist will receive a fatal wound to the head, but miraculously he will come back to life (Revelation 13:3), perhaps to simulate the resurrection of Jesus Christ. Will his wound be healed and life restored by human hands, or would extraterrestrials demonstrate their powers to heal and restore life by the god his fathers knew not? Certainly only God can create and restore life, so Satan would be at a disadvantage. Would it be a flesh wound or staged event intended to show the powers of this global leader? The options are open.

Dr. Lehman Strauss, who had been a theologian and Bible instructor for thirty-four years, saw as early as 1976 the opportunistic avenues for demonic influence in the areas of human enticement to come, such as notoriety, prestige, and control through politics or other positions of power. So it should be no surprise that much of what would be needed in enacting global colonization of the world's governments would result from political leaders linking arms in global policies and procedures.

Then what would compel every nation to comply with these global rules? Certainly not war. We've already seen that war begets war and sanctions achieve little. Would it take something so outstandingly ominous, so powerful, so intimidating that the world would be amazed? According to Bible prophecy about the coming of a new world order, that is exactly what would be achieved. "Who is like the beast? And who can make war with him?" (Revelation 13:4) Logically speaking, this could not be another politician acting on his or her own resources, or another country saber rattling in opposition, but something much different. If warnings from the space people have effectively saturated the minds of many people, such intervention into our world would not be at all unexpected—and perhaps would appear as an opportunity too good to pass up. Changes have already been taking place. Dr. Strauss saw early on what was coming: "A thorough brain-washing is in store for earth's population. Satan's antichrists, under the supervision of the man of sin, will control the news media totally. The presentation of news events will be tailored so as to control the minds of everyone. By seduction and ruse Satan will have all of humanity at his feet." [285] This was written in 1976.

One has to wonder why the Space Brothers and other non-Christians attempt to cover their bases with Bible prophecy? Why is there such a need to counter or reinterpret biblical scripture? Obviously they want to make it fit a cosmic Christ, a world teacher for humans and all the beings that serve him.

If Bible prophecy is of no value, contains no truth, and offers no warnings, then why are there such attempts to mimic, discount, or reinterpret them, and to play out an end-times scenario that is similar to them?

If you're using Bible prophecy to promote a false doctrine, then know this—and be careful what you wish for. Bible prophecy speaks of an Antichrist who will govern the world, and ultimately the world won't like it. Theologian Ron Rhodes makes this clear: "Truly he will be anti-Christ in every way imaginable. And as theologian David Jeremiah put it, 'There are more than twenty-five different titles given to the Antichrist, all of which help to paint a picture of the most despicable man ever to walk on the earth.' Woe to those who are on the earth during the time of his reign."[286]

It's time to pay attention.

CHAPTER TWENTY
Signs of the Times

And there will be signs in the sun, in the moon and in
the stars.

—Luke 21:25

And on the earth distress of nations, with perplexity, the
sea and waves roaring, men's hearts failing them from fear
and the expectations of those things, which are coming
on the earth, for the powers of the heavens will be shaken.

—Luke 21:26–28

"What rulers, what powers, what world forces, what fortresses, what
speculations, what lofty things, what spiritual forces of wickedness in
the heavenly places, are we warring against?" asks Dr. Stephen Yulish.
Dr. Yulish sees a strong emphasis being put on the many attempts to
downplay any sort of negative influence that would impede the creation
of a one-world, harmonious society. It's a deception. In his article on the
same subject, deception, he notes that it is not "little green men" we are
dealing with because he doesn't believe these little men exist—not in the
way society wishes to view them, anyway. He was on to something. Covert
forces are at work. "It is my firm belief that Satan and all his demonic
hordes are preparing to unleash one of the greatest deceptions on mankind
that ever has been undertaken,"[287] continues Dr. Yulish. That view is shared
by Bible scholar William Frederick in *The Coming Epiphany*, in which
he writes of potential reasons for a falling away from the faith, which we
know will happen before the official second coming of the official Jesus

Christ. One such theory he presents, interestingly enough, involves aliens. He says, "Specifically, I am talking about the theory that aliens are real space beings and are the originators of life on earth. While many believers may initially bristle at this outrageous suggestion, there is much support for this theory that 'another gospel' will come at the hand of what many mistakenly believe to be alien beings."[288]

Many theologians are quick to point out that there are some very obvious discrepancies between "extraterrestrial spirituality" and Christianity's beliefs. Obviously the extraterrestrials would have to change the way we think about God and especially what is written in the Bible. One goal in particular, Pastor Rhodes points out, is to replace exclusivist Christianity with a religion of universalism. He points to the fact that the aliens never affirm the Bible as being God's Word, never glorify Jesus Christ, never address the sinful nature of humans or a need for redemption, and never have anything to say about Christ's redemptive work on the cross.[289] We may be rolling up on a time when false prophets may appear wearing helmets and space gear or have no need for either one. Let's be prepared.

But according to the "unadulterated" Christian end-times prophecy, another very important event must take place before it can be fulfilled: the gospel is to be preached in all the world as a witness to all the nations (Matthew 24:14). Today more than ever the gospel has been spread around the world—even into space, as demonstrated in December 1968 when Apollo 8 astronauts Bill Anders, Jim Lovell, and Frank Borman read a Christmas message from the Bible over the airwaves while orbiting the moon.

Less encouraging are the predictions of wars and rumors of wars, with nation against nation and kingdom against kingdom, and the famines, pestilence, and earthquakes in various places—all of which we have seen in our current age. Additionally, believers in Jesus Christ have encountered and will encounter opposition to Jesus and the Christian faith; it seems to be a growing trend. "How long will I be allowed to remain a Christian?" was the question asked in an article by journalist Douglas MacKinnon that circulated around the web in April 2018. "To say that Christians and Christianity are under a withering and brutal attack in certain areas of the world would be an understatement," he writes. "In various parts of the Middle East, there is a genocidal cleansing of Christians being carried out. Women, men, and their young children are being slaughtered because of their faith and world leaders and most of the media turn their backs in bored indifference. Here in the United States, Christians and Christianity are mocked, belittled, smeared and attacked by some on a daily basis."[290] That includes harassment and attacks on college campuses.

"These are the times that try men's souls," wrote the American patriot Thomas Paine in 1776. The struggle for freedom back then can almost be compared to the fight to keep our freedoms today. And that includes religion. If that goes, how many more freedoms will follow? These may be difficult times, but they are predicted times as well. Certain events will take place, and certain signs will be seen.

Scripture says there will also be noticeable changes on Earth, in the sky, and in the sea that will catch our attention. Such signs are meant to be an indicator of the times leading up to the return of Jesus Christ and are something that believers should be alert to. Although many catastrophic events have already occurred on our planet, the indication is that they will progress as "birth pangs" and continue to grow more intense. Earthquakes, famine, pestilence, and signs from heaven will increase.

Columnist Ron Fraser, in writing about some of these increases, said, "The incidence of natural disaster has risen dramatically over the past twenty years." Aside from the doomsday predictors and kooks seizing onto every natural disaster as the "end of the world," there is some legitimacy in looking at the statistics, which Fraser did. In his 2010 article "Why Have Natural Disasters Increased?"[291] he noted the mounting evidence that disasters have indeed been on the upswing and wrote, "The facts are that statistics prove natural disasters have risen startlingly since 1990. In a law-abiding universe, there has to be a reason for this." That particular decade did prove to be one of the deadliest. Fraser cited data from the United Nations Center for Research on Epidemiology of Disasters in Geneva for the 1990s showing that 3,852 disasters killed more than 780,000 people over a ten-year period, with earthquakes by far the leading cause of destruction. Today, the stats continue to show massive destruction from disasters globally. Fatalities from earthquakes hurricanes, floods, and heat waves. Domestically, freezing temperatures and snowstorms pummel the United States, and hurricanes, floods, and tsunamis have made headlines. Tornadoes have been increasing in frequency, earthquakes continue to rattle parts of the world, and fires have raged in unprecedented numbers, causing massive destruction and loss of property and lives.

Uneasiness has set in around the world. Illness, hunger, pestilence, terrorism, strife, and natural disasters have added to the fears of many who now are on guard for something worse. Egypt and Saudi Arabia have been put on alert for swarms of locusts that wipe out their crops.

Even the secular realm sees it. The late radio talk show host Art Bell, whose topics often included UFOs and a variety of paranormal subjects, came to feel that "something" just wasn't right in our society. He referred to it as the "Quickening." Bell was no novice when it came to discussing the "strange and unusual." His guests came from all backgrounds and professions, from New Age to "newly abducted." Airtime was granted on just about any topic imaginable. And people were listening. He had one of the highest-rated talk shows in the country and an audience of millions. His radio programs *Coast to Coast* and *Dreamland* were broadcast over three hundred stations nationally. During his tenure on the radio, Art spoke with literally hundreds of people, many of whom had seen or had traumatic events in their lives, all of which seemed to be leading to "something" like a foreshadowing of fearful things to come.

What on Earth is happening? Literally. Signs and more signs appear to be growing around the world. Crop circles of enormous size and perfect intricacy continue to appear in fields, cattle mutilations go on unabated, and there are an increasing number of UFO sightings, plus strange lights in the sky, strange noises, and sounds and booms coming from the sky. The world of the paranormal is rife with psychics, ghost hunters, and ancient alien theories, and mysteries on Earth abound.

Of course, attributing all these changes and occurrences to climate change is one way to explain them away, but it's not all that easy. Where do you slot UFOs, for instance? Strange things are occurring on earth and in our skies and most likely will continue to do so if Bible prophecy is being fulfilled.

One other interesting if not ominous sign we may be seeing comes from scripture. "When He opened the fourth seal, I heard the voice of the fourth living creature saying, 'Come and see.' So I looked, and behold, a pale horse. And the name of him who sat on it was Death, and Hades followed with him. And power was given to them over a fourth of the earth, to kill with sword, with hunger, with death, and by *the beasts of the earth*" (Revelation 6:9–11 *italics mine*).

Now here is another very disconcerting situation. Clearly this scripture points to the time of the Tribulation that will take place before Jesus Christ's return, and no doubt strange signs are occurring something that is dramatically affecting our animal kingdom. Unprovoked animal attacks against humans are on the increase. Coyotes in neighborhoods are killing domestic animals and in some cases attacking humans, bears have become a concern after several attacks on humans in national parks, cougars have been reported stalking and killing humans on bike trails, polar bear, alligator, and shark attacks appear to be increasing, and human fatalities from aggressive dog attacks have become a real concern. Obviously some of the attacks could be caused by humans intruding on or carelessly exposing themselves to these dangerous animals, clearly that is not always the case. Do they serve as a warning? Writer Chris Capps asks an interesting question: "Perhaps the collective consciousness of all living creatures is operating differently in these recent days. Is it in response to something that has already happened? Or could it be in anticipation to something that has yet to occur?"[292]

And animals are suffering. The loss of animal life in massive numbers has been occurring all over the world. So much so that they have earned their own designated classification of the event. In 2014, *CBS News* reported a story about the inexplicably strange occurrence of mass animal deaths, scientifically referred to as mass mortality events (MME). Biologists around the world have seen and recorded a rapid increase in the incidents of MME over the last several years. Reporter Amanda Schupak brought the gravity of the situation to the forefront in her report appropriately titled *"Mass Animal Deaths on the Rise Worldwide."* "Thousands of birds fall from the sky. Millions of fish wash up on the shore. Honey bee populations decimated. Bats overtaken by a deadly fungus. Piglets die in droves from a mysterious disease,"[293] she said. The facts are the facts: these types of mass deaths are increasing, and no one knows why. According to her report, researchers from Yale University and the San Diego and Berkeley campuses of the University of California have tried to establish why it might be happening in numbers that threaten to wipe out some populations—some from disease, some from human causes such as chemical poisonings—but they haven't been able to account for the enormity of these events happening worldwide. The researchers have discovered that many of the mass deaths have occurred in populations of mammals, birds, fish, reptiles, amphibians, and marine invertebrates. These deaths are occurring globally and are ongoing— some even say in biblical proportions. Could this be God's judgment? Perhaps, but whether one believes in the end times or not, incredible losses of animal life are occurring and no one completely knows why, let alone how to prevent it.

The End Times Prophecy Group sees these massive animal deaths as a possible sign of what has been prophesied in the end times and maybe they're right. This group of ardent researchers has been documenting these mysterious deaths for over eight years on their website and has not seen a decline in the numbers.

Then we have the "human animal." Violent crime continues to increase; drug addiction, gang warfare, bigotry, political extremism, terrorism, rape, murder, racial conflicts, bullying, shaming, trolling, lack of respect for elders and educators, the law and leaders. All are all on the upswing. The Bible says that attitudes will take a turn for the worse, lawlessness will abound, and the love of many will grow cold. (Matthew 24:11–12).

"But know this, that in the last days perilous times will come. For men will be lovers of themselves, lovers of money, boasters, proud, blasphemers, disobedient to parents, unthankful, unholy, unloving, unforgiving, slanders without self-control, brutal, despisers of good, traitors, headstrong, haughty, lovers of pleasure rather than lovers of God" (2 Timothy 3:1–4).

We have to ask ourselves the obvious, are we becoming an immoral society of self-centered individuals without a conscience for our actions? Cruelty has reached unspeakable heights; animals suffer at the hands of humans; humans suffer at the hands of other humans; murder-suicides take out entire families; children commit heinous crimes; and shootings in schools, churches, synagogues, and mosques, and bullying to the point of suicide are some blatant examples. And perpetrators of crimes are becoming younger and younger in age. In October 2016, a ten-year-old special-needs boy was doused with gasoline and set on fire. His attackers were nine, ten, and eleven years old.[294] What are we becoming as a nation that we would see such cruelty? The very lack of conscience for the killing of babies has risen to the point of full-term executions. Have we gone back to the sacrifice of infants on the fire pits of Baal?

Something indeed is happening to our humanity. As we advance technologically we appear to be digressing spiritually. The downward trend grows every day, and those not wanting to hear the truth persecute those who choose to call out the evil.

What Bailey wrote under the influence of a spirit is nothing new. The assault against God's people is nothing new. The attacks on the Christian belief are nothing new. The spirits who wrote these directives through Bailey and Creme and all the others are nothing new. It is the same old devil at work. Spirit entities at enmity with God cannot present the truth of the Bible as it is, so they must twist the truth to meet their requirements of a world savior, a leader, or a world teacher. The stage is being set for a grand deception and those who remain alert to the signs will see it.

So, what parts will UFOs and extraterrestrials play? Will we see a cosmic Christ? The late pastor Ray Steadman saw a connection with UFOs and signs of the times. "Some preach that reality is made up of many dimensions or spiritual realms, from which UFOs, alien beings, crop circles, and other manifestations come ... Jesus says that some of these signs and wonders will appear so convincing so miraculous, that even Christians may be fooled by them."[295]

Perilous times will come, and already some can see the opportunities for our own destruction. According to the Associated Press, the *Moscow Times* recently ran a story about one church leader's concerns. *Russian Patriarch Warns 'Antichrist' Will Control Humans Through Gadgets"* read the headline. The leader of the Russian Orthodox Church is afraid that dependence on modern technology will result in the coming of the Antichrist. Patriarch Krill said that the collection of user data, including an individual's location, interest, even fears will make it possible for humans to be controlled by external forces. In fact he believes that control from a single point is a harbinger Antichrist. Krill told the state-run Russia-1 TV network on Orthodox Christmas Monday that he believes that the Antichrist will be a personality who will be at the head of the World Wide Web and ultimately control the entire human race. Thus, the Internet structure itself presents a danger, he advised them. The church leader was adamant that there should be no single [control and access] center. Although the church does not oppose technological progress it is concerned that "Someone can know exactly where you are, know exactly what you are interested in, know exactly what you are afraid of and that such information could be used for centralized control of the world." [296]

This being who is destined to fulfill Bible prophecy will cause all of humankind to receive a mark on their right hand or on their foreheads, "That no one may buy or sell except one who has the mark. Here is wisdom. Let him who has understanding calculate the number of the beast, for it is the number of a man: His number is 666" (Revelation 13:16–18).

But for believers in Jesus Christ there is much hope. The end is not the end. Difficult times may lie ahead, whether they come from land or sea or "sky," but it is important to remember what carries us along: our faith, our God, and the knowledge that all these things must come to pass, as Jesus told us. "Now learn this parable from the fig tree: When its branch has already become tender and puts forth leaves, you know that summer is near. So you also, when you see all these things, know that it is near—at the doors!" (Matthew 24:32–33)

But here's the upside to that: "Now when these things begin to happen, look up and lift up your heads, because your redemption draws near" (Luke 21:28).

CHAPTER TWENTY-ONE
Looking Up

He has delivered us from the power of darkness and conveyed us into the kingdom of the Son of His love, in whom we have redemption through His blood, the forgiveness of sins. He is the image of the invisible God, the firstborn over all creation. For by Him all things were created that are in heaven and that are on earth, visible and invisible, whether thrones or dominions or principalities or powers.

—Colossians 1:13–16

Let not your heart be troubled; you believe in God, believe also in Me.

—John 14:1

Incredible times lie ahead—challenging but exciting times as well, as we continue to look for signs of Jesus's return. This book has been a journey through UFO conspiracies, false doctrines, the supernatural, alien deception, and the means by which an enemy of God could assume leadership of the world. By now, you have seen that the paranormal is real and that UFOs exist. You have read of supernatural experiences, learned of the spirit realm, seen photographic evidence, paged through testimonials, and read the truth of the word of God through scriptures. You've seen how the enemy works and learned of a grand deception.

What was the number one warning Jesus gave? To not let anyone deceive you! God has a plan of His own, and He has been merciful enough to share it with us by giving us prophecies of the end times and the promise of all that is good that lie ahead for those who believe. What a blessing, to be alerted to all of this ahead of time and learn of the devil's plans before he carries them out. We need, as the scripture says, to be "wise as serpents and harmless as doves."[297] It is the ultimate heads-up from a loving God. Knowing this ahead of time should help give you peace in a chaotic world and make you wise to feigning visitors from afar should they appear.

You know now that there is an ongoing attempt to present to the world a new Christ and a form of global governance, whether that comes through peace or calamity. We can see a solid progression toward changes in our world on all levels—politics, religion, education, current affairs, and global policies—that can and will affect us all.

We continue to see unidentified objects in our skies, cross paths with them in the heavens, and seek them out on Earth. We are hurtling toward some phenomenal future event that will totally transform our world and our reality and challenge our very sense of being. It's time to keep our heads up in our own anticipation of what is to come, as Bible prophecy continues to unfold. We need not be fearful, we have been told, and although we do not know the day or the hour of the real return of Jesus Christ, we are commissioned to stay alert and continue to watch.

Many people will fall victim to a deceptively close encounter of another kind. Please don't be one of those people. We know that a rapture of Christians will happen, whether pre-tribulation, mid-tribulation, post-tribulation, or standing on Earth when Jesus himself returns. We know that at some point, we will be caught up to meet the Lord in the air.[298] But in the meantime, Christians have a responsibility to share the gospel, not in a controlling, condemning way, but in the manner God intended, humbly and freely. In a real sense, Christians are messengers. It is our job to throw out the lifeline of salvation to those who will receive it, those who have eyes to see and ears to hear. The good news of the Bible won't always convince or spiritually convict everyone, but our commission is to try. It is the Holy Spirit that works in the hearts of people, but the seed of faith needs to be planted. I can't help but wonder what would happen if we said nothing. How would the rest of the world react if the information was there but they never heard it because we never told them? More importantly, how would God react? For those who don't know the Lord who may be reading this, it may sound a bit preachy, but that's intentional. How else will you know? There is a broad road to destruction, but there's a way out and a way up for those who believe. If you don't know Jesus, I pray you will. Believe on the Lord Jesus Christ and you will be saved. If you want to know the truth, open your heart, ask forgiveness, and ask Jesus to show you and save you.

No doubt, challenging and amazing days lie ahead. Never have we been more taxed with conflicts and challenges. In all the unique events and experiences in my life, never have God, Jesus, and the Holy Spirit been more real for me, and I hope for you as well.

There are unidentified flying objects in our skies, although what or who they are, and how many, is yet to be revealed. Whether friend or foe, we know that spiritually there are those beings who come to our aid and those who come to destroy. There is good in the world, but there is also evil. We need to be alert to how this will all play out—not panicking, but with wisdom and the testing of spirits.

Therefore knowing by the evidence presented that these entities are real, we take comfort and encouragement in knowing that God is very real, Jesus is very real, and what He did on earth was very real—His miracles, preaching, pain, and suffering as evidenced by the wounds He carries in His hands and feet and side. So we press on toward the goal, knowing that at some time there will be a reunion with Him and all the heavenly hosts.

Keep looking up.

About the Author

Sylvia McKelvey has been a Christian investigator for over thirty years. She provided research materials for and appeared in the 1983 documentary *The New Age, A Pathway to Paradise?* produced by Christian television network WCFC in Chicago, Illinois. She has been an investigator for the Mutual UFO Network (MUFON) and has served as the MUFON state section director for Santa Clara County, California. She is a former petty officer of the United States Naval Reserve Hospital Corps and served on active duty during Operation Desert Storm. She lives with her husband in Northern California.

Endnotes

Preface

1   Michael Snyder, "More Americans Believe Aliens Have Visited Earth Than Believe That Jesus Is the Son of God," Signs of the Times, posted January 6, 2014, https://www.sott.net/article/271567-More-Americans-believe-aliens-have-visited-Earth-than-believe-that-Jesus-is-the-Son-of-God.

Chapter One

2   Alice A. Bailey, *The Externalization of the Hierarchy* (New York: Lucis, 1985), 916.

3   Alice A. Bailey, *The Unfinished Biography* (New York: Lucis, 1981), 162.

4   Dave Hunt, *Peace, Prosperity, and the Coming Holocaust* (Eugene, OR: Harvest House, 1983), 158.

5   Constance Cumbey, *The Hidden Dangers of the Rainbow* (Lafayette, LA: Huntington House, 1983), 111.

6   Alice A. Bailey and Djwhal Khul, *Ponder on This: From the Writings of Alice A. Bailey and the Tibetan Master, Djwhal Khul* (New York: Lucis, 1974), 140.

7   Benjamin Crème, *The Reappearance of the Christ and the Masters of Wisdom* (Amsterdam: Share International, 2007), originally published in 1979.

8   Bailey, *Externalization of the Hierarchy*, 55.

9   Bailey, *Externalization of the Hierarchy*, 59.

10   Shirley MacLaine, *Out on a Limb* (New York: Bantam, 1984), 164.

11   Giorgio Dibitonto and William T. Sherwood, *UFO Contact from Angels in Starships*, ed. Wendelle C. Stevens (Tucson, AZ: UFO Photo Archives, 1990), Introduction.

12   Benjamin Creme, *The Gathering of the Forces of Light: UFOs and Their Spiritual Mission* (Amsterdam: Share International Foundation, 2010), 18.

13   Gerard Aartsen, *Here to Help: UFOs and the Space Brothers* (Amsterdam: BGA, 2008), 160.

14   Scott Wood, "Waiting for Maitreya: Benjamin Crème Was a Great British Eccentric," Little Atoms, littleatoms.com/waiting-maitreya.

Chapter Three

15 Otto O. Binder, *Flying Saucers Are Watching Us* (New York: Belmont, 1970), 173.

16 Frank Scully, *Behind the Flying Saucers* (New York: Henry Holt, 1950), xv, 23.

17 Ibid., 59

18 George Adamski and Desmond Leslie, *Flying Saucers Have Landed* (New York: British Book Centre, 1953), 107.

19 Ibid.

20 Ibid., 167.

21 Ibid., 125.

22 Ibid., 158.

23 Ibid., 201.

24 Ibid., 203.

25 Benjamin Creme, *The Reappearance of the Christ and the Masters of Wisdom* (Amsterdam: Share International, 2007), xii.

26 Scott Beekman, *William Dudley Pelley: A Life in Right-Wing Extremism and the Occult* (Syracuse, NY: Syracuse University Press, 2005), 161.

27 Ibid., 162.

28 Andy Roberts, "In Advance of the Landing: The Findhorn Community," Magonia, posted September 8, 2009, http://magonia.haaan.com/2009/findhorn/.

29 Gerard Aartsen, *George Adamski: A Herald for the Space Brothers* (Amsterdam: BGA, 2010), 20.

30 Henry Dohan, *Pawn of His Creator*, quoted in Gerard Aartsen, *George Adamski: A Herald for the Space Brothers* (Amsterdam: BGA, 2010), 20.

31 Gerard Aartsen, *George Adamski: A Herald for the Space Brothers* (Amsterdam: BGA, 2010), 22.

32 Ibid., 23

33 George King and Richard Lawrence, *Contacts with the Gods from Space: Pathway to the New Millenium* (Hollywood, CA: Aetherius Society, 1996), 48.

34 Ibid., 50.

35 Ibid., 54.

36 Wikipedia, s.v. "Howard Menger," https://en.wikipedia.org/wiki/Howard_Menger.

37 Wikipedia, s.v. "Daniel Fry," https://en.wikipedia.org/wiki/Daniel_Fry.

38 Skygaze *Strange & Unexplained- Space Brothers* https://www.skygaze.com/content/strange/SpaceBrothers.shtml

39 Gerard Aartsen, *Here to Help: UFOs and the Space Brothers* (Amsterdam: BGA, 2012), 44.

Chapter Four

40   T. Alberto Tulli, "The Tulli Papyrus," Gregorian Egyptian Museum, Vatican City State.

41   Peter Brookesmith, *UFO: The Complete Sightings Catalogue* (New York: Barnes and Noble, 1995), 14.

42   Jacques Vallee and Chris Aubeck, *Wonders in the Sky*, (New York: Jeremy P. Tarcher/Penguin, 2009), 82.

43   Ibid., 195.

44   Wikipedia, s.v. "1492 Light Sighting [Christopher Columbus]," https://en.wikipedia.org/wiki/1492_light_sighting.

45   Wikipedia, s.v. "1561 Celestial Phenomenon Over Nuremberg," https://en.wikipedia.org/wiki/1561_celestial_phenomenon_over_Nuremberg.

46   Ibid.

47   Ibid.

48   Wikipedia, s.v. "1566 Celestial Phenomenon Over Basel," https://en.wikipedia.org/wiki/1566_celestial_phenomenon_over_Basel.

49   Dale Topping, *When Giants Roamed the Sky*, (Akron, Ohio: University of Akron Press, 2001) 23.

50   John LeMay, Noe Torres, Jared Olive, and Neil Riebe, *The Real Cowboys and Aliens: UFO Encounters of the Old West* (Edinburg, TX: RoswellBooks.com, 2014), 17.

51   Mack Maloney, *UFOs in Wartime: What They Didn't Want You to Know* (New York: Berkley Books, 2011), 18.

52   Ibid.

53   "Eddie Rickenbacker Quotes," AZ Quotes, https://www.azquotes.com/author/12335-Eddie_Rickenbacker.

54   Brookesmith, *UFO: The Complete Sightings Catalogue*, 31.

55   Ibid.

56   Wikipedia, s.v. "*The War of the Worlds*," https://en.wikipedia.org/wiki/The_War_of_the_Worlds.

57   Richard M. Dolan, *UFOs and the National Security State: Chronology of a Cover-up 1941–1973* (Charlottesville, VA: Hampton Roads, 2000), 6.

58   Ibid.

59   Jerome Clark, *Strange Skies: Pilot Encounters with UFOs* (New York: Citadel, 2003), 21.

60   Ibid.

Chapter Five

61   Renato Vesco, *Intercept UFO* (New York: Zebra, 1974), 57.

62   Wikipedia, s.v. "1952 Washington, D.C. UFO Incident," https://en.wikipedia. org/wiki/1952_Washington,_D.C._UFO_incident.

63   Kevin D. Randle, *Invasion Washington: UFOs Over the Capitol* (New York: Harpertorch, 2001), 40.

64   Ibid., 68.

65   "Mysterious Sky Riders Swoop Over Washington," *New York World Telegram and Sun*, July 29, 1952.

66   Ibid.

67   "The Daily Oklahoman," February 24, 1952.

68   Ibid.

69   "Two Saucer-Eyed Pilots Report 8 Flying Disks," United Press International, Miami, FL, July 16, 1952.

70   Frank C. Feschino Jr., *Shoot Them Down! The Flying Saucer Wars of 1952* (Morrisville, NC: Lulu, 2007), 3.

71   Ibid.

72   Gordon Cooper with Bruce Henderson, *Leap of Faith: An Astronaut's Journey into the Unknown* (New York: Harper Collins, 2000), 79, 80.

73   Casey McNerthney *UFO frenzy was sparked here 65 years ago* (Seattle Post-Intelligencer, June 27, 2012

74   Jesse Marcel Jr., *The Roswell Legacy* (Helena, MT: Big Sky, 2007), 29.

75   Ibid., 38.

76   Jerome Clark, *The UFO Book*, (Detroit, MI, Visible Ink Press, 1998) 353

77   John Spencer, *World Atlas of UFOs* (New York: Smithmark, 1991), 23.

Chapter Six

78   Gordon Cooper with Bruce Henderson, *Leap of Faith: An Astronaut's Journey into the Unknown* (New York: Harper Collins, 2000), 79, 80.

79   Ibid., 81.

80   Ibid., 83, 84.

81   Ibid., 84, 85.

82   Ibid., 85.

83   https://www.gravitywarpdrive.com/UFOTestimonies.htm

84   "NASA Astronaut and Russian Cosmonaut Facts," UFO Casebook, http://www. ufocasebook.com/nasafacts.html.

85   Astronaut Edgar Mitchell, post–Apollo 14 moon flight, 1971.

86   Cooper, *Leap of Faith*, 91.

87   https://www.gravitywarpdrive.com/UFOTestimonies.htm

Chapter Seven

88   *Close Encounters of the Third Kind*, written and directed by Steven Spielberg, 1977.

89   Department of Transportation, Federal Aviation Administration, Air Transportation Security, Form 1600-32-1, November 17, 1986.

90   Richard Haines, "Sturrock Panel Report," March 12, 1977.

91   Jimmy Carter, Campaign speech, Lions Club, Leary, Georgia, January 6, 1969.

92   "1974: Ronald Reagan's UFO Sighting," UFO Casebook, www.ufocasebook. com/2010/reagansighting.html.

93   Ibid.

94   Leslie Kean, *UFOs: Generals, Pilots, and Government Officials Go on the Record* (New York: Three Rivers, 2010), 24.

95   Ibid., 249.

96   Ibid., 254.

97   Wikipedia, s.v. "Stephenville, Texas," https://en.wikipedia.org/wiki/ Stephenville,_Texas.

98   William J. Birnes, *UFO Hunters: Book One* (New York: Tom Doherty, 2013), 292, 293.

99   Ibid., 293.

100 Ibid.

101 Gardiner Harris, "Two Police Officers Have Dogfight with UFO During Helicopter Patrol," *Louisville Courier-Journal*, March 4, 1993.

102 Tucker Carlson and David Fravor, *Fox News*, December 20, 2017.

103 Ronald Reagan, Speech to United Nations General Assembly, September 21, 1987.

Chapter Eight

104 Gerard Aartsen, "The Friendship Case: Space Brothers Teach Lessons of Brotherhood; An Excerpt," Share International Magazine (website), April 2011, http://www.share-international.org/magazine/old_issues/2011/2011-04. htm#correo.

105 Benjamin Creme, *The Gathering of the Forces of Light and Their Spiritual Mission* (Amsterdam: Share International, 2010), 13.

106 Bob Pratt, *UFO Danger Zone: Terror and Death in Brazil. Where Next?* (Madison, WI: Horus House, 1996), 57, 58.

107 Ibid., 13, 14, 15.

108 Ibid., xii.

109 Donald E. Keyhoe, *Aliens from Space: The Real Story of Unidentified Flying Objects* (New York: Doubleday, 1973), 20.

110 Pratt, *UFO Danger Zone*, xiii.

111 G. Cope Shellhorn, "UFO-Related Homicide in Brazil: The Complete Story," *International UFO Magazine*, http://www.newsnfo.co.uk. (Warning: graphic)

112 Peter Brookesmith, *UFO: the Complete Sightings* (New York, NY: Barnes and Nobel Books, 1995), 60.

113 "Sheriff Blinded by Light from UFO: Minnesota 1979," UFO Case Files, https://www.ufocasebook.com/minnesotasheriff1979.html.

114 "Robert Jacobs," Ufology, http://ufology.wikia.com/wiki/Robert_Jacobs.

115 Ibid.

116 http://www.ufoevidence.org/cases/case1017.htm

117 Ibid.

118 Ibid.

119 Brad Steiger and Joan Whritenour, *New UFO Breakthrough* (New York: Award Books, 1968), 16.

120 Ibid., 11.

121 Raymond E. Fowler, *UFOs: Interplanetary Visitors* (New York: Bantam, 1974), 308–309.

122 Ibid., 289.

123 Steiger and Whritenour, *New UFO Breakthrough*, 19.

124 "Child Burned in New Mexico," *Aerial Phenomena Research Organization Bulletin*, November 1964, available at www.openminds.tv/pdf/apro/apro_nov_1964.pdf.

125 Brad Steiger and Joan Whritenour, *Flying Saucers Are Hostile* (New York: Award Books, 1967), 68.

126 Ibid., 126.

127 Steiger and Whritenour, *New UFO Breakthrough*, 38.

128 Steiger and Whritenour, *Flying Saucers Are Hostile*, 8.

129 Steiger and Whritenour, *Flying Saucers Are Hostile*, 11.

Chapter Nine

130 Harold T. Wilkins, *Flying Saucers on the Attack* (New York: Ace Books, 1967), 63.

131 Brent Raynes, "Early UFO Cases with Paranormal Twists," *Alternate Perceptions Magazine* #170 (March 20, 2012), http://www.apmagazine.info/index.php?option=com_content&view=article&id=248&Itemid=53.

132 Ibid.

133 Jenny Randles and Peter Hough, *The Complete Book of UFOs: An Investigation into Alien Contacts and Encounters* (New York: Sterling, 1996), 66.

134 Stanton T. Friedman and Kathleen Marden, *Captured! The Betty and Barney Hill UFO Experience* (Franklin Lakes, NJ: Career, 2007), 34.

135 Ibid., 206.

136 Raynes, "Early UFO Cases with Paranormal Twists."

137 Lee Speigel, "48 Percent of Americans Believe UFOs Could Be ET Visitations," *Huffington Post*, September 11, 2013 (updated December 6, 2017).

138 "60 Percent of Americans Claim to Have Seen Ghosts," *Fox News,* October 18, 2018.

139 Amanda Woods, "Half of Humans Believe in Alien Life, Study Says," *New York Post*, December 8, 2017.

140 Kathleen Marden and Denise Stoner, *Making Contact: Alien Abduction Case Studies* (New York: Rosen, 2015), 93–94.

Chapter Ten

141 Brad Steiger and Sherry Hansen Steiger, *Real Aliens, Space Beings, and Creatures from Outer Worlds* (Canton, MI: Visible Ink, 2011), 146, 147.

142 Wikipedia, s.v. "Edgar Cayce," https://en.wikipedia.org/wiki/Edgar_Cayce.

143 Ibid.

144 Ruth Montgomery, *A Gift of Prophecy: The Phenomenal Jeane Dixon* (New York: William Morrow, 1965), 15.

145 *National Inquirer*, September 14, 1976.

146 Nicholas Redfern, *On the Trail of the Saucer Spies: UFOs and Government Surveillance* (San Antonio, TX: Anomalist Books, 2006), 33.

147 Uri Geller, *Uri Geller: My Story* (New York: Warner Books, 1976), 93.

148 Ibid.

149 Raymond E. Fowler, *UFO Testament: Anatomy of an Abductee* (Lincoln, NE: Universe, 2002), 28–30.

150 Ruth Montgomery, *Aliens Among Us* (New York: Putnam and Sons, 1985), 38, 39.

151 Clifford Stone, *Eyes Only*, (Clifford Earl Stone, 2011) 31.

152 Brad Steiger and Sherry Hansen Steiger, *Real Encounters, Different Dimensions, and Otherworldly Beings* (Canton, MI: Visible Ink, 2014), 343.

153 Brad Steiger and Sherry Hansen Steiger, *Real Visitors, Voices from Beyond, and Parallel Dimensions* (Canton, MI: Visible Ink, 2016), 329.

154 Ibid., 19, 21, 22.

155 Brad Steiger, *Gods of Aquarius: UFOs and the Transformation of Man* (New York: Berkley Books, 1981), 126, 127.

156 Ibid

157 Ibid.

158 Steve Barton, "Dread Central News, 9/12/12. dreadcentral.com.

159 Andrew W. Griffin, review of Operation Trojan Horse," by John A. Keel, *Red Dirt Report,* September 26, 2017, https://www.reddirtreport.com/rustys-reads/book-review-operation-trojan-horse-john-keel.

160 Raymond E. Fowler, *The Andreasson Affair* (New York: Bantam Books, 1980), 188.

161 Paola Harris, *UFOs: How Does One Speak to a Ball of Light?* (Cleveland, OH: Fenix, 2011), 295.

162 Ibid., 344.

Chapter Eleven

163 Katie Hall and John Pickering, *Beyond Photography: Encounters with Orbs, Angels, and Light Forms* (London: John Hunt, 2006), 130.

164 Wikipedia, s.v. "Plasma," https://en.wikipedia.org/wiki/Plasma.

165 Brad Steiger and Sherry Hansen Steiger, *Real Encounters, Different Dimensions, and Otherworldly Beings* (Canton, MI: Visible Ink, 2014), 75–77.

166 Ibid, 79.

167 Terry Ray, *The Complete Story of the Worldwide Invasion of the Orange Orbs* (Mechanicsburg, PA: Sunbury, 2014), 49, 50.

168 Hall and Pickering, *Beyond Photography*, 5.

169 Ibid., 173.

170 Ibid., 220.

171 Ibid., 230.

172 Elisabeth Haich, *Initiation* (Garberville, CA: Seed Center, 1974), 110.

173 *UFO Hunters*, episode 313, "Dark Presence," History Channel, 2009.

174 Ray, *Complete Story of the Worldwide Invasion*, 112–115.

175 Eltjo H. Haselhoff, *The Deepening Complexity of Crop Circles: Scientific Research and Urban Legends* (Berkeley, CA: Frog, 2001), 20, 22, 85.

176 Lynne D. Kitei, *The Phoenix Lights: A Skeptic's Discovery That We Are Not Alone* (Charlottesville, VA: Hampton Roads, 2004), 3–7.

177 Billy Crone, *UFOs: The Great Last Days Deception* (Las Vegas, NV: Get a Life Media, 2018), 114.

Chapter Twelve

178 Kris Vallotton, *Spirit Wars: Winning the Invisible Battle Against Sin and the Enemy* (Bloomington, MN: Chosen Books, 2012), 16.

179 Kris Vallontton, *Spirit Wars*, (Bloomington, MN: Chosen Books, 2012) 16.

180 Ibid., 47.

181 Ibid., 50, 51.

182 Brad Steiger and Sherry Hansen Steiger, *Real Visitors, Voices from Beyond, and Parallel Dimensions* (Canton, MI: Visible Ink, 2016), 34.

183 Robert C. Brenner, *Supernatural and Strange Happenings in the Bible: An Engineer's Study of Scripture* (San Diego, CA: Brenner Books, 2013), 471, 473.

184 Ibid.

185 Chip Ingram, *The Invisible War: What Every Believer Needs to Know About Satan, Demons, and Spiritual Warfare* (Grand Rapids, MI: Baker Books, 2006), Section 3.

186 "Raymond E. Fowler: Aliens, Abductions, and the Andreasson Affair," interview by Daniel V. Boudillion, The Raymond Fowler Alien Zone, August 2002, http://boudillion.com/interviews/fowler.htm.

Chapter Thirteen

187 Billy Graham, *Angels: God's Secret Agents* (New York: Pocket Books, 1977), 21, 22.

188 Susan Michaels, *Sightings: Beyond Imagination Lies the Truth* (New York: Simon and Schuster, 1996), 148.

189 James M. McCampbell, *UFOlogy* (Millbrae, CA: Celestial Arts, 1973), 34.

190 Ibid., 41.

191 Dina Dumezil, "The Humboldt Squid," http://fall11marinecology.providence.wikispaces.net/The+Red+Devil.

Chapter Fourteen

192 John 8:23.

193 John 18:33–38 (NIV).

194 John 18:36.

195 Mark 15:10.

196 John 8:23.

197 John 8:21.

198 John 8:14.

199 John 3:12.

200 Mark 1:24.

201 John 10:10.

202 Matthew 27:19.

203 John 19:8.

204 Mark 15:25.

205 Matthew 27:54.

206 Matthew 28:2–7.

207 2 Corinthians 11:14.

208 Matthew 16:13–17.

209 John 14:1–3.

210 Acts 1:9–11.

Chapter Fifteen

211 Stefano Breccia, *Mass Contacts* (Milton Keynes, UK: Author House, 2009), 171.

212 Raymond E. Fowler, *The Andreasson Affair* (New York: Bantam Books, 1980), 137.

213 Gary Bates, *Alien Intrusion: UFOs and the Evolution Connection* (Powder Springs, GA: Creation Book Publishers, 2011), 383.

214 Ibid., 384.

215 C. Fred Dickason, *Angels: Elect and Evil* (Chicago, IL: Moody, 1973), 223.

216 Ryan Pitterson, *Judgment of the Nephilim* (New York: Days of Noe, 2017), 47.

217 Ibid., 55.

218 Nick Redfern, *Secret History: Conspiracies from Ancient Aliens to the New World Order* (Canton, MI: Visible Ink, 2015), 82.

219 Ancient Aliens, *The Official Companion Book,* (New York, NY: Harper Collins, 2016) 98.

220 Brenda Denzler, *The Lure of the Edge: Scientific Passions, Religious Beliefs, and the Pursuit of UFOs* (Berkeley: University of California Press, 2001), 23.

221 "The Hybrids and the New Race of Children," The Hybrid Project, Hybrids Rising, http://hybridsrising.com/Hybrid-Project/Hybrids-Rising-Hybrids-New-Race-of-Children-HP.html.

222 Michael Salla, "Interview with Charles Hall: Motivations of Tall White ETs and Their Exopolitical Significance," December 26, 2016, ExoPolitics.org, https://www.exopolitics.org/interview-with-charles-hall-motivations-of-tall-white-ets-their-exopolitical-significance/.

223 Janet Bord and Colin Bord, *Mysterious Britain: Ancient Secrets of the United Kingdom and Ireland* (London: Granada, 1982), 252.

224 Denzler, *Lure of the Edge*, 119.

225 Colin Wilson, *Alien Dawn: A Classic Investigation into the Contact Experience* (Woodbury, MN: Llewellyn, 2010), 355.

226 David M. Jacobs, *Secret Life: Firsthand Accounts of UFO Abductions* (New York: Fireside, 1993), 316.

227 "The Hybrids and the New Race of Children."

228 Rachel Becker, "An Artificial Womb Successfully Grew Baby Sheep—and Humans Could Be Next," *The Verge*, April 25, 2017, https://www.theverge.com/2017/4/25/15421734/artificial-womb-fetus-biobag-uterus-lamb-sheep-birth-premie-preterm-infant.

Chapter Sixteen

229 "J. Allen Hynek: The Unexplained Column," interview by Allen Spraggett, November 8, 1975.

230   Michael Hesemann, *The Cosmic Connection: Worldwide Crop Formations and ET Contacts* (Bath, UK: Gateway Books, 1996), 95.

231   Raymond E. Fowler, *The Andreasson Affair* (Englewood Cliffs, NJ: Prentice Hall, 1980), x.

232   Brad Steiger, *Gods of Aquarius: UFOs and the Transformation of Man* (New York: Berkley Books, 1981), 214.

233   Linda Moulton Howe, *Glimpses of Other Realities: Volume I: Facts and Eyewitnesses* (Huntingdon Valley, PA: LMH Productions, 1993), 249.

234   Nick Redfern, *Secret History: Conspiracies from Ancient Aliens to the New World Order* (Canton, MI: Visible Ink, 2015), 35.

235   John Spencer, *The UFO Encyclopedia* (New York: Avon Books, 1991), 11.

236   "The Nachash in the Garden of Evil," Before It's News (website), December 18, 2014, https://beforeitsnews.com/v3/prophecy/2014/2466112.html.

Chapter Seventeen

237   John R. Sinclair, *The Alice Bailey Inheritance: The Inner Plane Teachings of Alice Ann Bailey, 1880–1949, and Their Legacy* (Great Britain: Turnstone, 1984), 112, 113.

238   Glenn McWane and David Graham, *The New UFO Sightings* (New York: Warner Paperback, 1975), 128.

239   Ruth Montgomery, *Aliens Among Us* (New York: G. P. Putnam, 1985), 88–89.

240   Brad Steiger and Joan Whritenour, *New UFO Breakthrough* (New York: Award Books, 1968), 15–16.

241   Paola Harris, *Connecting the Dots: Making Sense of the UFO Phenomenon* (Mill Spring, NC: Wild Flower, 2003), xvi.

242   Lynne D. Kitei, *The Phoenix Lights: A Skeptic's Discovery That We Are Not Alone* (Charlottesville, VA: Hampton Roads, 2004), 151.

243   Ibid., 134.

244   Benjamin Creme, *The Reappearance of Maitreya the Christ and the Masters of Wisdom* (London: Tara, 1980), 169.

245   Review of *A World Parliament: Governance and Democracy in the 21ˢᵗ Century*," by Jo Leinene and Andreas Bummel, 2018, 188–193, democracywithoutborders.com.

246   Ibid., 192.

247   Ibid., 223.

248   Ibid., 289.

249   Benjamin Creme, *The World Teacher for All Humanity* (Amsterdam: Share International, 2007), 77.

250   Dave Hunt, *Peace, Prosperity, and the Coming Holocaust* (Eugene, OR: Harvest House, 1983), 158.

251 "Difference between Socialism and Anarchism," Difference Between.net, http://www.differencebetween.net/business/difference-between-socialism-and-communism-2/.

252 Nick Redfern, *Contactees: A History of Alien-Human Interaction* (Franklin Lakes, NJ: Career Press, 2010), 42.

253 Brad Steiger, *Aquarian Revelations: Channeling Higher Intelligence* (New Brunswick, NJ: Inner Light, 1987), 117.

254 Alick Bartholomew, *Crop Circles: Harbingers of World Change* (Bath, UK: Gateway Books, 1992), 67.

255 Creme, *World Teacher for All Humanity*, 41, 64.

256 Patrick M. Wood, *Technocracy Rising: The Trojan Horse of Global Transformation* (Mesa, AZ: Coherent, 2015), xiv.

257 Beate Wilder-Smith, *The Day Nazi Germany Died: An Eyewitness Account of the Russian and Allied Invasion of Germany: An Autobiography* (San Diego: Master Books, 1982), 43.

258 Creme, *World Teacher for All Humanity*, back cover.

Chapter Eighteen

259 Brandon Ambrosino, "If We Made Contact with Aliens, How Would Religions React?" *BBC Future*, December 16, 2016, http://www.bbc.com/future/story/20161215-if-we-made-contact-with-aliens-how-would-religions-react.

260 Stephen Chen, "China's Giant Fast Radio Telescope to Join Hunt for Extraterrestrial Intelligence," *South China Morning Post*, October 31, 2016, https://www.scmp.com/news/china/policies-politics/article/2041602/chinas-giant-fast-radio-telescope-join-hunt.

261 Michael Hathorne, "China Removing Thousands from Homes to Hunt for Aliens," *Fox News*, February 17, 2016.

262 Ross Andersen, "What Happens If China Makes First Contact?" *The Atlantic*, December 2017, https://www.theatlantic.com/magazine/archive/2017/12/what-happens-if-china-makes-first-contact/544131/.

263 Ibid.

264 Steven Lerner, "Ex-NASA Scientist Says That UFOs Are Real and the Government Covers Up Alien Life," *Tech Times*, June 30, 2018, https://www.techtimes.com/articles/231514/20180630/ex-nasa-scientist-says-that-ufos-are-real-and-the-government-covers-up-alien-life.htm.

265 Lukas Mikelionis, "Harvard Prof Doesn't Back Down from Claims that Alien Spacecraft May Be Zipping Past Jupiter Orbit," *Fox News*, February 5, 2019, https://www.foxnews.com/science/harvard-prof-doesnt-back-down-from-claims-extraterrestrial-spacecraft-tech-is-flying-past-jupiter-orbit.

266 John Thomas Didymus, "SETI Scientist Warns World to Prepare for Alien Visitation but Admits Action Plan Could Be Like Neanderthals Preparing

in Case the U.S. Air Force Shows Up," *Inquisitr*, November 27, 2016, www.inquisitr.com/3748412/

267   John W. Traphagan, "Is Active SETI Really Dangerous?" *Huffington Post*, March 1, 2016 (updated March 2, 2017).

268   Ibid.

269   Ambrosino, "If We Made Contact with Aliens."

270   Arjun Walia, "NASA Brings Scientists and Theologians Together to Prepare World for Extraterrestrial Contact," Alternative News, Collective Evolution, September 25, 2014, www.collective-evolution.com/2014/09/25.

271   theeventchronicle.com, Editor, November 2, 2015 http://www.theeventchronicle.com/galactic/how-would-humanity-change-if-we-knew-aliens-existed/.

272   Chris Ciaccia, "Secret Pentagon Projects Reveal Gov't Looked into UFOs, Wormholes and Other Bizarre Anomalies," *Fox News*, January 23, 2019, https://www.foxnews.com/science/secret-pentagon-projects-reveal-govt-looked-into-ufos-wormholes-and-other-bizarre-anomalies.

273   Leonard David, "UFO Legacy: What Impact Will Revelation of Secret Government Program Have?" *Fox News,* January 11, 2018, https://www.foxnews.com/science/ufo-legacy-what-impact-will-revelation-of-secret-government-program-have.

274   David Wallace-Wells et al., "Reasons to Believe: How Seriously Should You Take Those Recent Reports of UFOs? Ask the Pentagon. Or Read This Primer for the SETI-Curious," *New York Magazine*, March 13, 2013, http://nymag.com/intelligencer/2018/03/13-reasons-to-believe-aliens-are-real.html.

Chapter Nineteen

275   Walter J. Veith, "Robert Muller's Global Education," Amazing Discoveries, April 22, 2010, https://amazingdiscoveries.org/S-deception_United_Nations_Muller_UNESCO_U-Thant.

276   "Could an Alien Deception Be Part of the End Times," GotQuestions.org, https://www.gotquestions.org/alien-deception.html.

277   Ibid.

278   Ron Rhodes, *Unmasking the Antichrist: Dispelling the Myths, Discovering the Truth* (Eugene, OR: Harvest House, 2012), 142.

279   Chuck Missler and Mark Eastman, *Alien Encounters: The Secret Behind the UFO Phenomenon* (Coeur d'Alene, ID: Koinonia House, 1997), 276.

280   Jefferson Scott, "Most Christians Don't Think About UFOs," http://www.jeffersonscott.com/nonfiction/ufos.htm.

281   Missler and Eastman, *Alien Encounters*, 285.

282   Ibid., 285, 286.

283 Tuella (Thelma Terrell) and the Ashtar Command, *Project World Evacuation: UFOs to Assist in the "Great Exodus" of Human Souls Off This Planet*, eds. Timothy Green Beckley and Tim R. Swartz (New Brunswick, NJ: Inner Light, 1993), 48.

284 Rhodes, *Unmasking the Antichrist*, 113.

285 Lehman Strauss, *Demons yes—but thank God for good angels*, (Neptune, NJ: Loizeaux Brothers, 1976) 79.

286 Ibid., 129.

Chapter Twenty

287 Stephen Yulish, "The Harpazo Deception," rapturenotes.com.

288 "William Frederick, *The Coming Epiphany: Your Guide to Understanding End Times Bible Prophecy* (Lulu.com, 2017), 24.

289 Ron Rhodes, *Alien Obsession* (Eugene, OR: Harvest House, 1984), 198.

290 Douglas MacKinnon, "How Long Will I Be Allowed to Remain a Christian?" *Fox News*, April 21, 2018, https://www.foxnews.com/opinion/how-long-will-i-be-allowed-to-remain-a-christian.

291 Ron Fraser, Thetrumpet.com, March 3, 2010.

292 Chris Capps, "Could Violent Attacks by Wild Animals Be Increasing Worldwide?" Simply Unexplainable, November 26, 2009, http://www.unexplainable.net/simply-unexplainable/violent_animal_attacks_worldwide_even_as.php.

293 Amanda Schupak, "Mass Animal Deaths on the Rise Worldwide," *CBS News*, January 16, 2015, https://www.cbsnews.com/news/mass-animal-deaths-on-the-rise-worldwide/.

294 "Special-Needs Boy, 10, Doused with Gas, Set on Fire in Texas Town," *Fox News*, October 6, 2016, http://www.foxnews.com/us/2016/10/06/special-needs-boy-10-doused-with-gas-set-on-fire-in-texas-town.html.

295 Ray Stedman, *What On Earth Is Happening? What Jesus Said About the End of the Age*. (Grand Rapids, MI: Discovery House, 2003).

296 "Russian Patriarch Warns 'Antichrist' Will Control Humans Through Gadgets," *Moscow Times*, January 8, 2019.

Chapter Twenty-One

297 Matthew 10:16.

298 1 Thessalonians 4:17.

Cluster of UFOs.

Unknown Object that hovered over us.

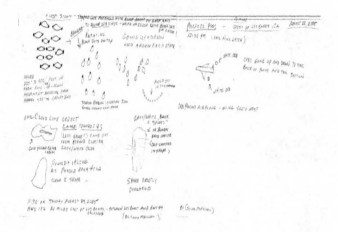

My drawing of the sightings.

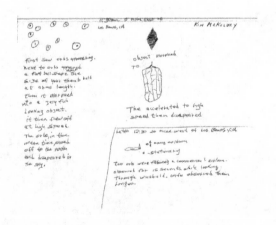

My husband's drawing.

Cat chasing orbs not seen visibly by us but captured with camera.

Left, plasma configuration, Right double orbs. Seen only with camera.

Left: Three objects caught off wing of plane flying over Arizona. Right: UFO in local neighborhood sky.

Extraordinary picture of unseen entities in kitchen reflected by the window.

Close up of entities.